Brecht, Music and Culture

RELATED TITLES FROM BLOOMSBURY
METHUEN DRAMA:

Brecht on Art and Politics
edited by Tom Kuhn and Steve Giles

Brecht on Film and Radio
edited by Marc Silberman

Brecht on Performance: Messingkauf and Modelbooks
edited by Tom Kuhn, Steve Giles and Marc Silberman

Brecht on Theatre
edited by Marc Silberman, Steve Giles and Tom Kuhn

Brecht in Practice
David Barnett

Bertolt Brecht: A Literary Life
Stephen Parker

*The Craft of Theatre: Seminars and
Discussions in Brechtian Theatre*
Ekkehard Schall

Brecht, Music and Culture

Hanns Eisler in Conversation with Hans Bunge

Edited and translated by Sabine Berendse and Paul Clements

BLOOMSBURY

LONDON · NEW DELHI · NEW YORK · SYDNEY

Bloomsbury Methuen Drama

An imprint of Bloomsbury Publishing Plc

50 Bedford Square	1385 Broadway
London	New York
WC1B 3DP	NY 10018
UK	USA

www.bloomsbury.com

Bloomsbury is a registered trade mark of Bloomsbury Publishing Plc

Original German language work by Hans Bunge entitled *Hanns Eisler Gespräche mit Hans Bunge. Fragen Sie mehr über Brecht.*
Copyright © by Deutscher Verlag für Musik, Leipzig, 1975

English language translation © Sabine Berendse and Paul Clements 2014

This edition first published in Great Britain in 2014 by Bloomsbury Publishing Plc

British Library Cataloguing-in-Publication Data
A catalogue record for this book is available from the British Library.

ISBN: HB: 978-14725-2435-5
PB: 978-14725-2841-4
ePub: 978-14725-3159-9
ePDF: 978-14725-3441-5

Library of Congress Cataloging-in-Publication Data
A catalog record for this book is available from the Library of Congress

Typeset by Integra Software Services Pvt. Ltd.
Printed and bound in India

Dedicated to my father

CONTENTS

LIST OF
ILLUSTRATIONS

NOTES TO THE GERMAN EDITION[1]

by Hans Bunge

From 1958 until just before his death in September 1962, I held a series of conversations with Hanns Eisler. They came about because I wanted to ask Eisler some questions about his collaboration with Brecht. The conversations were unstructured and not systematic; the content was not worked out in advance nor did we set out to prove anything. Eisler dealt with ideas with superior ease – he was an experienced, educated, engaged dialectician. His mind was indescribably agile and he bubbled over while linking ideas together. On those occasions his mind jumped from topic to topic in the belief that everyone could follow him. Impatiently he dismissed counter-arguments, returned to them, tested them, added to them, adopted them or rejected them altogether. His conclusions and generalizations were brave and often contradictory. He wasn't afraid of making mistakes, but if he didn't know enough about something he refused to make a judgement. Eisler described conclusions reached in discussions as preliminary conclusions. He liked being provocative and loved being provoked by others, but he drew the line at irony. He sowed the seeds of doubt, in himself as well. He enjoyed being didactic with other people and thought it important that his ideas would be preserved.

Discussions were such a great amusement for him that he, contrary to medical advice, stretched himself to the limit. And in so doing he laughed until he cried.

Hanns Eisler was an example of an artistic talent and a political position coexisting in one person. As a realist he thought reasonable compromises to be inevitable, in order to bring together in productive agreement intelligent, strategic and tactical procedures over political issues with progressive artistic aspirations. He did not allow himself to be pushed into passivity, but rather felt throughout his life that he belonged to the Marxist avant-garde. These conversations, in which Eisler never said what he thought others wanted to hear, demonstrate an implacable opposition to his political opponents and a friendly – albeit critical – position towards his political friends. Eisler was completely committed to the idea that the socialist system is the opportunity of the future.

We recorded several of our conversations on tape – fourteen in all. Eisler listened to the recordings regularly and commented on what he'd said. He regretted that these comments were not also recorded because he did not approve of everything he had said and some things he found 'stomach-churning'. Then he got worked up and did not conceal the vanity with which he observed himself. However, what he most enjoyed, when he heard what he'd said, was the sophisticated possibility of being able to experiment with ideas, noting down every passing stage of the conversation and using it as a hypothesis.

In 1958 when Eisler was looking through Houben's *Conversations with Heine*[2] again, he suggested that we should do 'Conversations about Brecht'. We changed the plan later, because, among other reasons, the content of our conversations was no longer exclusively Brecht. We were planning to compile a book of 'Eisler's Conversations'. We thought the transcriptions of the tape-recordings would be the raw material. It was to be completed over a period of time, and when we had sufficient material, we wanted to sort and edit it. We didn't get around to that.

The music department of Radio GDR 2 was interested in the material and between autumn 1965 and spring 1967 broadcast in twenty instalments nearly all of the conversations I conducted with Eisler. The publishing house Rogner & Bernhard in Munich published the transcript of the broadcast series in 1970 as a book with the title *Fragen Sie mehr über Brecht* [Ask me more about Brecht]. In the 1975 edition from Deutscher Verlag für Musik the conversations are published complete for the first time in their chronological order and their entirety.

To remain true to the experimental nature of the conversations, I treated them as a documentary record and left the few factual errors and repetitions as they were. Thoughts that were in full flow should not appear to be fixed, sudden ideas should not receive disproportionate meaning, detours and digressions as a result of the speaker's embarrassment should not give the impression that they were planned. The acoustic losses, which the reader has to accept, are considerable in any case. The captivating intensity of Eisler's way of speaking is lost, as is the humour, which comes from his intonation, and the atmosphere in which the conversations took place.

There are a few editorial intrusions, which do not affect the substance of the conversations and they are at no time the censoring of thoughts that he didn't complete or that he articulated and afterwards corrected. I have also condensed some of my questions[3].

Hans Bunge around 1954

TRANSLATOR'S NOTE

Translating the conversations between Hanns Eisler and my father, Hans Bunge, began at first as an interesting and stimulating hobby, but as so often, when one becomes more deeply involved in a project, the work evolved into a journey, a long-sought connection between my father and me. With British theatre director and drama educator, Paul Clements, I set out to undertake this intellectually and emotionally demanding, but also deeply rewarding, work.

The 1975 East German edition of *Hanns Eisler Gespräche mit Hans Bunge. Fragen Sie mehr über Brecht*[4] forms the basis of our translation. We have sought to achieve an English version that stays as close as possible to the original without compromising either the content or the flair of the conversations. Bunge added hundreds of footnotes to the conversations because detailed additional material was undoubtedly necessary at the time to inform German-speaking readers about topics with which they were probably unfamiliar and, further, for which research sources were scarce. Today, however, there are abundant reference sources to which the reader may turn. The publication of Brecht's *Journal* in English[5] also provides a wealth of material to which we refer the reader to illuminate the full text. Consequently, we have included only those notes which we think are essential. We have edited the content to produce a book that will present the best of the material, intervening in the conversations as little as possible. Cut passages are indicated by [...] and occasionally we have condensed some of Eisler's lengthier contributions to ease readability.

This long-overdue translation of the conversations will, at last, reach a non-German-speaking audience and will help the Anglo-Saxon world both to gain an insight into Eisler's astuteness and personality, and to develop a deeper understanding and appreciation of his enormous and diverse output. Eisler's intelligence, his cultural breadth and his sparkling wit and vivacity make this book a fascinating, entertaining and compelling read. It is a captivating personal overview of half a century of artistic and political turbulence with the protagonist usually in the thick of the action.

I would like to thank the Hanns and Steffy Eisler Foundation as well as the Goethe-Institute London for their generous contributions in support of the publication of this translation. Further thanks to Gudrun Bunge and Daniel Pozner (for the Bunge and the Eisler Estates), David Blake and Ian Wallace for their invaluable assistance with proof reading, Angela Jarman for her editing suggestions and, last but not least, our families. My special thanks are to my two sons: Tim, who helped with the translation of Bunge's foreword, and Felix, who generously understood how important this project was to me.

Conversation 1
9 April 1958[6]

14 Ways of Describing Rain – Meetings between Brecht and Arnold Schoenberg, Charlie Chaplin and Thomas Mann – Brecht and Music

I have to apologize again that we have to repeat the recording of 9 April because the tape was inadvertently wiped.

It's the story of my life.

I'd like to refer to an entry in Brecht's Journal of 20 April 1942 in which he states that you were your 'old self, in wit and wisdom' when you arrived in California and that you had received a grant from the Rockefeller Foundation for your project, 14 Ways of Describing Rain, *which he describes as taut music accompanying a film-clip of rain. Not without irony, Brecht mentions his own project: 'perhaps after all my tui-novel[7] is not totally…' The sentence is left unfinished.*

You have to see it like this: at that time I was a university professor at the New School for Social Research. The New School for Social Research, a university in New York, received grants from various institutions, such as the Rockefeller Foundation. And my director, the very kind Professor Alvin Johnson, offered me a project and I accepted it. We were in the middle of a war and I was a political émigré – what was I supposed to do? So, as well as carrying on my usual compositional work (which by the way doesn't deal with abstract things), I decided to research the relationship between music and film – a matter of dramaturgy, which was also of interest to Brecht. It was a job on the side. And, as you know, a university professor in America has also to undertake research if he wants to keep his chair.

What does 'research' actually mean?

Scholarly projects. A professor can't just teach, but must also carry out research into his subject. That's what academic life is all about – it's the same in Germany, incidentally. A professor who only teaches through seminars and lectures is immediately seen as inferior unless he does his own research as well. The Rockefeller grant works like this: some university professors get selected – there's even something of a regular cycle – and receive financial support to carry out research as well as their teaching. Of course it's a bit more complicated than this in practice.

The *14 Ways of Describing Rain* is only one of the theoretical as well as practical projects that I delivered. I'm very aware that my friend Brecht – albeit in a friendly way – mocked me about this. The world was complicated, the most dreadful war in world history was taking place and someone gives Eisler the opportunity to perfect his research skills and what does he write? – an assignment about *14 Ways of Describing Rain*.

When Brecht writes in his Journal: 'perhaps after all my *tui-novel* is not totally...' and then leaves a blank, which I'm filling in now by adding *'incorrectly conceptualised'* – he is right. To outwit the authorities – that means to get on with one's life and not to prostitute oneself, to continue to work in spite of things and deliver something worthwhile – was (a) the tui-attitude and (b) then again it wasn't. The sentence that follows this, in which Brecht describes me, shows that I wasn't a tui. But I have to admit, my position was...

You know, one should read again the Roman classics about the behaviour of Greek slaves in Roman domestic life. They behaved in a very similar way in imperial Rome, found all sorts of ways to support their own work and yet still delivered to the Emperor – in my particular case the university – what was required of them. It is not a very dignified attitude, I admit that, but it is one – *one* attitude. It at least permitted me to continue with my composing and what I composed at this time might perhaps turn out to be the best justification. You see how difficult it is, if you work only as a scholar, to find excuses for someone like me [Eisler's phone rings. After the interruption he says]. That's quite good, isn't it? We solved the case. Let us continue. Maybe I didn't express myself clearly enough when I added '*incorrectly conceptualised*' and it's not quite obvious that I spoke it in inverted commas. What Brecht wanted to say is: 'my *tui-novel* is indeed correctly conceptualised'.

Brecht writes in his Journal of 24 April 1942 that he is at Adorno's listening to recordings of Rain. *He likes them very much – they remind him of a Chinese ink-drawing. Then he refers to an ambush on Schoenberg and later quotes from somewhere that a clinical thermometer is one of the most important instruments for judging music.*

I remember that, yes.

One should immediately after listening to a piece of music take one's temperature to see whether or not it has remained constant or whether the temperature rises when the music is stormy, fervent or simply powerful. Brecht adds that as far as Bach is concerned, you will be left with no change in temperature: it will be the same even with the most passionate works.[8]

Brecht indeed listened to *Rain* a few times and was…quite content. He didn't write in his Journal, however, that he also cursed a great deal. He felt attracted to and repulsed by the work at the same time. What was attractive for him was what he called its Chinese ink-drawing quality: the delicacy of the music. But he was repulsed by a kind of tui-attitude. It seemed to him in some way immoral to devote oneself in such difficult times so intensely to rain – and not only rain but also the different ways in which it rains. Brecht didn't note this in his Journal. But I do know that he – and I say this very openly – raged about it behind my back. Which is perfectly all right, because friendships are not only about bestowing praise but also about being sharply critical of each other.
Brecht understood later that rain is also a symbol for grief. In many languages, rain is one of the metaphors for grief, being drenched in sorrow. Remember the magnificent rain poems by Verlaine, for example. It's also there, I think, in Rimbaud's poems, as it is in every great poetic tradition. Rain represents grief and in

a way, *14 Ways of Describing Rain* meant, fourteen decent ways to mourn. That also is part of art. I won't go as far as to claim that this is the central theme of the twentieth century – the anatomy of grief or the anatomy of melancholy – but it might have a place in one's work as well.

Brecht's clever remark about the increase in temperature through listening to music and the possibility of assessing music by this means is typical Brecht. Indeed, you can already find something similar in Goethe. Everyone knows about Goethe's dislike of Beethoven (maybe 'dislike' is too strong a word, rather a lack of understanding), because Goethe spoke of emotional confusion when listening to Beethoven's music. That meant it made him hot and bothered but with nowhere to go. It's like excitement *pour* excitement. If you can have *l'art pour l'art*, so you can also have fever *pour* fever. And that made an intelligent man like Goethe very irritable. It was the same with Brecht.

The medical profession has not yet conducted research into the physiological effects of music. This whole field in medicine has, as yet, not been ploughed, although some medical schools have studied how to improve, not heal, certain illnesses through music – which corresponds to ancient legends. As you know, music has always been considered to have mystical powers. Just think of the Orpheus legend. And if you haven't got anything better to do, have a look at Hegel's *Aesthetics*, in the section on music, and read the very amusing piece that Hegel wrote about Orpheus.[9]

What Brecht loved in music was clarity and the avoidance of feverish excitement. This isn't to say that Brecht's idea of the purpose of music was the same as what happened in France after the First World War when they tried to freeze out everything that had gone before.[10] Think of certain periods in Stravinsky's work.

Whether or not the normal body temperature stays at 37 degrees when you listen to Bach…I doubt that. First of all, I just have to think of the expression on Brecht's face to see how moved he was when I played Bach to him. It seemed to me that his temperature was significantly higher. Take, for example, the St Matthew Passion (the great E minor section at the beginning, 'Come you daughters, help me mourn') or the first twenty pages of the St John Passion. I don't want to cast doubt on my late friend, but I'm convinced his

temperature rose alarmingly, especially because he so admired Bach
for his great ability with narrative – think of The Evangelist in the St
John Passion, [Eisler sings] 'Jesus went with his disciples'. You see,
the alienation of the text because it is just recited – in all its great
beauty – always made a huge impression on Brecht.
We should draw this to a close now. We can only establish, what
I have often said: Brecht had an undoubted taste in music and an
excellent way of approaching this rather difficult art form.

Could it be that Brecht was interested in 14 Ways of Describing
Rain *because of its experimental method? In his theatre work there
are similar attempts to investigate a certain pattern of behaviour
from different angles.*

Certainly. To be fair to a dead man, a great man, who never put
on record that he *didn't* like *Rain*, I have to say that there were
times when he found it terrible.
When we lads were back in Berlin again and had become more
mature, he told me a few times that *Rain* was one of his favourite
pieces. Even so, there were occasions during the exile when he
found my preoccupation with rain to be somehow immoral. Brecht
wasn't into that kind of symbolism. That rain could stand for grief
was far too subtle for him. And Brecht, a typical Bavarian, had a
very healthy aversion to subtlety.

*On the other hand, Brecht knew perfectly well that you didn't
compose this piece just to please yourself, that you were fulfilling
a commission. Brecht himself was in a similar position. He notes
in July 1942, that he is constantly working with Fritz Lang on the
'hostage story' in order to make a living.*[11]

Of course. And I have to say that I believe that this piece of music,
looked at from today's perspective, is my best chamber work, and
has gained a certain reputation despite its only being written to put
bread on the table: and for that it's pretty outstanding – particularly
as it doesn't in any way try to cosy up to you. It is I think – and I can
say this now I'm old enough – really outstanding chamber music,
which will be listened to for some time to come. Unfortunately,
there was other breadwinning work I had to do – and it was the
same for our dear Brecht – which didn't always reach the heights
that the university work enabled me to achieve.

You weren't really a 'true' tui.

Tui as camouflage. I behaved like a tui in order to be able to compose. So I worked on *Rain* at the most for a few hours a day, leaving significantly more time for composing my other things. It's interesting: if we imitate the behaviour of a tui, without actually being one, we can get on with the things that really matter to us.

On 27 April 1942, Brecht writes about the 'tyrant' Schoenberg. It amuses him to hear how you confess to him with a smile that you tremble when you go to see Schoenberg, worry about your tie being straight or arriving 10 minutes too early. You told Brecht then that Schoenberg received Rain *with words of praise. That must have been very important to you.*[12]

That's right. My behaviour – not only mine but also that of such extraordinary musicians as Alban Berg, Anton von Webern, or my friend Steuermann or Kolisch (I mention after all two of the most significant composers of this century and two of the best musicians I have ever known) – we all were … how shall I say this … *Angst* is the wrong word … simply full of the highest respect. I think this tradition of loyalty of a student towards his teacher is to be found only in the working class movement. You understand what I mean: our great political functionaries, had they ever had the opportunity to meet Karl Marx personally, would have behaved in the same way as I did towards my teacher Schoenberg. Now, for God's sake, I don't want to compare the man Arnold Schoenberg with the man Karl Marx. I really admire Schoenberg but that would be taking it too far. Schoenberg's political point of view was that of a most dreadful petit bourgeois.

But you know, in music you still have this relationship between teacher and student. To show the student how to write good music, analyse the classics – that is a great tradition in music and something that hardly exists any more in literature or painting. On top of that, there is the tremendous gratitude that people like me have towards Schoenberg, because Schoenberg taught me free of charge.

I often lived with him for six months at a time and he gave me money because I was a very hard-up young student – it was like a father-son relationship, if you like. Schoenberg's care for me went well beyond the lessons. He actually supported me for many years and made a musician of me – which wasn't that easy since I was quite a rebellious lad. That was really something.

On top of this kind of humble respect for Schoenberg, there is something else, in that I had two, three – I remember two at least – terrible rows with him, which can mainly be attributed to my political views and which led to the breakdown of the relationship between the Schoenberg and Eisler households for many years. Affairs were always restored, though, by dreadful events – especially the time of exile. But these disagreements always lay dormant in the background (one didn't talk about them). I tried desperately not to talk to Schoenberg about politics, since nothing could be achieved by it. Besides, the man was ill.

So, you see, all of this explains the way my behaviour culminates in an attitude of admiration and shyness – which I…you know…somehow put on. This is how I wanted Schoenberg to see me; he wasn't supposed to think me arrogant or to say: 'He's a know-all'. Actually, I felt I was better off than Schoenberg. You had to make everything 'just so' for a petit bourgeois like him. Short and sweet: all of that led to my adopting an attitude of utmost respect and admiration and, as I remember, Brecht absolutely understood this. I don't know how Brecht would have got on with Frank Wedekind if he'd had a chance to meet him; it could have been the same kind of relationship because, as everyone knows, when he was a young man Brecht learned a lot from Wedekind.

I remember Brecht saying at the opening of the master classes at the Academy of Arts that he could happily have sought tuition from Georg Kaiser in the same way that others are now coming to him.

So, I felt admiration, veneration, and I should mention the word 'gratitude' here too, for a master, a twentieth-century giant like Schoenberg, whose weaknesses were historically determined and don't indicate a lack of genius. You can't step outside your own time; indeed, an individualist like Schoenberg even helped produce the stupidities of his time, the consequences of which you can, unfortunately, see by looking at exceptionally foolish and downright dreadful people nowadays. Everyone nowadays takes on that individualistic attitude of Schoenberg's, especially in West Germany, and the outcomes speak for themselves. Brecht has captured this very accurately and it is the absolute truth.

It would be great if you could use this opportunity to tell us something about Brecht's attitude to Charlie Chaplin and to Thomas Mann whom he also met in California.

Brecht's attitude to Chaplin was certainly different from my attitude to Schoenberg because Brecht wasn't Chaplin's personal pupil and hadn't been supported by Chaplin as a young man. But there was something of this in that relationship. Brecht consciously adopted an attitude of listening respectfully to a great theatrical genius – perhaps the greatest theatrical genius of the twentieth century. I have seldom seen such an attentive and sincere listener to the many stories that Chaplin always used to tell us. And really the loudest laughs came from Brecht... and me. Let me tell you a story.

Chaplin invited 200 of his friends and acquaintances to see his movie *Monsieur Verdoux* in a private showing before it was released to the public. Among them were very wealthy people – the whole great film industry – and there were some bohemian friends, to whom Brecht and I must have belonged, since we had nothing to do with the film industry. In certain scenes – for instance when the bankers jump out of the window and shoot themselves during the economic crisis (there is a short sequence in this movie) – you could hear two people sitting a long way from each other laughing very loudly. That was Brecht and me. Everyone else kept silent because there were bankers in the audience watching the film too. So you can see, we were of one mind here, Brecht and me. We were the most perceptive laughers. Of course, we only laughed at those of Chaplin's jokes that had a social meaning, so that Chaplin – to whom it was very important to be admired for his jokes, at the dinner table too, and rightly so – clearly understood that those two people are laughing most at the jokes with a social bite. As a result, he became more radical in our company.

Unfortunately, at other times Chaplin didn't know what to make of Brecht who he thought was a highly interesting man. Chaplin didn't speak German and Brecht's plays weren't translated into English. He was at the very first performance of *Life of Galileo* with Charles Laughton as Galileo. I don't think that Chaplin really understood the play. He was somehow impressed by it, but didn't know what to make of it. We sat together at the play and afterwards went to dinner. He thought that Brecht was a wonderful man, to be sure, but – then he became very embarrassed – he didn't understand what he'd just seen. The most important thing for him was that the play wasn't theatrical enough for him – he thought it should have been fixed up in a completely different way. When I explained to him, that

Brecht didn't want to 'fix' anything 'up', he had no idea what I was talking about. I dropped the subject very quickly then. There was respect, but it didn't get as far as comprehension. On the other hand Brecht was a Chaplin expert *par excellence*, one of the best.[13] We spent evenings together, when we regaled Chaplin with all the little details from his movies and we all laughed like madmen – what entertaining evenings. 'Charlie, do you remember in *Modern Times*...' – and then we told him the effect it had on us; it kept us going for at least three hours.

We were rather modest as émigrés.

And Thomas Mann?

With Thomas Mann it was the opposite. First of all Brecht didn't read the kind of novels Mann wrote, although I tried over and over again to make him. The word 'friend' is a little too intimate for the relationship I had with Thomas Mann, which was more one of respect from a distance, but you could call it a kind of fatherly affection: there were the visits from house to house, the families knew each other, I was often at Mann's and he often came to me. Brecht didn't like that at all, this intimacy with the Manns. He was far too polite to say anything about it, but he saw it as a kind of treason – actually that's the only word for it. I was exceptionally amused by Thomas Mann, by the whole family. Mann's interest in music – you know, all the old favourites like Pfitzner's *Palestrina* and especially Wagner's music – stimulated some wonderful arguments, so much so that we have a few good stories to tell. Emigration evenings on the whole are dull, but a good dinner at Thomas Mann's plus a conversation about Wagner – that was very enjoyable. Incidentally, Thomas Mann made some nice notes – he even published them. You can find conversations with Eisler in his diaries. Mann enjoyed those evenings too.

When Thomas Mann came to visit my house, I tried repeatedly to get Brecht to come as well. And Lion Feuchtwanger. You see what problems one had – whom to invite? Such trivialities actually existed. Brecht was against Thomas Mann in such a way I can only call...obstinate! In the difficult times of war, you do have at least a few anti-fascist Germans and, to be fair, you have to credit Thomas Mann with being an anti-fascist – I'm already talking like Brecht – you can't conjure anti-fascism out of Thomas Mann! But Mann's hesitant, indecisive behaviour when Brecht made controversial statements (statements that he always wanted everyone to agree with) made Brecht's blood boil.[14] In short: from distrust, via obstinacy to raucous viciousness, this made a get-together between Thomas Mann and Brecht pretty uncomfortable. Mainly no allowances were made for Thomas Mann's age. Mann was already past the age when it would have been legal to shoot him. So why did Brecht behave like that? What was the point?

Well, Thomas Mann knew a few plays by Brecht. Brecht knew Thomas Mann's works, I think, only from my reports. Brecht very much liked this kind of literary reporter. For I also read very fat books – I don't mind as the evenings are often long and I can't compose at night – and it was then that I told Brecht about the great passages in *The Magic Mountain*. He was always astonished that it contained such good things and thought that one really ought to look through it, but he never did. For example, in *Magic Mountain*, Settembrini's views on music are very similar to Brecht's. The way both of them look at art is from a Jacobin point of view. As is well known, Settembrini says in *Magic Mountain*: 'Music as an art is politically suspect'. That means music is protean, is so capable of assuming many forms, is so unprincipled, that for the Jacobin Settembrini – you could also call him the 'enlightener', although I don't want to go into an analysis of his character now – music becomes 'politically suspect'.[15] That could have come straight from Brecht. Settembrini's dislike of music – because it is so long-winded and so non-committal – is a truly puritanical enlightenment point of view. (You know that the great Protestant sects wanted to eradicate music altogether – just think of the Geneva period!) Even so, Brecht did think about music. He just couldn't get to the bottom of it.

Very maliciously, Brecht called Thomas Mann 'this short story writer'. He insisted that it would be useless for Mann to try to write long novels as he simply didn't possess the skills. He could only write very short novellas – that's about it. For his part, Thomas Mann called Brecht 'the unfortunately gifted Brecht'. We – incidentally you're much younger than me – have to understand that in cultural history, as written, literature takes up a more complicated position. There are many such anomalies. And Thomas Mann, at the time of the Weimar Republic, didn't have any knowledge of Brecht's works. He only knew that Brecht was a significant person. Besides, the family didn't like Brecht either, especially Klaus Mann, unfortunately now deceased, who had written a few spiteful things about Brecht in a travel book.[16] Brecht didn't represent that well-brought-up, gently dying bourgeoisie with that great insight into its own demise; he was an extremely rebellious man. And this didn't sit comfortably with the well-bred manners of this family of senators.

I can give more precise details of the story about the mutual enmity between those two men. Therese Giehse, who was friends with Brecht as well as with Thomas Mann, gave the play Mother Courage and Her Children *to Thomas Mann. She said he had to read it. Once he'd read it Thomas Mann said: 'The beast has talent!' Giehse, who sometimes came to Berlin, told Brecht about it. Brecht smiled, flattered and returned the compliment: 'Actually I always quite liked his short stories'.*

I have to say that Brecht overlooked a true humanity in Thomas Mann. I don't only mean in his books but also in his whole behaviour. I would like to mention – in fairness to dear old Thomas – how positively he behaved during my rather despicable political scandal in America.[17] He was courageous and decent. A support committee for me was set up in his house using his own letterhead. I want to make this clear because Brecht, at this point, became distrustful of Thomas Mann, although he eventually acknowledged that the Manns really took enormous risks for me and my wife, for which I am deeply grateful and indebted to them. You can't just say that Thomas Mann was a quiet citizen who enjoyed the demise of his own class. It isn't that easy; that wouldn't be dialectical.

I found a note in Brecht's Journal in which he states that he wrote some notes on film music for you. This was on 2 May 1942.[18]

Yes, I wrote a little book at that time, which has since been translated into a few other languages, and asked Bert for some notes. Brecht wasn't interested in this topic at all. In my book – you should look it up – I'm sure you'll find a few things about Brecht. I think his notes on film music are identical with his general theories about theatre.[19] Although it wasn't actually anything I could make use of, he certainly wrote a few sentences and it would be a shame if I couldn't find them again. It is possible that a former pupil of mine in Vienna[20] – he has an archive with letters and notes – might be able to retrieve it. It was at the most half a page because Brecht didn't have anything directly to do with film.

But even so, he worked with Fritz Lang, for example.[21]

That was such an ordeal for Brecht, I can tell you! It was just so terrible.

In an entry on 9 May 1942, Brecht observes that you don't seem to like the song 'Ballad of the Soldier's Wife' because of the supposed sneer in it. Brecht quotes you as saying: 'and what if i did send my mother a piece of salami from italy in 1917? the generals purloin pianos and carpets, the privates take the chance to buy shoes for their wives. that's what they get out of the war, not much'. He goes on to say: 'it is a difficult one. i could say that i did not make him send his wife food, just clothes, looted junk. but that doesn't really make much difference, she needs that too'. Brecht then wonders if he could have written the poem if the widow's veil had come from Paris but it still begs the question: 'how can i support the people's claim to lead and at the same time condone its irresponsibility?' Brecht says, when he wrote it he was probably thinking what the SA-man's wife would have got in the mail. Which is why he gave it that title.

That's right. I remember this discussion, because of the disrespect for humanity in it that Brecht certainly did not intend. I dug out a letter for you that I once wrote to Brecht[22] in which – from an admirer's point of view and because I liked this fabulous ballad – I criticized exactly such disrespect in *Mother Courage* where the dehumanization of the 'little' people is marvellously depicted. In *Courage*, the poverty of the poorest – except for the field colonel – is shown in precise detail. I spoke with Brecht about that too, and you'll find it in Brecht's notes. He took down what I said when we were in Buckow.[23]

Once, when I told him he shouldn't delude himself that he had portrayed the character of the mother as a monster, he asked, 'Why?' 'It doesn't work because of the length of the production' I told him. 'Because it's so long, the mother becomes likeable'. Brecht was beside himself with rage; I had introduced a concept he hadn't reckoned with at all. I said: 'If, as is the case here, you put a woman on the stage for three hours, with all the nuances of her behaviour, you make her – whether *you* like it or not – likeable. The length brings her closer to the audience'. He probably made a note of that. That's in no way a criticism of this magnificent play, but you have a similar factor in this ballad as well. There isn't mockery in the play – there isn't mockery in the ballad either – but in my opinion, the oppressed are called to account.

Certainly, Brecht could have said: 'If I'm pursuing an idea, I can't keep referring to oppressed people in every scene, in every verse'. But that somehow leaves an aftertaste. He sharply criticized the lower class although anyone who knows a single line of Brecht knows that he was in no way less critical of the upper class. But while I'm not asking that every sentence or every scene has to replicate the pattern of the behaviour of the upper or lower classes, certain artistic means could lead to things to which I have a certain antipathy. And with reference to the passage that you quoted from the Journal, I had to make my antipathy known – and not just because I'd been a soldier during the Great War. I didn't think that was the most important thing. There had to be something more. Now it would have been quite correct – only poetically not so good – had Brecht written: 'And what did the mail bring to the SA-man's wife?' That those little Nazi-PGs [party comrades] also tried to get rich themselves – that would top everything, wouldn't it? Because from the start they were involved in the war, which they then imposed on their own people. They were the ones shaping the masses who were driven into this war. These are such hair-splitting questions, which today are made irrelevant by the beauty of the poetry. Let's consider it only for the oddness of our discussions. At least it's good that two Marxists like Brecht and – from a respectful distance, so to speak – I, had no greater concerns than to rack our brains about such questions. Certainly, discussions of this nature are the prelude to honest art. That's all I've got to say about this.

In fact the importance of this discussion for Brecht is revealed when, on the same day, he writes that you are quite correct in recalling the danger that exists when purely technical innovations, unconnected to a social function, are put into circulation. Stirring music was at that time the imperative. He continues by saying that stirring music can be heard on the radio in the US countless times a day in jingles that seduce people into wanting to buy Coca Cola. A desperate Brecht even goes so far as to call for l'art pour l'art and continues by reporting a conversation with Adorno. Brecht ridiculed the abnormal declamation of texts by the Schoenberg School, characterized by extreme and rapid intervals, which Adorno

defended as being part of music's development. Brecht concludes that
it is *'exclusively constructional, almost mathematical considerations
and postulates of pure logic in the assembly of tonal materials that
force musicians to whinny like dying horses...'*[24]

Brecht has two thoughts here which one has to keep separate.
The first is what Adorno is trying to defend concerning large leaps
in the intervals of the vocal lines in so-called modern music and the
second is Brecht's remark about the rousing music.

That Brecht even goes so far as to call for *l'art pour l'art* – if
that comes from a man like Brecht, who was made physically ill by
the idea of art for art's sake – that shows what kind of damage this
popular music can cause. Music for advertisements, for example,
inviting you to buy things, is written in the style of light music. I feel
it's the same even with our broadcasting stations, which are forced to
play, I don't know, twelve hours of music every day. They produce an
enormous amount of trashy, banal music, which attempts to express
the thoughts and ideas of the working-class movement mostly by
using military-type motifs and the like. I gradually develop such an
aversion to the whole system that when by chance I hear three bars
by, for example, Schoenberg, I suddenly think they are the greatest
expressions of humanity. Why? Because with Schoenberg there
will at least be an expression of grief or lamentation, not all this
liveliness, this false enthusiasm, this pathetic zest for life expressed
in a waltz, or a jolly polka – nor, indeed, the foolishness of my young
colleagues who, with the best intentions try to write something for
the working-class movement. It is simply unbearable. So, here is a
serious challenge for our people: to try to write in popular genres
that don't have this terrible, hackneyed banality, this conformity to
the past of which Brecht was acutely aware.

During the Weimar Republic, we always took care that music
should be fresh, rousing. But the question is – and here I come back
to Settembrini's statement that 'music is politically suspect' – what
is rousing music for? So in order to clarify our political purposes,
music has to have special artistic means and tight corsets, crutches
too or a backbone – even better when it is a backbone.

The second question, which Brecht touches on, is Adorno's
comment. This metaphysical, blind belief in 'the development of
music' produces results, which are entirely detached from the social
circumstances of the people! If only Adorno would understand once

and for all that music is made by people for people – and that even if it develops, it is not abstract but can be connected in some way to social conditions – he wouldn't have uttered this abstract nonsense. Brecht was quite right to be sharply critical, and his last sentence ...

'...to whinny like dying horses'.

Yes, but it's not about warhorses – horses that go into battle – but about horses that will be carted off for slaughter at the knacker's yard.[25] Adorno is thinking of the warhorse. But it's not the thoroughbred that goes down in battle, pierced by an arrow and neighing for the last time; it's the worn-out old nag going off to be turned into sausages and which, before he's made into sausages, lets out a cry of horror. Adorno defends a different kind of music historically. So, you have to be careful: there's more than one kind of horse. Brecht, as a Bavarian, was certainly referring to the slaughter horse, the old nag and the sausages. The dying horse of the knight – that is long gone.

On 12 May 1942, Brecht mentions in his Journal a lunch with you at Horkheimer's and that after lunch you suggested a plot for the Tui novel. It was to be the story of the Frankfurt Sociological Institute. A wealthy man dies – Weil, the wheat speculator – leaving money in his will to establish an institute to investigate the causes of poverty. The cause is, of course, himself. The Institute conducts its business at a time when, in the face of popular unrest, even the Emperor wants to know the source of all evil. The Institute itself then assists in the investigation.

And the source of the misery proves to be the wheat speculator. The scholars of the Institute can't publish that, of course. Well, as you know, Max Horkheimer – he is today, I think, Rector at Frankfurt University – was then the director of this strange Institute. The Frankfurt Sociological Institute has an endowment from a big wheat trader – I would say the biggest of the whole of the wheat trade – Weil, *hermanos*, that is the Brothers Weil.

This is a real name?

Yes. With head offices in Argentina and in Frankfurt. The big wheat traders. And the father did indeed make a huge donation at the end of his life: an imposing building with lots and lots of rooms in it. It invites erudition, and for forty years now people have been asking themselves, 'Well, how's it all going?' Of course, the way I express myself is from a plebeian perspective. Serious ideas are, certainly, generated there, but I think the way I refer to it hits the nail on the head.

Brecht thought this suggestion was great fun. Otherwise, he wouldn't have written it down. I can only lament over and over again: if only he had written this novel, it would have been an enormous contribution. You will, by the way, find a few beginnings for it among his papers.

Yes, there is a lot of material about this.[26]

Also, how the wheat trader Weil travels from village to village and, as a consequence of meeting a few shady characters, decides to found this institute. This is quite an extraordinary institute. And I can see that after Brecht's death nobody will have the intellectual stature to describe the dirty dealings there.

Brecht notes on 30 May 1942 that you introduced him to Clifford Odets. What's your comment on this?

Clifford Odets is a highly regarded American playwright. Today his reputation is somewhat diminished. I would say he's a kind of American Chekhov, without his ever having achieved Chekhov's significance. His plays are studies of the Jewish working-class milieu in New York, and the transition of these classes to the petit bourgeoisie. His portrayal of the despair of these classes during the great American crisis was very interesting. Linguistically he was especially gifted, you know – he had a linguistic talent for a sort of argot. His theatre works with Chekhovian technique and the actors were directed in Stanislavskian style – a very attractive combination, with the addition of Broadway slang. I was good friends with him. Clifford Odets was nice and decent then.[27] He never knew what to make of Brecht. Indeed all the other American playwrights and theatre people – Charles Laughton was one of the few exceptions – acted towards Brecht with rudeness and a complete lack of interest. Clifford Odets later behaved – I think in 1951 – very badly. He was called before the House Committee on Un-American Activities – the same committee where Brecht and I, and also my brother, appeared. His behaviour there was pathetic and since then I have no longer associated with him. He is morally outraged about this but that's his problem. I don't therefore know what's happened to him. I think he writes films and so on in Hollywood.

Anyway, since that time he hasn't produced anything special. Originally he had talent – a strong talent with a popular touch. He did have a little talk with Brecht about the filming of *Fears and Misery of the Third Reich*,[28] for which he had quite a good idea. But, as usual, the film wasn't realized. It just remained a plan. That's all I can say about Odets. You can find everything of relevance in any modern American literary history. He is very well known.

On 5 June 1942, Brecht mentions this plan about which you've just spoken. He says that there was a working lunch at Fritz Lang's when you, Odets and Brecht came up with draft ideas for making a film of Fears and Misery.

That's the 'little talk' between Odets and Brecht I was referring to. Did Brecht use this idea? I can't remember now if that's the one by Odets or it could just as well be one of Brecht's – anyway, that's beside the point.

First, you have soldiers driving up in a tank and then the story of each individual soldier will be told. This means that there's a tank heading for the Soviet Union and you have to find a way to get all these people together in that tank. That was the premise – a very good idea. As each one steps out of the tank, the scene changes – now we see the scene with the teacher whose son is a spy, now we see the SA-man...– you know, each has a back story. Finally you have them all put into the tank together to send them East. That was the concept. A shame that it was never taken on.

Explicit details can be found in the Aurora-edition of *Fears and Misery of the Third Reich*, which I can show you, because Brecht also wrote some verses about it. When we were in the sleeper train from Los Angeles to New York to attend the rehearsals, Brecht was forever composing verses for 'the tank' during meals. In his little pocket book, he enthusiastically drafted verses for the soldiers in the tank. The only one I remember is: 'and ... dee dom dee dom ... and Krupp puts the wheels on ...'[29]

The verses you find there were mostly written for this proposed film. There was eventually a performance of the play in New York, directed by Berthold Viertel. It was again one of our striking failures. It was terrible.

Do you mean The Private Life of the Master Race?

It was a terrible failure. Brecht was not so much sad as embarrassed about it. If you have a flop like this, it really is awful. Berthold Viertel did try his best. But the critics and the audience just didn't know what was going on. Brecht had this fantastic idea of putting white make-up on a black actor. The theatre critics in New York thought this was immoral. Well, it was a depressing business. It was the third setback for Brecht in America. Second was *The Mother* and before that, in 1933, *The Threepenny Opera*. Since then, as we all know, Brecht has been fantastically rehabilitated; *The Threepenny Opera* has now already run for 11,000 consecutive performances, I think.

In his Journal entry of 16 June 1942, Brecht records a Frankfurt Institute Seminar that took place at Adorno's, attended by Adorno himself, you, Horkheimer, Nürnberg, Pollock and Ludwig and Herbert Marcuse. Is that a branch of the Institute for those who emigrated to America?

You couldn't call it a branch. It was the centre. They had an office there in Hollywood and another office in New York because Paris was occupied by the Hitler gang. They set up a discussion evening – a seminar it was called – and I was invited to it. They wanted someone to give them credibility. And here was a man who still had close connections with Germany's Communist Party in exile. By inviting me, they secured a guarantee they stayed loyal towards the working-class movement and that, in particular, nothing anti-communist would be discussed. I took great pleasure in attending. Unfortunately, Brecht was not invited because they were afraid of him. If he had been there, they wouldn't have dared waffle on as they sometimes did.

Horkheimer is the director of the Institute. Pollock, whose work was less scholarly, more about housing and property speculation, is economic director of the Institute. Ludwig Marcuse is still living in Los Angeles today. He's written a book, something like 'In Praise of Pessimism'. He was on to something there: that pessimism is the best. Optimism is bland, pessimism is the best. Thus humanity only comes into the foreground when you're a pessimist. Tricksy stuff like this could have been written by my friend Adorno too. There is another Marcuse called Herbert Marcuse, a very decent man who has written a level-headed study of Hegel. Nürnberg is a former journalist from Berlin who has since died; a man of no significance whatsoever.

On 29 June 1942, Brecht writes that you had set to music most of his Finnish poems in a 'Hollywood Song-booklet'. You sang them to Odets, who said: 'That's the kind of thing you can only do when you're poor'. There's another note in relation to this nearly a month later on 26 July 1942 when you told Brecht that you had completed the last of the Finnish poems. He quotes you as saying how much the poems gained the more you worked on them. He compares your settings to the performance of a play: the ultimate test. Brecht admires the precision of your reading when, for example, in the last poems you objected to the word 'work' and weren't satisfied until Brecht had replaced it with 'poem' or 'verse'. Or, again, in the poem 'In the Willows at the Sound' you omitted the words 'about those in power' on the grounds that this made the poem cleaner. Brecht isn't convinced that the resultant cleanliness is not itself beyond criticism because he fears the poem might lose what he calls its 'historical self-sufficiency'. He notes that you also criticized the title of the third poem in the cycle '1940, Fog in Flanders', because you found it didn't make sense and that you weren't happy until he had renamed it 'Flanders' Landscape 1940'.

Very good. Yes, I have to say that 'about those in power' was too abstract for me. Different people rule for different reasons and at different times. That was too abstract for me. There's nothing else I can say about that.

And what about: 'That's the kind of thing you can only do when you're poor'.

That's the typical *parvenu*. My former good friend, Clifford Odets, came from a poor middle-class family and at that time he was earning $3000 a week. He was a very rich man but he hardly ever behaved like one. He was a good comrade, a friend. But this thing – money – spoils you. In America, artists are spoiled because they earn money too quickly.

I have one more question for today. What was the extent of Brecht's influence on the music for the plays you worked on?

On the work I did, unfortunately not enough. Maybe some of it could have been better – I mean, he was just very satisfied when I composed something. And he was very sweet; he picked out certain poems that I might set to music. For example, he repeatedly asked me right up until just before he died: 'Please at long last set "Freedom and Democracy" to music for me!' I really must get down to it. It was his most cherished wish! It would be so important now. The piece is only half finished, and I really should complete it because he never stopped asking for it.

Then there were the poems – like the 'Children's Songs' – that he especially wrote for me, and when I didn't set them to music quickly enough, he was a bit disappointed. He also insisted that these pieces were to be both performed and published. He wanted certain music for theatre to be – how shall I put it? – humorous, funny even. That's about as far as his influence went. With one wonderful exception:

I was in Vienna when he was rehearsing *Katzgraben*,[30] and I composed a little song to the poem 'The Old Times are Now Gone'. It was a very simple thing. He wanted children to sing the moral at the end lightly – it's an important line in the poem and I thought the simpler the better. The gestus is childlike. When I returned and went to the rehearsal, I saw and heard – with great pleasure, by the way – our excellent actor Franz singing 'The Old Times are Now Gone' an almost demonic melody, in a strong voice. I said to Brecht: 'That's just wonderful, who…?' 'I did', he answered. 'But how did you do it?' I asked, to which he replied: 'I always remember that, in certain compositions, you use the contrapuntal technique of inversion, you invert a theme. So, I took the trio in Chopin's *Funeral March* and inverted it and this melody came about'. I really liked that a lot although, I always had to smile to myself when I heard this particular song, especially as it was sung so superbly by Franz, and with such a demonic gestus. I said to Brecht: 'Of course, you also added to your composition a melancholy, a regret about the old days being over'. At first, Brecht liked this idea very much since there is always cause for regret when something comes to an end – for an ending can also be very painful. Later he changed his mind and unfortunately discarded his melody and went back to my insignificant tune. I promised myself never to make such a remark again. Brecht is too big a character; you can't tell him anything, even if it's the truth, without his challenging it. So, I noted down Brecht's tune – it really is excellent – and I will keep it.[31]

By the way, as you know, the first edition of the *Domestic Breviary* contains Brecht's own melodies. Some of them made it to the stage, as for instance the beautiful melody in *Mother Courage*, which is an old French sailor's song [Eisler hums the melody]. I think Brecht found it somewhere. I have to repeat once more: Brecht was a highly musical man. Had he not been a great author and playwright, I should have liked him to have composed a little bit more music. That would have been wonderful for all of us. A quite astonishing musical talent.

But this talent was theoretical – reading music only went as far as his guitar music.[32]

Yes, he could only play the guitar. He couldn't read music – or he'd forgotten. But that doesn't matter. A lot of people in the world know how to read music, you know. But Brecht's musicality was an enormous musicality without technique, in the same way that he had a special mathematical talent without mathematical technique. That's how it is. And I prefer someone like this to some mediocre professional musician. Yes, he had huge musicality. Of course, Brecht, for all his accomplishments, wasn't able to tell me how I should compose: although there's nothing I would have liked better, it never materialized. I don't think Brecht intervened in that way with anyone.

Conversation 2

13 April 1958

Galileo – *Hollywood Elegies* – Brecht and Feuchtwanger – Brecht and Music for the Theatre – *Schweyk in the Second World War*

Yesterday I got hold of the programme of Irmgard Arnold's 'Liederabend' [Evening of Songs] at the Deutsche Staatsoper. In it your song 'The Durable Grey Goose' was given a new title – 'The Fuellable Grey Goose'.[33] *In the meantime, I heard that Irmgard Arnold's housekeeper dictated the running order to the dramaturgy department over the phone.*

[Eisler gives a pained laugh]

Perhaps I can make a statement at this point. There is an interesting little book by Houben, *Conversations with Heine*.[34] It keeps up a tradition probably started by Eckermann. Looking at the abundance of Brecht's Journal entries 'Conversations with Brecht' would be a literary sensation, in the most positive sense, a sensation because one could publish all those brilliant comments, thoughts and insights. I think that 'Conversations with Brecht', published in the right way, using what's there, is a task that could secure a man's place in literary history. You can't, of course, expect completeness with such things. It might turn out to be a thick book. Editorial comments would have to be kept to a minimum in order to hear Brecht's actual voice. (In this respect I'd suggest that you look at Houben's book – it's been published in the GDR, so you should be able to get hold of it.) To publish such a book, and the sooner the better, would be wonderfully enriching and something of enormous significance. It's impossible to overestimate the value it would have. Just think of the enormous influence – although, sadly, unfavourable – that Eckermann's conversations with Goethe have had on German literature; one still reads today about Goethe's meeting with Hegel, for example.

In those conversations with Goethe, you can find some of Hegel's ideas that don't appear anywhere else in his work. Take, for example, the famous statement he makes while dining with Goethe, that actually, as in dialectics, everything in the nature of mankind is based on the spirit of contradiction – dialectics, as it were, in biological terms, the striving of man towards contradiction. A very naïve point of view, but he was trying to make his dialectics palatable to the suspicious Goethe; and Goethe took it in with 'Yes' and 'No' and a lot of reservations. You should read this passage. But that apart, one shouldn't ridicule all of Eckermann's contributions. You can also find classical ideas of Goethe's, new ideas, in those conversations – Eckermann was a very honest man. I don't think that being compared with Eckermann poses any danger to a literary scholar like you. Eckermann, by the way, became very famous, something I'd wish for you too. 'Conversations with Brecht' would be a real achievement.

Yes, if you could unearth as much as Eckermann…

I guess it was easier for him, because Goethe and he always…Goethe made him his secretary for this very reason: he wanted to have his conversations preserved. Can I also remind you of Martin Luther's *Table Talks*.

I have to say a project like this could be crucially important – I can't overestimate its importance – and you could publish it together with Brecht's Journal entries. What would you say, for instance, if I suggested a large-scale project that required you to be sent to Los Angeles, as long as you could get a visa? Are you a member of the SED?

No.

Anyway. Do you have a GDR passport?

Yes.

You wouldn't get a visa if you wanted to see Feuchtwanger.

Yes, it's very unlikely that I'd get a visa.

Feuchtwanger has treasures – I mean with regard to memories. That's common knowledge. Memories from the early days. I want to draw your attention to Arnold Bronnen as well. Bronnen has thirty highly interesting letters from the young Brecht – I've seen them – which are not in your Brecht archive. They're handwritten; you should have a look at them.[35]

I talked to Bronnen. He's agreed to give us the letters.

To photograph them, yes.

He wants to publish them himself.

And so he should, I suggested that to him. But it's not only about publishing these letters. Bronnen, who's a writer himself, told me he was doubtful; he didn't want to ride on Brecht's coat tails. I talked him out of those reservations, said that we'd all be enthusiastic to see a little book telling us about this period of Brecht's life. He just didn't want to make capital out of it, as he put it. But he knows a lot about those very difficult years of 1922 and 1923 in Berlin, which none of us know much about.

I have already recorded similar conversations with Jacob Walcher and Günther Weisenborn.

Weisenborn probably isn't a mine of information.

He talks mainly about the collaboration on The Mother.

Yes, that's right. Working on *The Mother* that was Weisenborn, me – and who else was there?

Slatan Dudow.

Yes. Weisenborn didn't play a big role, because at the time he simply wasn't able to learn from Brecht's way of working.

He admits that openly.

He's a decent bloke. But that'll make him more colourful.

I think it would be really interesting if someone were to write or say: 'Although I made a contribution, I had no idea what Brecht was about'.

Weisenborn had no idea.

It was also only because of Brecht that I learnt something about Marxism.

Weisenborn didn't have a clue. He made the most ridiculous suggestions. Often we just all roared with laughter, especially at the speed with which he came out with these banal ideas, snapping them up at the same rate as a tit catching flies on the wing. But let's get back to Brecht's Journal.

In Brecht's Journal entry of 29 July 1942, he writes about you both attending a lecture on modern composition given by Arnold Schoenberg at UCLA...

That's a university in California.

...and his impression of Schoenberg was that he was very lively, with a polemical attitude. He admired his discourse about freeing music from dissonance. He also records in detail Schoenberg explaining that some of the brevity and emotional excesses of the early compositions by members of his school were attributable to the extremely demanding and undeveloped musical technique of these early works. Although Brecht admits that he didn't understand the parts of the lecture concerned with musical technique – and regretted that musical education these days is lacking, to the extent that one isn't even able to understand what one doesn't understand – he found that Schoenberg gave the impression of being completely clear. Afterwards, you both went to Schoenberg's house on Sunset Boulevard. Brecht observes the little children all clustered around Schoenberg whom he describes as 'a seventy-year-old, rather bird-like man who has great charm and is agreeably dry and sharp with it'. Brecht goes on to say that when you tried to persuade Schoenberg to complete two of his great unfinished works – one of them an opera – Schoenberg replied that his works wouldn't be performed anyway, as long as the wrong playing techniques dominate the American music scene and then goes on to demonstrate, in a comical way, the great efforts of a wind-player and a cellist. Brecht writes that Schoenberg didn't care for Shostakovich's Leningrad Symphony, which had been broadcast on American radio, because he thought it was too long, with twelve minutes of material stretched out to thirty-five.

Later Schoenberg told the story of how he bought good-quality equipment in the army – the uniform, shoes and especially a pair of fine leather gloves – and how the corporal was a spiteful piece of work who made them practise repeatedly 'going face down' in the mud. When someone who had seen Schoenberg taking off his gloves every time they did this asked him why, Schoenberg replied in a dry manner: 'My hands belong to the Kaiser, but the gloves are mine'.

Finally, Brecht recounts a nice little story of yours. When Schoenberg's son had an operation, you contributed $300 towards it. Schoenberg was reluctant to accept the money and offered to repay it in small instalments. As a joke, you told Schoenberg that you'd take a few lessons from him instead. Schoenberg's quick response was: 'If you still haven't learnt it, I can't teach you it'. Brecht writes that he liked Schoenberg very much because he thought Schoenberg was able to see himself in a historical context; when somebody mentioned to Schoenberg that another composer had completed Schubert's Unfinished Symphony *for a competition, Schoenberg said that he could have done it better but that he wouldn't have dared.*

Very nice. Well, that's a brilliant, exact description of our meeting with Schoenberg. All I can say is, that's just how it was.

In his Journal entry of 13 August 1942, Brecht recalls a discussion at Adorno's of Aldous Huxley's novel Brave New World. *As well as you and Adorno, Horkheimer, Pollock, Marcuse, Stern, Reichenbach and Steuermann were also there.*[36]

That's a strange work of Huxley's, whom Brecht – and, I too, by the way – met at Chaplin's. It is about a pessimist utopia, an accurate and most bizarre vision of decline. Utopias are usually projected dreams of what the world should look like, but in this book, it's the opposite. In a way, it's a depiction of the complete dehumanization of the world. Strangely enough, my friend Adorno and also the very astute Professor Horkheimer saw something progressive in it, while I argued against it – at least as far as I remember. Brecht must have been there too. But Steuermann, for example, wasn't invited to that peculiar debating society. It is one of the oddities of this Frankfurt Institute that they see all signs of disintegration as progressive from a semi-Marxist point of view. It can only be progressive if you're able to assess the bourgeoisie as being in decline and anticipate its further decline with satisfaction.

In the absence of a true polemic and a true battle against the bourgeoisie – theoretical as well as the practical – you can't observe the signs of decay and happily call them progressive. Nor can you use them as arguments against the attempts of bourgeois ideologists to dress up this decay as something else. Certainly, in this idiotic theory – which sees in capitalism the best of all worlds, some sort of capitalist *Candide* – you can call Huxley's utopia the dystopia or even a move towards the abyss. What you can't do is identify this move as progress. That is how I thought then, and how I still think about it today.

I think Brecht would certainly have agreed with me. What they're lacking, these 'Frankfurturists', as Brecht called them, is a genuine anti-bourgeois position. You can't be a Marxist without politics – that's one of the great pieces of wisdom that everybody should really bear in mind today. Even now when I read some of the Frankfurturists' pamphlets, they still suffer, as far as I can see, from the central dilemma: wanting to be cleverer than the bourgeois theorists but not wanting to fight against them. They're the privileged pupils of the downfall.

Can you tell me something about Reichenbach?

The physicist Reichenbach, Hermann Reichenbach?[37]

Yes, who often met with Brecht and, to the best of my knowledge, advised on the presentation of the scientific problems in Life of Galileo.

I met Hermann Reichenbach many times at Brecht's. He was actually, if I describe it correctly, a Neo-Mach, something like that – or you can call it the Vienna School. But unfortunately this gifted physicist (I loved his popular and informative little books on Einstein's relativity theory) subsequently became a philosopher and pursued philosophy in such an outrageous positivistic way, it was enough to make my stomach turn. Brecht, who detested metaphysics, found the way in which the most vulgar positivism was presented as philosophy refreshing, in that it could be used as a weapon against metaphysical methodology. Brecht, who had nothing of a positivist in him, liked to use certain scientific questions to support his point of view, especially in the Vienna Neo-Mach circle, whose magazines he very much enjoyed reading. And as Reichenbach taught at the University of Los Angeles, Brecht was very interested in him. It's a known fact that the scientific advice Brecht needed for *Galileo* he sought from Niels Bohr's assistant in Denmark.

He didn't ask Niels Bohr himself?

No, just his assistant. That wasn't a problem at all; Bohr is a big man with a big institute – one of the younger staff members was sufficient. It was about basic questions of physics and for that you don't need a modern atomic physicist.

21 August 1942: an evening with you, Morgenstern and Gina Kaus and a conversation about Skivers in the Great War.

'Skivers' are people, who through intelligence, audacity and cunning, avoided having to serve in the war.

Let me first say something about Morgenstern. His full name is Soma Morgenstern; he is a Doctor of Jurisprudence and, originally, when he was a young lawyer, he wrote theatre criticism in the *Frankfurter Zeitung*. He lived in Vienna and, both there and later during the emigration, had already started to write novels. They weren't at all bad and were mostly set in an eastern Jewish farmer milieu. There are farmers among the eastern Jews whom he contrasts in a very interesting way with emancipated Jewry. He's still writing today, by the way. He's very intellectual, and a great admirer of Brecht. Gina Kaus is a famous novelist.

So, famous anecdotes were told about how you could avoid military service – for which you had to have a lot of nerve – and that was very interesting to both Mrs Kaus and Morgenstern who, by the way, was a lieutenant in the k.u.k. army[38] in which I also served. I'm sure other people must have been there as well, like Gina Kaus' husband, a certain Doctor Frischauer, who also used to be an officer. There are brilliant stories about skivers. One of them…I don't know if you've ever heard this one; if you'd like, I could tell it to you.

With pleasure.

Well, it goes like this. The only thing I had to contribute was my fear because I didn't have the courage to avoid military service, but one of my friends, an artilleryman, a young man with socialist inclinations, didn't want to go back into battle after being wounded.

So when he was released from hospital and was due to report back for duty, he had an idea. He wrote a letter, a direct appeal, to the Kaiser. Well, it's not customary to write directly to the Kaiser; you have to go through official channels. When you are a lieutenant you can only write to your commanding officer: a plea to the Kaiser should go first to the battalion command, then to the regimental command, then on to the brigade, to the division, from the division to the army corps and, finally, from there to the chambers of the Apostolic Majesty of Austria. It's not as easy as you'd think. But my friend Karl – I don't want to divulge his surname – did it differently. He wrote directly to the cabinet chambers of the Kaiser – the salutation alone was outrageous. He wrote:

> Dear Kaiser! I've come back with honour from the front, wounded – I'm better now – and I think the war is just and that I have actually achieved the aims of the war already. But I'm also determined to continue fighting. What's more, I received two medals and am content. I only want to ask for one little privilege. Since I'm an especially good artilleryman, I should be permitted – by highest decree – to wear, while I'm on duty, a top-hat as well as my military cap. I sincerely hope that you, dear Kaiser, will grant me this wish. Your brave artilleryman, Karl'.

Because of this plea, the man was, with immediate effect, sent to the asylum; a man who does something so bizarre can't be a normal skiver. The idea with the top-hat was just too shrewd – even if you only know a tiny bit about the military then you know what a totally absurd proposal this is. And the whole letter oozed such patriotism. It was just a little request, so easy to grant because, militarily it wouldn't have caused anyone harm. So what if an artilleryman wore a top-hat while shooting at Italians. But it was enough to keep the man out of the war until the end…first for observation for a few weeks in the asylum and then he was released as mentally ill. He spent the last two years of the war in civilian clothes. This is an especially ingenious, heroic example of the art of skiving, and of luck at having escaped a hero's death. Not everybody had such shrewdness, intelligence, mental ability – and, most of all, character; you'd have to have an iron character to copy a thing like that. It belongs to the most famous heroic deeds of the Great War. Such things amused Brecht extraordinarily.[39]

I refer to the following entry in the Journal of 20 September 1942 on the subject of the Hollywood Elegies, *which Brecht wrote for you. He says that Winge, who was working in an underwear factory in downtown Los Angeles, visits him at least once a week and, on one occasion, reads some of the* Hollywood Elegies. *Winge says that, 'it's as if they had been written from Mars'. Brecht and Winge agreed that the sense of 'detachment' in the poems is not attributable to the writer but a quality of Hollywood: nearly everybody here possesses this quality. Houses in California don't become the property of their owners by being lived in, but by the exchange of a cheque, it seems. People don't so much live in them as 'have them to hand'; also, the houses become merely extensions of garages.*

In this gloomy, everlasting spring of Hollywood I said to Brecht, shortly after we met up again in America: 'This is the classic place in which to write elegies'. There are the Roman elegies by Goethe, which are one of my favourite works – Brecht admired them a lot as well. I said: 'We have to do something similar. There's a price to pay for living in Hollywood. You have to describe both sides of it'. Brecht promised to do it and brought me, I think, eight *Hollywood Elegies*, which are published by the way in the second volume of my *Songs and Cantatas*.[40] There really is an extraordinary detachment in those poems. Brecht describes magnificently how the houses are extensions to the garages and that one inhabits them rather than lives in them. Well, there's nothing more to say. I set the poems immediately and often performed them at my home to Brecht's and my other friends' delight. Even today, they still belong among my favourite poems by Brecht.[41]

On 3 October 1942, Brecht writes of your playing the Elegies *and some of the* Finnish Epigrams *for Winge and Herbert Marcuse. Brecht says that when you talk about these compositions (although not when you're working on them), you're either unable to free yourself completely from the conventional view that they are small, somewhat inconsequential, occasional pieces, like the jottings in someone's diary, or, that perhaps you're simply hoping that, by speaking in this modest manner, someone will contradict you by saying, for example, that the composer might think these important pieces are trifles, but not us! (Brecht calls this 'Bruckner's gesture of modesty'.) Brecht adds, however, that these pieces are also important as music that emphasizes the importance of the epigrams – the music compels people to read them and to study them in depth. Brecht says that: 'these are full-scale poems, the fact that they are laconic does not mean they contain any less than a long poem'.*

Had I really adopted 'Bruckner's gesture of modesty', I wouldn't today have any problem admitting it; it wouldn't discredit me. I also have my vanities and set the greatest store by them. But no, at that time, I really wrote a 'Hollywood Songbook', a title that I subsequently dropped. That means, every day I wrote at least one song – sometimes more – to texts either by Brecht or by Hölderlin (I set a lot of Hölderlin to music) or something from a text by Pascal, for example. I had a big folder and wrote on the cover: 'Hollywood Songbook' or 'Hollywood Diary' – I don't remember which – and said: 'That's just to pass the time, something I do alongside my actual work'. I wrote a variety of things while I was in Hollywood, especially orchestral pieces. So, I really didn't intend to sound too modest because I know how important such song cycles are in the history of music and what a significant role they can play.

Anyway, it so happened, that my then friend, Adorno, begged me to let him write the Foreword to the songs when they were eventually published. I didn't remind him of this when I saw him last in Frankfurt in order not to embarrass him; he wouldn't be seen in public with me, let alone associate his name with mine. Looking back, I have to say that it is a strange and inspiring work – especially the *Elegies*. It is astonishing how such an enormous subject can be encapsulated in four lines. Brecht has replicated this same clarity in other works. In a way he learnt from his conciseness. You'll find in there certain four-liners about drinking tea. Or look at the *Buckow Elegies*.

Or the War Primer *poems.*

Yes. This dreadful idyllic Hollywood landscape, probably the result of a land speculator's brainwave more than anything else, had nothing in itself to offer. If you turned off the water there for three days, the jackals would come back and so would the desert sands. The whole place is one huge, manufactured property swindle that has paid off in a big way. So, in such a strange, tainted idyll you had to express yourself concisely. Unfortunately, because of the sea climate, you also suffer badly from poor concentration.

Brecht complained about his health. Everything would be too tepid, too mild for him; there would be no difference in the seasons and everything in flower all the time would only make you want to throw up. In a nutshell, he felt bitter; he was completely embittered by this experience and that was also a reason why he used this taut and terse style of writing, as an antidote. 'No matter what, you can't let yourself go when everything is so balmy'.

I wanted to ask you about Wexley. On 2 November 1942, Brecht wrote that you had dinner at Wexley's and then brought him over to Brecht's.

John Wexley is, I think, a very brave and courageous man ... up to this point, as far as one can say from so far away. A dramatist, whose play *The Last Mile*, about a man sentenced to death, was a hit on Broadway when he was young. He couldn't repeat that success; a one-play-man. He was a bit narrow-minded as well, and ungenerous.

He worked with Brecht on the script for the Fritz Lang film *Hangmen Also Die* – the only film script Brecht wrote in Hollywood. I probably dragged Wexley there because Brecht needed someone – and he was forward-thinking and at least spoke good English. He also knew something about the workings of Broadway and was therefore just about suitable as a collaborator with Brecht. It didn't work out though. It has to be said at this point that Wexley behaved badly towards Brecht in the same shoddy way that the entire American intelligentsia behaved towards Brecht. It even came down to an arbitration decision by the Hollywood Writer's Association about the screen credits. It might sound grotesque but Wexley wanted to push himself into the foreground, and Brecht, for economic reasons ... if he was doing only that one film, he didn't want his name to appear in a subsidiary position. But above all, it would have been grossly unfair because the whole idea came from Brecht.[42] To cut a long story short, it came to this arbitration decision where Lang and I appeared as witnesses and spoke strongly against Wexley. It led to a colossal falling out, and also put an end to the relationship between the Eislers and Wexleys.

It took its toll on Wexley. From this point onwards, he went downhill, step by step, as you say. I don't know what he's doing today. His political viewpoint is decent, though. I saw him once in

Vienna in 1948. He was in love with a beautiful Viennese woman and was suffering like an animal. So he did get his punishment in the end.

I'd like to bring up a few more names. At Christmas and on New Year's Eve 1942, Brecht mentions evening get-togethers at his house: you and your wife, Reyher, Lion Feuchtwanger and his wife, with the Homolkas arriving later. And, again, an evening at the Kortners with you and your wife, Viertel, the Henreids, the Thörens and the Donaths.

Right. First Reyher. He's an American writer without a big name, but who's witty and clever, spoke German and had already met Brecht in Berlin during the Weimar Republic. I think his full name is Ferdinand Reyher. He tried to earn a crust as a novelist but to no avail. I think he was also a journalist – a very decent man, although I haven't heard from him in the past fifteen years. He was a devoted friend of Brecht's and always tried to write those famous film scripts with him. Nothing ever came of it. Nothing was ever sold to anyone. 'Nothing ever came of it', in Hollywood terms, means that you put it on the market but there isn't a buyer. It obviously wasn't written to become an end in itself! That's him.

Then there's Robert Thören, who died recently. He used to be an actor – smallish parts – under Reinhardt. He became a screenwriter during the emigration period and had quite some success. He knew who Brecht was, visited often, sat modestly at the feet of the master – and then went back to writing his trash in different film studios without ever trying to help Brecht. None of those people, with the exception of Reyher, would have put in a good word for Brecht; that would have been too complicated. It was a crazy fight for survival.

Homolka is the famous actor, Oskar Homolka, with whom we were very great friends and who, after our American scandal,[43] didn't even contact us once.

Didn't Brecht think later of giving him the role of Schweyk to play?

Yes. But Homolka, the very rich Homolka – by inheritance – broke off all relations with us after our appearance before the House Committee on Un-American Activities. Especially with

Brecht. Homolka used to be at my place two, three times a week and the rest of the time he was at Brecht's. But then – nothing. He's a master of the art of survival.

Berthold Viertel was a remarkable theatre director and a poet of great distinction. He was very hard done by in Hollywood – it was just awful.

Ludwig Donath, an actor from Berlin, was – in contrast to Fritz Kortner, for example – the only actor, among all the others, who had a year's contract with the Columbia Film Company where he played small roles, mostly SA-men. That was the period of anti-fascist movies. He also played Hitler in a small movie and was kept on as a character actor. I don't know what became of him.

Paul Henreid[44] is an Austrian actor who didn't have much success in Vienna. He was a very good looking man. He was called to London to play the role of Prince Albert in the hit movie *Queen Victoria* – he obviously looked like him and spoke English with a refined German accent. He later had a huge success on Broadway and was a star for a few years. He was the only one who made it in America. He used to work in the operetta chorus of a theatre in Vienna – supremely untalented – and was discovered in America as a big star. He received hundreds of letters a week from female fans and he also somehow presented himself as a Baron – 'von' Henreid. But that was just fine; in America they love those 'vons'. Unfortunately, we couldn't carry that off; we couldn't very well say that Brecht was a Baron, now could we? Prince Eisler? Impossible! But von Henreid succeeded. He had an elegant house – we had great dinners there, Brecht as well – in this desolate Hollywood. Sometimes we visited Henreid although Brecht and I had an agreement that we would never watch any of the films he was in and that when we were present, there wouldn't be any talk of art in general, cinematic art or the parts he played. And since he also had a very nice wife, our agreement was respected. You could eat very well at Henreid's, talk about politics and general matters, but not about cinematic art – especially not about Henreid's appearances – and it was generally accepted, as a matter of principle, that we would never watch his movies. In that respect he was a pleasant host and had a really charming way towards Brecht. He played the attractive, admiring Viennese Baron with a weakness for great art, and we let him play this role. On top of that, he was one of the few people who had Scotch whisky – although this didn't interest Brecht as much as me – because he was very rich. Whisky was scarce at that time in America, so to have a drink or two at Henreid's bar was an evening activity I often sought.

That leaves Feuchtwanger and Kortner.

They're old friends, Feuchtwanger and Kortner. They got along with each other too; that's what you did in those days: you got along with each other. Feuchtwanger regularly invited his acquaintances – I can't say that I was a friend of Feuchtwanger – so he invited his acquaintances. I knew him from my time in Berlin. Sometimes he read to us, which was unfortunate because, although I enjoy reading his novels, to hear them read aloud... well I just don't hear them. He didn't do it to Brecht. He simply never invited Brecht along to those readings, but I had to endure them often. And Fritz Kortner as well. There were no excuses. You just had to keep quiet. He read very well, by the way.

Kortner was in a really wretched situation. He did some casual work as a screenwriter and played tiny little roles. It was a time of deepest humiliation for him. But he was an intelligent man, and he entertained Brecht and me on those dismal Hollywood evenings by telling us enthusiastically about the humiliations he had to go through – and believe me, they were enormous. It's astonishing how much you can humiliate someone. For example – this is unforgettable and made a deep impression on Brecht (you might even find it in his Journal) – Kortner, who was always waiting to be cast in something (he had to earn some money to pay the rent; it was always a matter of life and death) finds himself in the following situation. A film agent comes to him and says: 'Well Fritz', – in America you're on first name terms immediately – 'here is the chance!' (I say it in German although it all sounds much better in English.) 'Fritz, the chance of your life has come. Zanuck...' – that's the powerful film mogul of Twentieth Century Fox, one of the big film studios – '... needs someone. I think you're exactly the type. Right, into the car at once! The man is already waiting for you. This time you'll make it big'.

So Kortner accompanies him to the film studio. First they have to wait for an hour in the outer office. Then – and Kortner tells this incomparably – the door opens. He's led into the room and sees only the soles of Zanuck's shoes; he has his feet on the desk. As soon as Zanuck sees Kortner, he just says, 'No!' Finished! Incredible. Kortner told us this and other such stories in the evenings – the abominable treatment doled out to the great star Kortner! Actually, Kortner was rehabilitated in an incredible way when he became what you might call Munich's art dictator. That amused Brecht extraordinarily too. We all experienced humiliation and had a hard time of it, Brecht included, but Kortner's experiences were also quite funny.

In the way he described them?

Yes, in his description. He told those stories wonderfully. When Kortner is next in Berlin, I'm sure he'd like to talk to you about Brecht. He was friends with Brecht; they made plans together. Kortner always wanted to play Galileo. So when Charles Laughton appeared, some kind of estrangement took place and Kortner became jealous and so on. But he always behaved impeccably towards Brecht. Kortner was actually the one who organized the money for Brecht to flee Finland; he really played a great part in bringing Brecht to safety. I'd like to make that clear here.

Did they have any contact later?

Yes. When Kortner came to West Berlin, he and Brecht met. These two great men met at some pub close by the train station Zoo, just the two of them. Brecht always wanted Kortner to play at the Berliner Ensemble. It was the same with Elisabeth Bergner who was often there. But, alas, they didn't want to.

I remember a nice little anecdote. Kortner calls up Brecht. Somebody supposedly has found out that Hitler was a second Napoleon. He, Kortner, became angry and thought about it. He knew now what group to put Hitler in. He's a second Mussolini.[45]

Very good.

Could you tell me more about the collaboration between Brecht and Feuchtwanger?

Yes, but I was never there. I have to say that Bert – and he must have had his reasons – never invited me to those meetings. I was busy with my own work anyway, but he never took me along. I was fine with this. Brecht often came to me with the scenes from *Simone*[46] beforehand and argued over a few small points with me – nothing significant. In Brecht's notes you'll find the few small suggestions I was able to make. But he really did this with Feuchtwanger. I only know that Feuchtwanger complained bitterly – to me! – about Brecht's obstinacy with regard to his epic theories. Brecht was totally relentless in advocating – with, as Feuchtwanger put it, brazen persistence – his theatre theories, which Feuchtwanger didn't share at all. I only remember Feuchtwanger triumphantly telling me that when Brecht started again with his epic theatre, he said: 'Well, with those theories he can kiss my arse!' But Brecht wasn't at all concerned and in the end, the play was written in the way Brecht wanted it. In this respect, Feuchtwanger and Brecht had very different approaches; their collaboration *was* an argumentative one. Feuchtwanger actually wanted to create a realistic and naturalistic play and Brecht didn't. Feuchtwanger himself wrote about this, but I never was part of it.

Earlier you said something about the significance Feuchtwanger had for the young Brecht.

I only know this: Feuchtwanger discovered this young man from Augsburg. The title of Brecht's first play, *Drums in the Night* was provided by Feuchtwanger. Brecht originally called it 'Spartacus', but I can't say more about it because, at that time, I was a student in Vienna. But it must have been a very interesting period. Arnold Bronnen will be able to say something about this. When Bronnen was young, he treated Brecht very well; Brecht was always telling me about this – Bronnen supported him. When Brecht was in hospital with kidney stones, Bronnen was the only one who visited him and brought him the things that he needed. Brecht talked with great fondness about his friendship with Bronnen.

May I come back to The Vision of Simone Machard? *Brecht noted on 28 May 1943, that – even though you had written a wonderful piece of music for the angel's first appeal – you criticized the character of Simone for being too much of a 'natural patriot'. Brecht says that you want to see the role of the book expanded. As Simone is the victim of a patriotic education, she should only do those duties that are required of her. Dutifully she saves France (the property of the possessors) by defending it against the Germans but then fails to save it (again the property of the possessors) by handing it over to them. According to you, the ending should be changed and all mention of the free French eliminated. Simone is then demoted, has to give back her book and her apron and join those with the big heads. Her friends are not allowed to speak up, and so have lost the battle.*

I would suggest that your influence on Brecht regarding this play can't have been as small as you made it out to be earlier. You're presenting yourself too modestly.

It's not a question of whether I think Brecht is a genius, but a question of my friendship with him. You know, it's really easy, if you're not completely daft, to suggest things to a man of significance like Brecht; I don't see anything special in that. Any sensible person could have made similar suggestions, as long as they were Marxists' suggestions; patriotism isn't hereditary. Brecht acknowledged my objections straightaway; he didn't really need me to point them out. But when you're working, you often lose sight of things and somebody from outside with a fresh mind is able to say, 'What's going on? How can the child be so patriotic?' I also understood that there had to be brutality in the play. Brecht, this great humanist, is acutely sensitive. He immediately understood that I found the way in which this young girl gets mixed up in strange conflicts and eventually caves in tremendously brutal. I said: 'She's also a victim of patriotic education'. As you know, Simone is modelled on Jeanne d'Arc and I saw her as a victim.

It must be fascinating for a dialectician. The thought: 'What does a patriotic education do to a poor child?' has to be an integral part of the play as well. One effect is that it makes a child a victim. This was a different side of the same coin and Brecht grasped it. Nevertheless, in my opinion, the issue doesn't surface in the play. When I recall all this now – it's partly Feuchtwanger's fault, don't you think? – this victimization doesn't come out so well. Maybe it could be emphasized through a careful production. I've only seen it once in Frankfurt and then it wasn't made clear. It seems too heroic to me – do you know what I mean? The play is too heroic for me.

Simone Machard is one of the plays that Brecht never directed himself. All this would probably have come out and been developed during a production.

Yes, particularly this problem. He probably left it as it was because he didn't want to argue constantly with Feuchtwanger.

I know Brecht. He would have put it right later because, as you could see, he immediately grasped what I meant – my objection was self-evident. When you see a fourteen-year-old girl on stage, she has also to be a victim. Patriots ought to be a little bit older. I mean it's simply abominable what this girl has to go through. My objection, which even people who aren't Marxists would share, is a simple human response. That's the other side of the coin, and under Brecht's direction, it would certainly have surfaced.[47]

Brecht let the girl become younger and younger.

Yes, the girl is in a horrible situation, and on top of this is the way in which she is so atrociously exploited in the tavern. This delicate little thing has to carry heavy washing baskets, or the vendor's tray loaded with all sorts. She already works – and Brecht did this on purpose – like a grown-up; she has to for the family's sake. So that they don't starve, she becomes an object of exploitation; according to modern law child labour is illegal and should be non-existent. But in the countryside, where the law isn't enforced, or where officials turn a blind eye, child labour is still commonplace. Today, under capitalism, children still work on farms or in other isolated, undeveloped areas, even though every capitalist law book will tell you child labour has been abolished. The battles to abolish child labour were long but they needed to be fought. What hasn't been abolished yet is the patriotic education of children – a false patriotic education because it's a bourgeois patriotic education – which turns them into objects of political exploitation. In the same way that the young girl has to flog her goods, which are far too heavy for her, to the refugees, and has to carry heavy washing baskets, she also has to carry the heavy burden of patriotism. This is an atrociously barbaric process and one you can't glorify. If you were to omit the burden of patriotism then the play would be merely heroic. And this is the point at which today's all-too-popular dialectic comes into existence. It's crystal clear what's meant by it. Do I take it you've only seen the Berlin production?

Yes. I think your objections would have been confirmed.

I thought Buckwitz' direction was splendid and the performance was magnificent. But it was a hero's glorification for me and that's wrong. I don't need to tell you how far that contradicts Brecht's whole style; that's also something I learned from Brecht. You see, I'm applying everything I learned from Brecht, to whom I owe all I know about theatre. I'd like to add here that I'm only applying what he taught me.

Please tell me something about Brecht's understanding of music. Did he prefer a certain type of music? For example, I read on 8 June 1943 that he had listened to the final act of Don Giovanni *on the radio and thought it unsurpassable, and was astonished that it had been created so early.*

Brecht never went to concerts because you weren't allowed to smoke there, and besides, he had a lot on – although I have to admit he did make exceptions. If a concert piece by one of his friends was performed, he suddenly appeared – I never sent him an invitation – and listened to it. He did this because, as I said, he possessed a Chinese politeness. His taste in music was excellent – with one weakness. You have to understand that Brecht saw all the arts, equal as they all are, from the viewpoint of a playwright, a dramatist. Art only existed for him in terms of its usefulness; this is what he was interested in. He found the music of Johann Sebastian Bach useful and he also looked for this quality in music beyond the context of the theatre. Furthermore, he admired Mozart very much. He liked certain Turkish, Chinese and Algerian music; flamenco, as in folk music; or the ancient and stylistically formal music of ancient China. I once played him a record – 'The Virgin on the Seven Stars', or was it 'Seven Virgins on One Star'? – which thrilled him because of the way in which the texts were recited. And he admired Spanish flamenco.

He never knew what to make of Beethoven. I wrote something about this in the commemorative issue of the literary journal *Sinn und Form*.[48] He couldn't come to terms with it. Brahms – out of the question; also Strauss – quite impossible. Schoenberg he found too melodious; that's not just a frivolous, witty remark – no, that music made him hot and bothered. He often said: 'it's a kind of broken Lehár', or 'it's like Lehár' – which it really isn't at all. You have to understand that Brecht protected himself in a way by getting involved with music only insofar as it was useful to him.

Indeed, he also read for the most part only what he could use. As he got older, Brecht, who was a highly educated, brilliantly educated man (his education in some areas was astonishingly deep),

read only those things that he could use, either for information or
as a stimulus to thought. He read certain academic books for this
purpose alone. Brecht wasn't an 'art for art's sake' reader; even
crime novels, which he read with touching dedication, interested
him like a game of chess – how do you weave together the threads
of a story? Brecht studied crime novels in order to answer this
question, and he always complained loudly to me if he found out,
in the middle of a book, that he had already read it three times and
had just forgotten it. He'd put it aside. It was an eternal battle:
'Aren't there any new crime novels?' was Brecht's almost daily cry
and all his friends were continually on the lookout.

Apart from that, he also read very difficult things. He was very
interested in physics and had a strong mathematical ability even
though he didn't have any formal training in mathematics – it was
the same in music. Brecht obviously never showed an interest in
mathematics while he was at high school. Unlike me who should
have become a mathematician, according to my mathematics
teacher, although I don't understand it anymore; I've forgotten
everything I knew. But Brecht had this odd, quite astonishing talent
for mathematics. But I couldn't pin down what this talent was. We
must ask Professor Reichenbach, who is a mathematician, about
the origin of this ability that Brecht had for abstract thought, and
which comes from mathematics. 'Out-mathematicising a topic', is
the expression Brecht used, in other words selecting a topic, cutting
it up in into different sections and assessing what it is that connects
them all.

At that time, twenty years ago, Brecht must have seemed like
a madman to a conventional literary scholar or run-of-the-mill
dramatist – either a madman, coining phrases like that, or a
completely hopeless fantasist! But the producers of conventional
literature are defeated and Brecht triumphs. And I think that is
exactly as it should be. Even someone like Ernst Toller, who certainly
admired Brecht, didn't have a clue; in fact he never understood what
Brecht was after. Even today I believe Feuchtwanger still doesn't
get it, although he is a very intelligent man – and there are other
people who still don't understand. Kurt Weill never even came close,
although he instinctively knew that what Brecht produced was very
effective because he's a highly talented man. Weill only saw the
effects of originality. The actual process he didn't comprehend.

It's still like this in the theatre.

Yes, you're right it is. But tell me, why is it that everything by Brecht is still so original? Why does everything sound so fresh? Why doesn't it sound hollow like the sounds you hear so often, especially in plays by progressive writers? Like, for example, the very commendable Friedrich Wolf or others who achieved important things – they're not to be underestimated. But, unlike them, Brecht is still so fresh, original and important – he's simply unique.

Someone seeing a Brecht play for the first time is particularly gripped by its originality and, were he to learn how this originality comes about – that is through the most rigorous thought, the most thorough and relentless analysis of a situation or the behaviour of a person in certain circumstances – he would be astonished, because it is originality that is the result of rigorous thought. Strangely enough, originality only happens when it's made concrete. That wasn't a problem for Brecht. He'd say: 'You know, once we've got the framework, the rest is nothing; I'll do it in no time'. For months, he was interested only in the construction of a play; the production, which today dazzles people so much, he saw as by-product, as an extra.[49] His unmistakable instinct for German phrases, for the German language, was innate and he used it so freely that he was never aware of what virtuoso work it was. But having the ability to use the German language to produce real images can't be separated from his ability to analyse a situation. The reverse is also true: only such an uncompromising view of human behaviour leads to such original linguistic creations.

It's an astonishing case. I've thought about it long and hard and I think it comes out of the fact that Brecht skips over a whole period of German literature – the whole so-called High German period, which led to a language of officialdom or, actually, what you call the classics. Brecht doesn't follow on from Lessing or Goethe but from Luther; he skips the classic period. I told him that a long time ago, and he agrees. It's a strange step back. And just as Luther himself takes as his starting point the vernacular ('to watch the people's mouth' is one of his most famous remarks), so Brecht, too, takes the true people's language as his own. High German attained a certain cultural status as a result of Goethe's achievement – but also a certain smoothness. It's no coincidence that, from the linguistic point of view, literature – with the exception of Heine and his political writings – deteriorated after Goethe's death. Goethe's influence on German literature was lost. Goethe was unsurpassed as a linguistic virtuoso, but Brecht never entered this classical virtuoso world at all. Brecht's relationship to the classics was more or less the same as his relationship to Thomas Mann – he always called them 'the Goethinger' and 'the Schillinger', changing their names into the Bavarian dialect by putting an -inger at the end. Although he admired Goethe's linguistic virtuosity, it just didn't do anything for him.

That a fairly young man can proceed in this way with such power and can be driven by such tremendous poetic genius, is absolutely astonishing; it's one of the few such cases in literature. Brecht was stimulated, though, by Kipling, by the Chinese, by Grete Reiner's (I think that was her name) translation from the Czech of Schweyk.[50] You'll find that Mother Courage has echoes of Schweyk, absorbed it from the translation of Schweyk, which was written in Prague-German. These inspirations are so inimitably original – it really is astonishing, quite astonishing. Someone should write about it – maybe Walter Benjamin already has, we should have a look – but that 'someone' should not be a composer who would obviously have very limited knowledge of such things. No, it would have to be a really talented literary expert. If Hans Mayer – he's a very intelligent man – wasn't always writing about other things, he'd be the best person. Alas, he's forever doing something else (I don't know what) but he could certainly do it.

To the reception of the classics I can contribute an anecdote. It's well known that Therese Giehse directed Kleist's The Broken Jar for the Berliner Ensemble and Brecht attended the final rehearsals. He made a few changes and afterwards we called the play 'Die Zerbrechte Giehs-Kanne' [The By-Brecht-Broken Watering Can].[51] Brecht thought highly of Kleist, but Giehse adored him. She whispered continuously into Brecht's ear while he was sitting beside her, 'Isn't this wonderful?' – 'Yes, yes' said Brecht, 'This verse is brilliant'.

Well, if you didn't see Brecht during the rehearsals for Urfaust, you haven't seen anything – how the infuriated Brecht cut those parts of Goethe's text that he thought were rubbish! Really, only someone like Brecht could get away with that. Don't try it yourself.

I continue with the Journal. On 9 June 1943, Brecht reports that he had just finished the first act of Schweyk in the Second World War and that you, Kortner and Viertel spent the evening with him. Viertel told a story about a film director who, having complained about something, was persuaded by the Studio to go off and get some food. Coming back from the restaurant, he found that he'd been replaced by another director and even had trouble recovering his hat. Kortner then told the story of how a friendly producer had advised him that, in the Studio, it's best not to describe someone as 'brilliant', but as 'a swell guy, easy to work with'. Finally, Brecht mentions your beautiful settings of 'One Stormy Night', 'German Miserere' and 'March of the Sheep'.

They weren't originally written for *Schweyk*. Brecht often took something that existed already and put it into his plays. He had already written 'March of the Sheep' in Paris. 'One Stormy Night' was written about one of Stalin's sayings. 'German Miserere' and 'Ballad of the Soldier's Wife' were also written earlier[52] and then included in *Schweyk*. That he composed these poems in such dark times, even before the battle of Stalingrad was over, is an indication of Brecht's great fortitude. Originally, Weill was supposed to write the music – he was commissioned to do it – but after a lot of trouble, poor Bert received just 500 dollars, only for Weill to turn it down. It didn't suit Broadway.

Do you know anything about the poem 'Moldau Song'? There's only a title in Brecht's manuscript. We haven't yet found the text. [53]

I know it. It goes like this:

The stones of the Moldau are stirring and shifting
In Prague lie three emperors turning to clay.
The great shall not stay great, the darkness is lifting.
The night has twelve hours, but at last comes the day.

That's the song. The stage direction says: 'All sing it', although first of all it is sung alone by the landlady after the Gestapo have smashed up the whole tavern. It's a particularly beautiful poem.

I remember reading somewhere in Brecht's notes that he was unable to write it.[54]

That was probably before he had it all together. It's a magnificent poem, one of Brecht's most beautiful ballads.

It seems you're the only one who's had the text.

Yes. With Brecht's agreement I repeated these four lines. Then comes the middle part: 'The times are changing, the bloody ones' etc., and then it's repeated once more: 'On the bed of the Moldau'. I made an A-B-A out of it, which Brecht agreed to, but I only set it to music when I was back in Berlin, at his request. I was able to play him all the *Schweyk* music before he died. Isot Kilian was there as well – you can ask her about it too. Brecht enjoyed it very much.

Do you remember the evening when you came to visit Brecht and he told you that the first act of Schweyk *was finished? Did he read the play out loud to you?*

He gave it to me to read. I only remember that I queried some of the things that Bullinger says. I asked Brecht to soften Bullinger's language when he's interrogating Schweyk – there were words like 'bullshit' and so on appearing far too often – not that Brecht had to clean it all up, but it was borderline. Otherwise I didn't have anything else to say.

Conversation 3
5 May 1958

Brecht on Arnold Schoenberg – Gestic Music – *The Caucasian Chalk Circle* – Döblin's 65th Birthday Party

May I again read you this note from Brecht's Journal on 29 July 1942. He gives an account of a visit, with you, first to a lecture by Schoenberg and then to Schoenberg's family home.[55]

I remember the lecture very clearly – it was really marvellous. Schoenberg, a composer regarded by the public, the musical public, as a complete anarchist, impressed Brecht with his clarity and logic. A rigorous logic and clarity of thought that astonished Thomas Mann and made a profound impression on him too.[56]

As you know, when discussing music the term 'madness' is often used. Brecht was amazed that you could meet such an outstanding man who was not only capable of analysing his own work with such precision but who, on top of that, could write such extraordinarily original music. I won't talk about Schoenberg's lecture (it's published, by the way, in Schoenberg's philosophical and theoretical works, I think by Schirmer in New York).[57] You should read it so that you have a better understanding of Brecht's reaction to it. Schoenberg made an enormous impression on Brecht. I'm not sure if that comes through in Brecht's Journal.

I just want to set the record straight, my dear Doctor Bunge. Before I took Brecht to Schoenberg, I said to him:

> My dear friend, I'm about to introduce you to Schoenberg. He's a very strange man. He's a genius. He'll talk a lot of nonsense, and you might feel the urge to be rude to him – I know you. He'll spout the greatest nonsense about politics, as only a petit

bourgeois can. But because you're a dialectician, you'll understand that this doesn't invalidate his enormous musical achievements.

I told him: 'If you lose control of yourself and are rude to Schoenberg, then I have to say, in all friendship, I'll immediately break off all relations with you – you are not allowed to behave like that'. (I laid it on a bit to rein Brecht in.)

So then we won't be friends any more. Schoenberg is my old, sick teacher – very sick indeed – and I won't have a single rude word from you. If you can't stick to this, you'd better not come. If you want to get to know him, I'll take you – but there's not to be so much as a single vicious sentence!

I said all this because Brecht could often be astonishingly vicious – to blockheads! It wasn't hard for Brecht to recognize, of course, that this bird-like old man was not a blockhead but a petit bourgeois genius.

Helene Weigel, my old friend Helli, was also there during this warning talk. As I've just described, I really spoke to him sharply and Brecht accepted it with a certain satisfaction and respect, as in 'Eisler defends his teacher so well before I've even met him that I can't help but be polite now'. I have to say that Brecht stuck to the agreement. There was no rough or – and I'll deliberately use a 'high society' expression – discourteous word. Brecht listened to Schoenberg with the greatest respect and there was no trouble: quite the opposite. Schoenberg, who had no idea who Brecht was, observed this strange-looking man with some interest. (Brecht looks like a cross between Ignatius Loyola and a Roman Consul in Bavaria, don't you think?)

Anyway, back to the story. Schoenberg's house, which wasn't on Sunset Boulevard as Brecht says, but in Brentwood (I'm just being pedantic), was absolute pandemonium. It was a private hell. It was also a twelve-tone hell in domestic terms. Of course, if a seventy-year-old man has an unbearable six-year-old son ... No, he was a very sweet boy, and I'm not just saying that, he really was an especially nice boy ... This mixture of a disorganized private life with small children ... His oldest daughter was forty-four, his youngest son six ... So this twelve-tone family ... For example, the children of the forty-four-year-old daughter had to address the little man, the six-year old, as 'uncle' – it was just simply hell. And Brecht could see that too.

Well, Brecht was immensely impressed by Schoenberg's astuteness. I mention in the commemorative issue of *Sinn und Form* how I encouraged Brecht to write a cantata in honour of Schoenberg's, I think, seventy-second birthday which I set to music. I hope I can find the sketches for it, by which I mean that I hope my dear friend, Professor Notowicz, will find them. The cantata is called: 'Ich habe von einem Esel gelernt' [I Have Learned From A Donkey][58] – you should read the text. I met with Mrs Schoenberg in August in Salzburg in Austria. She couldn't remember it but I'm convinced that if she looks hard enough, this unpublished poem by Brecht could be found. Schoenberg left a huge amount of unpublished work.[59]

Could you please help me back on track? There was the lecture at the university; Brecht's behaviour at Schoenberg's house (I think it was the first or the second time for him at his house, and I brought him there trembling because I didn't want my teacher to be insulted); and then there was the discussion in which I asked Schoenberg to ... You know with how much respect I undertake certain things – I always encouraged Brecht, too, to finish projects – and much good it did me. For example, there was a play about the man who was a great furnace builder, the hero of labour, Hans Garbe. And when Brecht told me, just before he died, of his plans for a play about Einstein, I urged him to write that too. I did the same – I ought to put this down on paper one day – when he told me of a third project about Mother Germania who breastfeeds her sons, the wolf cubs. Helli Weigel was also there when we discussed that; however, I don't think that there are even any notes. But now I've completely lost my thread. Let's get back to where we were.

You wanted to talk about how you encouraged Schoenberg to finish his opera Moses and Aaron.

Well, the opera was never completed. But what do the admonitions of a pupil mean to the master! *Moses und Aaron* (with a dreadful libretto that Schoenberg wrote himself) is at least performed as a fragment. It was a huge success and made an enormous impression on Brecht. But the second work, *Jacob's Ladder*,[60] wasn't even performed as a fragment, so at least the opera I urged him to finish has become one of the most magnificent fragments of modern musical literature. Talking about it once again moves me very much. You know, I'm not a young man any more, and I do get emotional sometimes. Remind me, what else does the Journal say?

The anecdote about Schoenberg's gloves.

Now, in this instance, I can add something about Schoenberg in the military. This isn't exclusive to the Brecht-Archive as I've already told my friend Notowicz about it. Schoenberg in the military was a very odd fish. In 1915, he was conscripted to a very famous Viennese house regiment, the 'Infanterieregiment Hoch- und Deutschmeister No. 4'. The officers knew that he was, in some way, a very famous musician but that he was also regarded as mad, and was generally despised by the music critics. So the Commanding Officer called for him (do you know what k.u.k. commanding officer were? – they were gods whom we hardly ever saw!) and said to him: 'Tell me, soldier, are you *the* Schoenberg?' to which Schoenberg replied, 'Well yes, sir – certainly sir'. (How on earth did this little Commanding Officer know…?) – 'Nobody wanted to be Schoenberg, but it had to be someone, so I offered myself' – that's classic Schoenberg, and also gives a Marxist great pleasure. May I add that Schoenberg composed a military march for this regiment that was never performed because the Bandmaster rejected it as being too dissonant. His estate will have it. So there!

And in return, what kind of impression did Brecht make on Schoenberg?

Schoenberg said to me: 'I know you wrote this play *The Measures Taken*, with him in Berlin during the Weimar Republic but I've never listened to it. My pupils said it wouldn't be worth it – although none of them was there for the performance – it wouldn't be interesting enough and not worth listening to'. Whereupon Schoenberg told me he made a huge scene with one of his pupils, one of the younger ones, and said: 'That really is the limit: you don't want to listen to the work of one of my best pupils?' So the students, thinking they'd flatter Schoenberg by telling him that they didn't listen to my work anymore, got into huge trouble with him instead.

Schoenberg had no idea about Brecht, so I just told him Brecht would be the greatest poet of the past fifty years. 'Well' Schoenberg said, 'let's hope so'.

*In connection with that, I'd like to refer to a passage from the
Journal from the end of October 1944 when Brecht, you and your
wife, and Dessau all had dinner at Schoenberg's. Brecht describes
Schoenberg as surprisingly lively, and his figure Gandhi-like, because
of the blue Californian silk jacket he is wearing. He calls him
'a mixture of genius and craziness'. Schoenberg complains about
the shortness of copyright for intellectual works. (He says that
when his son is forty-five he won't receive any more royalties and he
makes it sound like a monstrous injustice.) And then, half teasingly
half not, he says that he sometimes finds that his own works sound
awful; of course he meant in contrast to other composers (but not
all that many of course). Schoenberg admits that he sometimes finds
it hard to understand his own compositions and has to study them
laboriously. Brecht partially sympathizes with Schoenberg when
the latter complains that music lacks purely musical conceptual
material. Schoenberg defines form as 'the repose between two forces
acting on one another (seemingly a field concept)'.*

Marvellous! Schoenberg's last sentence is simply genius, as is
nearly everything that this man has said. In fact, it's astonishing
that a musician, who was a petit bourgeois politically, comes up
with such refined thought originating solely with reference to his
own sphere.

Was there anything else in this Journal note? Is there anything
else in this passage that you want me to talk about?

Perhaps the shortness of copyright?

Yes, that's something I find very grotesque. I remember that I often
walked with Schoenberg in his garden in Brentwood, California,
where he explained to me that he had finally to accept – this was in
the depths of the war and Schoenberg had been forgotten then – that
there was an international conspiracy of autograph-collectors who
bribe maidservants to seek employment in the houses of the greatest
thinkers of our time so that they could steal their manuscripts. He
insisted that it would be an international ring like, for example, an
opium ring or girl trafficking. I looked at Schoenberg – because of
the isolation he really was on the verge of paranoia. And I thought
to myself: wouldn't it be nice if we had indeed reached the point
where a criminal ring had been formed to trick their way into
stealing Schoenberg's manuscripts. His manuscripts had no value

whatsoever at the time; thank God they do have value now! – because since then, after all, Schoenberg has been rehabilitated. But these talks in the garden about the lengths to which malicious criminals would go to steal Schoenberg's manuscript of the Piano Pieces op. 19[61] were extraordinary.

By the way, I know from a private conversation that Schoenberg was actually shocked at first by his own music. You may know, perhaps, that Schoenberg suffered a deadly heart attack in 1946 or 1947.[62] So, I have to say – he was dead. But through an injection into his heart, he was brought back to life and with oxygen and very good care he lived another six years. He was actually dead for fifteen minutes but, as you know, there are these famous injections directly into the heart. The first piece he wrote after convalescence was a string trio, which I regard as one of the most beautiful compositions he ever wrote – and not just me, so does the whole world of music. When Schoenberg showed me the manuscript, I said: 'But Mr Schoenberg, that's an absolutely magnificent composition'. He replied: 'You know, I was so weak, I don't know how I wrote it. I just put something together'. But then he showed me how every chord represents an injection.

Well, that has nothing to do with Brecht. Let's get back to Brecht. Don't ask me so much about Schoenberg, otherwise I'll forget all about my cherished old friend Brecht. Ask me more about Brecht.

I read Brecht's note about Schoenberg to you once before. All you said then was: 'Very good, that's correct!'

Well then, you can see how much you inspire me.

I'll continue. Brecht mentions on 25 June 1943 that you wrote two magnificent cycles for the Hollywood Songbook containing poems by Anacreon and Hölderlin.[63] Brecht seems to like them, because he thinks dramatic choruses have become possible since the pieces are now entirely gestic.

That's a remark by Brecht that of course honours me greatly; I hope he's right. But I can't possibly say any more about it.

In that case, shall we repeat it another time, Professor?

Oh well, maybe I can say something then. Brecht was surprised that, in this difficult time of our lives, I was setting his poems to music and working on my orchestral works and, well... well suddenly, I astonish him with settings of Anacreon. Brecht would never have thought of Anacreon, let alone Hölderlin; the fact that I suddenly chose Anacreon really baffled him. Brecht is a very generous man. He would, of course, have preferred me to set his poems, but, because he was magnanimous, he was astounded that, in 1943, in the middle of the turmoil of this awful war, I withdrew for a few days and set Anacreon to music. Today, I'm also surprised that I did it – I have no idea what made me do it – and I read through the old manuscripts with a certain pleasure.

It's well known that Anacreon is a poet who describes the pleasures of everyday life although, funnily enough, Eduard Mörike's excellent translations of the Anacreon poems I chose have nothing in common with this definition. I also rewrote parts of the poems – that was the greatest fun for Brecht. He also praised me, and I say this with the greatest satisfaction, for taking certain Hölderlin poems and (to quote Brecht) 'freeing' them of 'plaster'. I had 'de-plastered' Hölderlin, by which I mean that I was always only setting fragments from Hölderlin poems (I have to say I'm quite astonished that it worked at all). Brecht's praise makes me enormously happy. It also shows his objectivity because he always wanted his own works to be set to music. 'Music preserves my verses like a fly in a piece of amber', he said – a beautiful sentence! – 'For that reason, I want my poems to be set not only by you, but by as many other composers as possible'. It's a classical tradition; you know that Goethe's poems have been set by hundreds of composers and it's the same with Heine and others. And that is absolutely as it should be.

Brecht saw it as my individual achievement that, during the world war, suddenly this Anacreon appeared. But, the way I interpreted Anacreon (probably to every Greek-professor's horror) amounts to a malicious desecration – that's all I can say. It just occurs to me – about fifteen or twenty years later – what an incredible thing it is for political émigrés to set Anacreon. You should look at the second, fourth and fifth volumes, also in the first volume, of my collected works to see what I was composing at that time. These are some of the most bitter songs I have ever written – adapted from 'the effusive aesthete',[64] as he is known.

I'd like to refer back to Brecht's statement about the fact that dramatic choruses have become possible since the pieces are now entirely gestic.

Brecht's theory about gestic music goes back to his youth. 'The gestus' is one of Brecht's brilliant discoveries. He discovered it in the same way as Einstein, for example, discovered his famous formula. It already existed in great literature from Homer to Shakespeare; where literature is great, its language is gestic. Where you have great music, by Bach, for example, it's gestic. What Brecht means by this is simply that the music also brings into being the attitude of the singers and the audience – 'the gestus' is the term this is known by. And these poems – you'd have to analyse them now – bring out the concept of gestus in music (a concept that I heard Brecht talk about for the first time in 1924[65]) especially vividly. He wouldn't otherwise have described them in this way since he was a very sharp critic, including of my own works.

In a conversation like this, I can't give a more adequate explanation of the term 'the gestus in music'. It needs practical demonstration. For example, at his request, I repeatedly played Brecht the Evangelist's recitative from the St John Passion. [Eisler sings] 'Jesus went with his disciples over the brook Cedron, where there was a garden in which Jesus and his disciples walked'. This is where Bach quotes from the Bible. By the way, the tenor is pitched so high [Eisler imitates] that expression, and consequently bombast and a super-abundance of feeling, is impossible. It can only be declaimed – the text is reported. And because of that, the Evangelist's gesture is also communicated.

[Eisler sings] 'Jesus went with his disciples over the brook Cedron'. The locality of the brook is identified exactly; Brecht thought that was a perfect example of gestic music – and so it is. You can find other similar examples in Monteverdi or in the oldest church music.

I should remind people, if anyone is interested in this topic (although I think I'm speaking here to listeners a hundred or two hundred and fifty years hence), to read the chapter on music in Hegel's *Aesthetics* in which he discusses the terms 'objectivity' and 'subjectivity' in music and explains the differences between them. So: 'Crucifixus est' in certain masses is composed objectively because the crucifixion is performed as a real action – the death on the cross is demonstrated for the listener. In contrast, subjectivity in music is when the listener feels sympathy. Well, those are certainly refinements, but we Marxists love refinements, but not all of our Marxists have caught on to that fact yet. Except the great ones.

So, for that reason such judgements are very difficult to make. You ask too much of me. I would enjoy talking though, if I'd more time, about gestic music in the Brechtian sense, gestic speech and gestic declamation.

Take this example. Brecht was delighted when I brought him a little book – well, I think that I probably talked to him about it because he almost certainly didn't read it – about the punctuation in Shakespeare, in the quarto editions and of Pope's *Collected Works of Shakespeare* (as you know, there are different editions of Shakespeare's works). I told Brecht enthusiastically that Shakespeare's punctuation in the first quarto edition isn't in accordance with grammatical rules, but is gestic. This means that the punctuation (dashes, full stops, colons) wasn't set according to grammatical rules but followed the raising and lowering of the voices. The famous monologue in Hamlet, 'To be or not to be, that is the question' has, in this first Shakespeare edition, a completely different punctuation from the lacquered, distorted edition by Pope. As you know, Pope is the great – well, you can call him a court poet. His 'Essay on Man' is still readable today; except that you have to read it in English because the translations are catastrophic.

I remember too, in Hollywood at this same time, Brecht and I discussing for hours on end the punctuation of Shakespeare's quarto editions. I say this as a tribute to Brecht. Under those miserable circumstances – and the younger generation may learn something from this – such questions were at the centre of our elaborate discussions; they were our main interest other than the victory news. When the Russians were beating the fascists at Stalingrad, we were preoccupied with commas in Shakespeare's quarto. Those are correlations, not contradictions. The battles were fought so that we could diagnose the commas.

I'm going to ask Paul Dessau himself but maybe you will also be able to tell me something about the music for Chalk Circle. *There are two versions in existence.[66] The second version, in my opinion, contains a lot of that gestus which you have just explained in the example of the St John's Passion. Especially in Gruscha's journey.*

Dessau will be much better at explaining this than me. I also made some sketches myself for *Chalk Circle*, which I will publish sometime. Well, I can't say much about this. Clearly, my friend Paul Dessau came from a completely different milieu compared to mine (he couldn't help that!) – he just wasn't trained to any great extent to work things out intellectually. But he could find his way amazingly quickly, and Brecht certainly discussed with Dessau the question of gestic theatre music. I'll have to stop here and you'll have to ask Dessau – and maybe the assistants who were also present at these discussions.

Brecht dreamed of a real Chinese music as the old Chinese music is very gestic. Brecht said he wished for music to which long epic stories could be told. Homer's epics were sung, for example. Brecht was always saying: 'Can't you write music or create cadences to which I can tell an epic story for two hours?' That was his ideal. Unfortunately I'm not sufficiently talented to have achieved this; most of the time after a few minutes of merely *thinking* of an epic, I'm already out of breath. But there is something 'right' about Brecht wanting this – Brecht's ideas *were* right. One has to say that the epic is no longer a modern form.

Unfortunately, industrial capitalism – or actually feudal capitalism before that – has destroyed the ability to foster great epic stories as popular art. Brecht was chasing a phantom, the illusion that the great epic, with its thousands of verses, is a popular thing – as it is today with the fairy-tale tellers in the market place in Algiers, or with the great operas with their incredible stories (all of them sung by the way) in China.

That's what Brecht needed for his dramas. I wasn't able to deliver this for him in any way, and Dessau could only do it to the best of his ability. It's embarrassing that we couldn't do it. Perhaps in another twenty, thirty, fifty years there'll be a better way of composing an epic drama. Let's wait and see but it'll remain a difficult question. Brecht's thoughts were absolutely right; it's very complicated to transpose these thoughts into our obsolete music language – even Schoenberg would be out of date. I have to say that Brecht had the courage to look into the future and give the old, popular traditions – including those from the Orient – a new purpose. That was his great wish but we could never actually deliver this, or at least I couldn't.

I'm gradually recognizing that we'll have to speak about all the other entries in Brecht's Journal as well. Up to now, I have only selected the days – sporadically, I admit – on which your name was mentioned. But of course the collaboration also existed when your name wasn't mentioned.

We lived in very close proximity, you know, and there wasn't a day when I didn't see Brecht at least once. Usually I came over at lunch time for half an hour and/or in the evening; I came to him, or he came to me. Looking back (I feel as if I'm an old man already) I have to say it was an astonishing time, a time full of contradictions. And I can't imagine anything more beautiful. Regardless of all the scares and the wretchedness and the difficulties we had, it was a magnificent time. I'd wish every young artist something so productive – and we *were* productive! We were in fact very diligent; if there is one thing to praise in this particular past, then it would be our diligence. We also had a true conviction that what we were writing only for the desk drawer, the unperformable things, would one day become the greatest performances. That's what's happening to me at the moment; all my works written for the desk drawer twenty-five years ago are now published and performed.

Brecht is on an even higher level. At the moment, he's world-famous through plays that nobody at that time wanted either to see or to perform. If you speak about art, you have to have what's called in English 'stamina', not a 'real belief in yourself' – that's romantic – but a belief in the usefulness of your work. We all believed in that, not just Brecht and I. And there were many more people who have never been published nor had their works performed during this time. We're writing things that are useful, and that's the reason why we're doing it. I remember certain times during winter on the Danish coast, on the island of Funen, when I composed in the mornings in my house 'like a wild man' as we say in Vienna – and Brecht wrote verses 'like a wild man'. Hopeless! If a petit bourgeois had seen us, he would have said: 'These two men are complete maniacs or idiots'. But we didn't believe only in ourselves, we believed in our cause, and all we had was the optimism of the progress of time.

You have to admit that, for works started in 1934, which are subsequently performed in 1950 or 1960 in Brecht's case – and maybe in mine in 1970, if I'm lucky – you have to have staying power. Staying power is not talent, diligence or genius but an unwavering conviction that, if you have something truthful to say, it will survive. Something just has to happen – well, history happens. The word history derives from 'happening'.[67] I think that is all I have to say to you today.

But wouldn't you add that it wasn't easy to write only for the desk drawer?

It was extremely easy, believe me, because what else was I to do from eight in the morning during the emigration except compose? Tell me, what else could I have done with my day? Brecht and I were productive in order to escape boredom. May I suggest to you, dear Doctor Bunge, since you're going to become a very famous literary scholar that you read Goethe's *Venetian Epigrams* – incidentally, I even set a few extracts from them to music. Goethe adds to the nine muses, who are, as you know, the inspiration for the arts, a tenth one: the Goddess of Boredom. He addresses her: 'You, Goddess of Boredom, you are actually the motor of my productivity. I bought this little book out of boredom, I write verses in it out of boredom'. I read that as a boy and never understood it and it was only when I sat on this island – the sea before me, the Nazis behind me, and ahead of me maybe some shoddy professorship in America – that boredom drove me to productivity. Brecht was so susceptible to boredom! For example, when we met up and had fifteen minutes with nothing to do, he'd say: 'For God's sake, what shall we do now!' He was in despair – he either had to create something, or read, or speak. A fourth activity, such as idleness, didn't exist for Brecht. Boredom made him physically ill.

So, to sum up: for émigrés who had nothing better to do than look at themselves for twelve hours a day, the greatest inspiration during the emigration wasn't our understanding of the circumstances of class, nor our true and, I hope, decent fight for socialism against fascism, but just this tormenting – as a Marxist I ought to say 'reality' – this tormenting boredom. This is the origin of productive power.

These days, we're producing much less because it isn't boring at all in the GDR. We have so much to do that we don't get any work done; because we're too busy we haven't written enough. Brecht and I have never in our lives been as productive as we were during the emigration. That doesn't mean that we recommend exile as a source of productivity, but it should at least be mentioned.

There was a joke going round that Brecht needs a new emigration for him to find time to write. Of course, he was also tremendously productive here.

Tremendously. I would like to criticize my dear friend Elisabeth Hauptmann here a little. See, I don't understand, for example, why she hasn't included Brecht's adaptations of *Antigone* and *The Tutor* in the Collected Works, the ten-volume edition, because, I think they belong there. Those are final and brilliant achievements, outstanding adaptations. And I also think that there's nothing as good as how Brecht 'doctored' (my word) Hölderlin's *Sophocles* – Hölderlin's brilliant lines and his brilliant translation – by rearranging the over-elaborate verses; nothing has ever topped that. Today Lenz's *Tutor* without Brecht is unconceivable; both are equally valued adaptations. Dear friend, can you tell me who else can achieve something like that? – give me the name of one dramatist who could do it. Brecht's work is underestimated.

Or take the magnificent adaptation of *Coriolanus*, which is not even published yet; if someone had done only this one adaptation, he would have become immortal, and justly so. Brecht has made three adaptations, which are among the greatest achievements German literature has to offer. Why are we so modest? What do we ask of our old Brecht? One hundred and fifty plays – right? Just think how much there is that's weak in Shakespeare. *The Two Gentlemen of Verona* is one example, and *A Winter's Tale* another; these strange comedies in which one never quite knows what is going on – so-called farces that we can no longer understand.

I've also suggested to Hauptmann and Weigel that after the four volumes of poetry which are being prepared at the moment, they publish…

Immediately! The three plays *Coriolanus*, *The Tutor* and *Antigone*[68] need to be published immediately. I tell you – and you have to admit that I'm a literary expert – that would be sufficient for me. If a man reaches the age of fifty-eight with this achievement behind him, that's enough – I wouldn't need anything else. We Marxists have to take care that our people get some culture, whether they want it or not. We Marxists have to stuff culture down the people's throats, you know what I mean? It's a matter of some urgency now.

I would like to get back once more to the collaboration while you were émigrés in America. There is the music to Chalk Circle, *by Paul Dessau, which Brecht accepted and also recommended for other productions. There is no doubt about the quality of the music. But why didn't you write the music when Brecht asked you to in America?*

Yes, that really was my mistake. I had made a few sketches. I can't compose theatre music if it's not going to be performed and besides, I had my own work to do. But it probably was a mistake. By the way, Brecht's plays work with good music, with mediocre music and with bad music. I am a musician. I don't over- or under-estimate this. I had far too much work on. If today I look at the scores of my orchestral works, which are now slowly beginning to be performed, I have no regrets. There's one of the scores lying over there. I have no regrets. I'm sorry that my name isn't associated with the wonderful play *Chalk Circle*, but I think Dessau's music is excellent. It's good, don't you think? And why? Why not? When it came to the production in Berlin, I wasn't even there – I was in Vienna; I had other things to do. That's why I didn't get round to it. I'm absolutely fine about it. And believe me it wouldn't make any sense to me, as a composer, to hang on to the coat-tails of the fame and genius of my friend Brecht. His plays work perfectly well without my music. And, in all modesty, I can say my music also works pretty well without Brecht's plays.

What was Brecht's own opinion of the value of music in his plays?

He found the music enormously valuable! He even overestimated its value. He was too modest. Strangely enough, Brecht attached huge importance to the music in his plays – on a level with costumes, décor and lighting. That's wonderful for us musicians. So, I'm going to say something completely heretical, un-Brechtian here: the plays also work without us – I mean, we're not the essence. Of course it's good if Brecht gets wonderful music, of course it's marvellous, but they also work without marvellous music.

There are different views on this matter. Some musicians believe they should be entitled to more royalties.

That's absolutely fine. If I receive a set amount of the royalties for *Galileo* – music which I wrote in two weeks (Brecht on the other hand worked for three, five years on the play) – I have to say, I get far too much money. It's out of all proportion. I wrote the music to *The Mother* in ten days. There's really no equivalent. We musicians work in a different field. For heaven's sake, I think Brecht always overpaid me – don't tell anyone! I can say I received the normal percentage of royalties as composer for Brecht's plays; it's nearly always the same amount – for *Galileo* I get a bit less, for *The Mother* a bit more. This is how it is and I'm happy; I'm absolutely satisfied with this arrangement. And when I compare the work that I put into it with Brecht's – well, I'd be able to learn a thing or two from him.

I'm referring to the Journal again where, on 25 July 1943, Brecht notes an evening with Kortner, Tsiang, Winge, Steuermann, Kaus and you. The radio news is about Benito Mussolini's resignation, 'who ... has now fallen back into the gutter he came from'.[69]

I can't remember this. I think we were delighted that this bandit had stepped down. And we hoped – I'm reinventing this now – that this resignation was a kick in the teeth for him as well. He was a total gangster. We of course enjoyed that.

May I ask you to say something about the names which were mentioned? We've already spoken about Kortner. What about Tsiang?

Tsiang was, I think, a Chinese cameraman. Nice guy.

And Winge?

I think Winge is a crook – all I can say about him is that he's a crook. I can't tell you any more than that. A petit bourgeois crook who smarmed up to Brecht.

Was that your opinion at the time? Or is it still your opinion?

It was my opinion then – I had a brief change of mind in the meantime because I can be influenced – but from today's stand point, I seem to have been right all along. He was, and is, a crook.

But there were regular conversations between Brecht and Winge.

Not only that. You know the word 'smarmy'? Well, during the emigration, Brecht used to like someone sitting at his feet listening to his words because he was stimulated by discussions – not that I hold that against Brecht. Winge was then a little man – and he always remained one. Today he's not a little man, but a downright … I'd like to say 'crook' or 'traitor' – also a Brecht-traitor. After Brecht's death, there was just one journal in Europe that published a shameful article about Brecht – you know, it just wasn't on to write a dishonourable article about Brecht after his death. It is a journal in Vienna called *Forum*, published by crooks – it's something like the Austrian version of *Monat*. Winge was the only ex-communist (he resigned from the party in Vienna) who worked for *Forum*. That fact alone is enough for me – he's a crook.

Next is Steuermann.

One of the best musicians I ever met in my life – Eduard Steuermann, born in Sambor in Galicia. He was a pupil of Arnold Schoenberg; his sister was married to Berthold Viertel. He's about eight or ten years older than me. He is a magnificent pianist and an absolutely brilliant musician, incorruptible, loyal and productively devoted (not devoted like Kurvenal in *Tristan*, but productively devoted) and committed to Schoenberg. He's a musician of true genius – actually I've never met a better musician in my whole life. He's still alive, thank God, and lives in America but I'm not able to keep in touch with him. In my field of music, I have never found anyone better than him and probably never will. He's a composer as well – he even dedicated three of his songs to me. I've got them here. I'm very proud of them. Steuermann is a pianist and teacher, and absolutely first class. But he's more than a pianist – he's a musical genius. I don't care whether he's famous or not – I'm not interested. Fame is common, genius is rare.

Then the name Kaus is mentioned.

She is a popular female author with Ullstein publishing house.

Ah, Gina Kaus?

Yes.

Then I will carry on with a story that is similar to one that you once told me. It was about Döblin's sixty-fifth birthday, which Helene Weigel organized. The entry is from 14 August 1943. Brecht recounts how Heinrich Mann greeted Döblin with a wonderful speech, followed by Kortner, Lorre and Granach who read from

*his books. There were Berliner songs from Blandine Ebinger and
Steuermann played one of your piano compositions. At the end,
Döblin made a speech in which he spoke against moral relativism
and was all in favour of fixed, religious standards. He didn't seem
to notice that with these remarks he was hurting the irreligious
feelings of most of the guests.*

*Brecht says there was some kind of awkwardness coming over
those listeners who were more of the rational kind; an awkwardness
not unlike the sympathetic horror that is felt when a fellow prisoner
talks under torture. Brecht reminds us that Döblin had experienced
some great losses in his life: his two sons were killed in France; no
one wants to publish his 2400-page epic; he has angina pectoris (that
great saver of souls); and he is married to an extremely brainless and
philistine woman. Brecht then wrote about a revealing slip made
by the reciter Hardt at whose house Döblin and his wife had just
spent the weekend. Hardt recited Kleist's 'Zoroaster's Prayer' and,
instead of saying 'May I have the strength to disregard the errors
and idiocies of my life', he substituted 'wife' for 'life'. Brecht then
goes on to tell how Döblin started to describe that, like many other
writers, he too was to blame for the rise of the Nazis – ('And did
you not, Mr Thomas Mann, say that he's like a brother, albeit an evil
one', he asked of the front row) – and doggedly went on asking why
that was. 'for a moment' Brecht writes, 'i had the childish conviction
he would go on and say, "because i covered up the crimes of the
ruling class, discouraged the oppressed, fobbed off the hungry with
songs" etc., but all he did was to announce stubbornly, with no sign
of penitence or regret, "because i did not seek god"'.*

So that's the reason why the Nazis came to power! Well, it
really was a wretched situation because Döblin, an old friend of
Brecht's, of course, and also a good acquaintance of mine, really
was in a terrible situation; it was awful. But Brecht was a truly
wonderful friend. This celebration of Döblin's sixty-fifth birthday
only came about at all because the Brechts – Bert and Weigel –
got on the telephone and said to me, for example (I only played a
small part): 'For God's sake, we have to do something for Döblin's
birthday – could you contribute something?' So, what did I do?
I knuckled down and wrote a piano piece[70] and persuaded my
friend Steuermann (who was also in California at that time) to play
it, even though he had nothing to do with Döblin. And Thomas
Mann probably joined in, Heinrich Mann and Feuchtwanger too.

We were all very touched and wanted to celebrate this good old man Döblin, to whom we all felt close from our time in Berlin. And Brecht's house was the nerve centre of 'Organisation Döblin's Birthday Party'. We threw ourselves completely into this, trusting in the ideas of our cherished master Bert. It ended in catastrophe. That I spent three or four days composing, with my friend Steuermann practising for a week in order to perform it, only to hear…I feel I have to paraphrase this: we're always called 'base materialists' but that's completely wrong – the real phrase is 'base idealism'…the base idealism of a God seeker personally makes me sick.

I have to add – and this is the reason why Brecht noted it in his Journal – that I probably became, well, almost, rude. I said that this was too much. They banged on my door and I composed a piece of music for this fool; my poor friend Steuermann, instead of relaxing at the beach, learned it – and then, I hear I should seek God! That was too much for me. I didn't create a scandal in the room, but got up from my chair noisily and publicly – Brecht called 'Shhh!' after me – and I left causing what you might call 'an unpleasant scene'. It was such a pathetic affair.

All this shows, though, that the Brechts – especially Bert but also, to her credit, Helli – are really loyal to their friends. But there are many friends who disappointed Brecht and Helli, in particular among them this unhappy Döblin, who also died a very sad death. I have no idea how his works are to be rescued if they're so full of this nonsense.

Then there's an important entry on 26 September 1944, where Brecht records an evening conversation with you, Helene Weigel, and his son Stefan about the prologue to Chalk Circle.[71]

Yes. I only had one comment. I liked the prologue to *Chalk Circle* very much. I think it makes the fable more concrete. But I had one comment and Brecht agreed to change it. I said: 'It's impossible to name a goat-kolchos[72] after Rosa Luxemburg! In Berlin-slang, (I remember this conversation) "goat" is an ugly term for a woman. What a goat!' I said: 'The Berliner proletarians will laugh when the "goat-kolchos Rosa Luxemburg" is mentioned'. I was really horrified about this lapse, and Brecht was the first to agree. 'It's impossible' I said, 'you can't say "the society of the bearded Karl Marx", although that's more likely. But "goat-kolchos Rosa Luxemburg"! To describe one of the noblest women in human history by this slang term!' Well, Brecht understood immediately; I think the whole conversation was just about the goat. Brecht was so horrified by my comment that he tried to defend himself for over an hour. I seem to remember that he accused me of thinking – in a bad sense – in too plebeian a way. But in the end, I think, he changed it. I'm convinced that if you see a performance of *Chalk Circle* today, you won't hear the words "goat-kolchos Rosa Luxemburg". These are my great achievements on behalf of German literature.

It was only changed for Brecht's first production of the play in Berlin in 1954; in 1948, when it was first published, it was still called that.

Bert probably forgot to change it. I just want to put it on record. It's the only real accomplishment of mine in the cause of German literature: that crooks aren't able to mock a passage in one of Bert Brecht's plays. Because there are crooks about – I reckoned on them. Brecht didn't; Brecht is much nobler than me. I'm prepared for the worst.

The entry under this date in September 1944 is also important to me for a different reason. The West German press claims that Brecht only added the so-called 'Prologue' – it was later retitled the 'First Scene' – after he came to Berlin, but the note in the Journal proves conclusively that the Prologue already existed in America.

I'll be happy to witness this. By writing this prologue, Brecht shows his true proletarian solidarity with the fighting Soviet Union, although in reality the proper rational conditions didn't yet exist there. I think that writing this prologue as the first scene is one of Brecht's most brilliant strokes of genius – political genius. The whole concept of the play proceeds on the basis of the prologue as the first scene; he would never have written the play otherwise. As you know, it's based on this famous Chinese classic play, *Chalk Circle*.[73] There is a rather ordinary adaptation by Klabund, which we all saw in 1925 with Bergner in the main role. And only because of the prologue – because of the idea of the prologue – was Brecht able to rewrite the play. Anyone who claims otherwise is talking nonsense. And it's not only me who can witness this, but also Helli and everybody who lived in Hollywood then. I think that for the prologue alone, Brecht deserves a monument – if you consider the time when Brecht wrote it.

Were you aware that the prologue's meaning wasn't understood in our production? Fritz Erpenbeck only mentioned it in two of his reviews of, or rather his polemics against Brecht's play, published at the time in Theater der Zeit, *in which he said: 'There are three fables if you count the prologue as well'.*

You see, Erpenbeck [...][74] didn't understand it. He didn't understand that Brecht could only present the fable in a concrete setting; Brecht couldn't very well all of a sudden start 'In Georgia in 800 AD...!' Is there any better way of seeing the fable objectively than having it performed for us? The only reason for performing the play is so that we can recognize our own problems. In a nutshell, the prologue is the audience. That's what the audience is supposed to see; the members of the collective farm have their own problems – and the actors show them, through their performance, how their problems can be resolved. Who is the audience for the prologue? It's us, sitting in the theatre. I mean that's not too difficult for someone to understand, or is it?

I don't see how someone can't understand that. 'The times are changing', Brecht says; the times *are* changing – it *will* be understood. Believe me, the prologue to Goethe's *Faust* was eventually understood and there are many other prologues. Homer *used* to be understood, yet today you know how difficult it is to understand him. But although Homer isn't understood now, he will be again, eventually. Under communism, reading Homer will become as popular as reading the *Berliner Zeitung*. And that's what I call true communism.

It was better understood in the West, although it wasn't even performed there. They immediately recognized the class question.

But my good friend Erpenbeck, who obviously only understood Chekhov (and I'm not even sure about that), didn't get it. As you know, the ownership of large estates can be abolished administratively by decree; it's possible to abolish a big industry or the private ownership of the means of production. But to abolish stupidity by decree – that's something we haven't yet succeeded in doing, and perhaps never will. It would certainly take some time, especially stupidity in the field of art. You can't very well say that Erpenbeck is a stupid man but you can say that, as far as *Chalk Circle* is concerned, he behaved like a stupid man – which he really isn't. What I mean is this: art can't be regulated by administration. It's a crying shame. It would be much easier if, for example, we had as a fundamental law … Remember what the Bolsheviks did in 1917? Law number one was: the land is, from now on, expropriated and handed over to the people for all time. Could we make a law like: art is expropriated from idlers and parasites and handed over to the people for ever? We couldn't even formulate it, let alone carry it out. The land was taken from the farmers. Who is taking care of the art? Besides the artists themselves – nobody. Therefore, it will take time.

This entry, from 6 November 1944, is about your many conversations concerning music with Brecht and Dessau (in connection with the Goliath *opera). Brecht's impression of Dessau is that he's much less developed and seemingly preoccupied with routine. Brecht goes on to describe how modern music converts texts into prose, even verse texts, and then poeticizes that prose and at the same time makes it psychological. The rhythm is lost (Stravinsky and Bartók are exceptions). Brecht adds, 'for the epic theatre this is useless'.*

That's a brilliant observation – all I can say now is that it's brilliant. I'll keep it in mind to reflect on another time as I'm too tired now. I have to admit that this opera *Goliath*, which we started in Denmark, in Skovsbostrand, was … We wrote the text and music for one act at the Danish Sound, and then … oh this damned emigration! Suddenly I had to go to America and Brecht to Stockholm – we were 8000 kilometres apart. That's no way to write an opera. And so it stayed as just one act. Brecht did sketch an aria for the second; we already knew exactly what the story was going to be – you'll find the whole thing in the archive. I can, by the way, tell you the complete story. I'll do it when I feel fresher.

Conversation 4
6 May 1958

Music for *The Private Life of the
Master Race* – Prologue to *Galileo* –
Eisler and the House Committee on
Un-American Activities – *The
Mother* in New York – Brecht and
Stefan Zweig – *Bajazzo*

*Yesterday I quoted Brecht's Journal of 6 November 1944 in which
he describes how modern music converts texts, even verse texts,
into prose and then poeticizes that prose and at the same time
makes it psychological. The rhythm is lost (Stravinsky and Bartók
are exceptions). Brecht adds: 'for the epic theatre this is useless'.*

That's right. Bartók comes from the Hungarian folk music
tradition and folk music doesn't make texts so psychological in the
way the late romantics or Schoenberg's compositional technique do.
It's obvious: an over-composing, an elaborate over-composing,
of a text has nothing to offer the theatre. On the contrary, it
takes it somewhere else. What is also missing in the music is the
Zeigefunktion [directional purpose], as Brecht called it. From the
point of view of the epic theatre, Brecht is absolutely right in his
analysis here. But, unfortunately, you can't see music only as a
component – albeit a component of equal value – of theatre. There's
much more to music than that.

A 'by-product' that emerges from Brecht's analysis is his distinctive
aesthetic judgement concerning pompous, false and artificial
gestures, pathos and sentimentality – and this is of outstanding
importance. Brecht's opinion about music often seems to some of

us a bit too narrow. This indeed might be the case, but what this narrowness specifically guarantees is the raising of standards with regard to taste. You can find out a lot about how Brecht applies music, but you'll never find bad taste. That's all I want to say about that for now.

Then there's a note of 20 July 1945. I gave you advance notice of it, when you mentioned that, out of loyalty to friends, Brecht removed some offensive passages from his Journal.

So here comes an offensive passage – that's something new. Right, let's have it!

In this entry, Brecht writes about your trip to New York together to write the music for The Private Life of the Master Race *and 'to keep an eye on things'. Immediately after you arrived in New York, you received a telegram from Los Angeles ordering you back to the Studios straightaway. Brecht describes your obedience as unseemingly hasty because he thought you had been given leave of absence. He records that you wrote the music while waiting for your return ticket but that he thought the result 'film kitsch' and insisted that you write something else. This time he liked it very much and called it 'brilliant theatre music'. He then goes on to describe how Paul Dessau is now complaining that, when you returned to Hollywood, you called Dessau and asked him to write some twelve minutes of film music for the Studio because you didn't feel well. After agreeing that you would split the cheque ($1000) with him, Dessau wrote four minutes of music. But when you recovered, you found you couldn't use Dessau's music. Brecht then writes that Dessau, of course, insisted on his money (and that you were astonished by that); he should have received $200, which was the usual price, but was content with $100. Dessau, who was very hard up at this time, waited four weeks for the money and Brecht claims you knew it. The entry finishes with Brecht saying: 'sitting in my study with Dessau in the kitchen, Eisler complained that Hollywood music was ruining his ear'.*

Yes, but I do have something to say in response to this, which unfortunately is not in the Journal: that the cheque for Dessau was posted and then one of those rare cheque thefts occurred – apparently, a man must have taken it out of Dessau's letter box or from somewhere else. The cheque was signed by about four names that I didn't know and the bank sent the counterfoil back to me. So Dessau didn't get the money – instead it was nicked. I made it up to Dessau after that. In those four weeks poor Dessau was waiting, the cheque disappeared – I'm sure he'll remember how it was. So, I entered this story like Pontius Pilate entered the Creed. It was one of the rare cases where a cheque in an envelope was nicked and came back with strange signatures. When my then wife showed this to Dessau, he understood that it wasn't carelessness on my side, but...

It's good that I've read you that passage. You can now set the record straight.

Well, I could also be mean and stingy, dear Doctor Bunge. Dessau was really living a dog's life, whereas I at least had a contract. But the stupid thing was... Now the story *still* isn't quite right. I really was totally overworked, and it was torture for me to have to compose long scores for sea battles – it's terribly boring even if you feel fresh. And whatever happened, I wanted to get Dessau to help me because he needed the money. This is not to disparage the talent of my friend Dessau. Today I am particularly close friends with him, but the music was neither useful for a film nor anything else. Dessau was overworked too and so wasn't able immediately to compose something that had to have this disgusting blandness in order to be acceptable to the studios in the first place. Furthermore, it wasn't even an interesting scene, but a very conventional sea battle. I could never do this sort of thing to save my life (it was always torture; I could even feel it in my wrist). My friend Paul was in the same position; he couldn't do it either. If the music wasn't any good, then it should at least have been my music that wasn't any good (incidentally, I don't think that my music was any better). But that was a depressing episode. And it shows what terrible working conditions there were in Hollywood.

Of course, my friend Brecht was mistaken. He said, I think, something about the first version, which I did indeed write in a single morning in New York.[75] The second version was virtually the same as the first but I might have played it to him too expressively, such things often happened with Brecht. Brecht was quite rightly hurt that I went back to the studios at once and interpreted it, understandably, as a kind of treason. He also quite rightly criticizes me for not sending Paul his 100 dollars, although he was clearly oblivious to the fact that, if I didn't fulfil my contract, I would stand there *vis-à-vis de rien* – i.e. without any money because the studio would have stopped my wages. I had to go back. The film was just an unbearable pile of rubbish.

What was that awful epic called again, in which my friend Paul Henreid played the main character? Something like...?[76] It was a wretched adventure movie.[77] The only reason I could do it was because the plot is about some brave sailors who rebelled against the Spanish rulers. And since, at that time, Spain meant Franco, that more or less justified my working on it, although it was a terrible movie. But I had to compose – in an astonishingly short time – eighty minutes of music: that's one hour and twenty minutes. And it had to be a whole score! That means, you can ask any musician, it can only end in a nervous breakdown, not for psychological reasons, but just because you had to sit up all night long at the desk without enough sleep. One often had to ask for help in such circumstances. My friend Ernst Toch, for instance, was always helped by somebody else in such situations, because it's murderous work and one isn't that young anymore. And the recording dates were inflexible.

So all we need to say in this particular case is that this 'glossy' music was neither for Dessau nor for me. Where there was a scene that suited gestic music, then it was possible, even in this adventure movie, to compose something sensible. But as soon as there were battles involved – you were lost. I can remember, for example, Stravinsky once signed a contract for a Norwegian adventure movie set during the anti-Hitler period when there was a Norwegian underground movement against the fascist oppressors. Stravinsky, who also seemed to be short of money at the time – Europe as a source of money was out of the question – signed the contract on conditions that: he wouldn't compose love scenes; there would be no battle scenes whatsoever; and he wouldn't write any title music, by which I mean those glittery tunes when the credits roll. Apart from this, he would compose everything. The rest he asked a good friend of mine, a French composer, to do for him – but again, it didn't happen and the film was never made. All the same, that's the reason why we now have three Norwegian dances[78] by Stravinsky, which were originally written for this film. The title music and some awful battle-scene music were composed by – what was the name of that Polish-French composer...?[79] He'll probably have kept the score. You see, in order to fulfil an awful task you have to enter into some strange symbioses (a biology term, where plants cling protectively to each other). Unfortunately, I have to say that nobody could help me with my terrible film, and nobody did.

I think it's odd that Brecht wrote about this money business at such length and so cuttingly in his Journal when he usually suppressed such personal things. He was probably annoyed with you.

And he was right, he was absolutely right. It's like this: if one reads this passage today, one would say that Eisler was a stingy man; he returns to the big studios in the evening of the same day, having just arrived that morning in New York. The whole day long he's sitting in his room, like sitting an exam, working his fingers to the bone – by the way it's quite a nice score for the short eight-hour shift I spent on it. From today's perspective you wouldn't understand it: what could an idiotic film mean as compared to a brilliant play by Brecht? Today I would thoroughly disapprove of myself for doing this – but one mustn't forget: I had rent to pay, I had to live.

But I also want to mention here something honourable I did, something that Brecht unfortunately omitted to mention. I received a fee of 500 dollars for this composition,[80] and because I composed it but then couldn't stay, I returned the 500 dollars to the theatre, which meant that I had written the music for them *gratis*. So there you have a mismatch between my meanness towards my, then, poor friend Dessau, and my generosity in delivering a composition and returning the fee because I couldn't stay. Sadly, Brecht omitted this detail and I only mention this so that I won't go down in history as a Harpagon figure – not that it would do my reputation much harm.

Our great masters, Beethoven, for example, were terrible skinflints. The rows Beethoven had with his maid over two spoonfuls of coffee have gone down in music history. And the fuss my respected teacher Schoenberg created in his house with his theories about the maids stealing – well, that's another story.

I want the truth to be known simply because I'm much too careless and irresponsible a man to set great store by money. That's not nobility in me, just sloppiness, irresponsibility. Brecht always was a good provider; he was never miserly, rather very exact when it came to his financial affairs. One can't say that about me. Anyway, this story belongs to one of the unpleasant episodes with Brecht. He was looking forward to travelling with me to New York – and I go back after only eight hours. It was absolutely idiotic, you can't excuse it. What is rent compared with art!

You need somewhere to live to create art.

That's a very good and proper thought from a dialectically educated person, but with incidents like this, Brecht was never able to see the funny side. Leaving him in the lurch – he didn't like that. He was far too emotional in these matters. He couldn't see reason. We had a terrible row because of my going back. He didn't grasp that I could have been fired.

And that's the reason why he pinned that money story on you in his Journal.

Yes, but he didn't mention that I paid back the 500 dollars.

No, not that, nor that the cheque got lost…

Here, the great Brecht is in the wrong, but since my friend Dessau now lives happily in Berlin, one could ask him about the whole wretched episode. It certainly *would* be very mean, first to ask a colleague: 'Help me out, I have no time, you do the sea battle'; and then, when he brings the sketches, to say: 'Yes, well, dear friend, I can't use them, please don't be angry, it's impossible'. It doesn't mean that it was bad music, it simply wasn't usable. Indeed, had it been bad, it probably could have been used. Maybe it was too original – although it wasn't – I only say this retrospectively in order to restore Dessau's honour. Let's just say that it was too original for me.

On the 1 December 1945, Brecht reports that Galileo *(he meant the American version) is now finished, except for the ballad. Charles Laughton gives a reading at Brecht's house in front of Helene Weigel, you, Reichenbach, H. Viertel…*

That's Hans Viertel, the son of Berthold Viertel.

…Salka Viertel, Brecht's son Stefan and one of his friends, as well as the young physicist Würtele, Feuchtwanger, and Brush.

Brush was, I think, Professor of German at the University of California.

I would like to read to you the Foreword, *which Brecht put into his Journal but which is not yet published.*[81]

Respected public of the way called Broad –
Tonight we invite you to step on board
A world of curves and measurements, where you'll descry
The newborn physics in their infancy.
Here you will see the life of the great Galileo Galilei,
The law of falling bodies versus the gratias dei
Science's fight versus the rulers, which we stage
At the beginning of a brand-new age.
Here you'll see science in its blooming youth
Also its first compromises with the truth.
It too must eat, and quickly gets prostrated
Takes the wrong road, is violated –
Once Nature's master, now it is no more
Than just another cheap commercial whore.
The Good, so far, has not been turned to goods
But already there's something nasty in the woods
Which cuts it off from reaching the majority
So it won't relieve, but aggravate, their poverty.
We think such sights are relevant today
The new age is so quick to pass away.
We hope you'll lend a charitable ear
To what we say, since otherwise we fear
If you won't learn from Galileo's experience
The Bomb might make a personal appearance.

But that is magnificent. I certainly hope it will be included in the annotated edition of Brecht's complete works.

Yes of course, it will be included. But I regret that we didn't use the poem in the stage production, maybe it could have gone in the programme.

Yes – as you can see, I have completely forgotten it.

Everyone's forgotten it.

Even Brecht had forgotten it. I remember, by the way, that every now and then when I visited Brecht, he was always writing something on his typewriter. When I asked him: 'What are you up to'? He

replied: 'I'm just writing something in my Journal'. 'Oh dear!' I said
to myself – and to him I said: 'Brecht, I know I'm not going to come
out of this well'. We were always having disagreements of one kind
or another then. He said: 'We'll see' and then we didn't talk about
it anymore. It made me uneasy to hear that he kept a Journal; I was
full of dark forebodings.

You see, you were mistaken.

Ah well, Brecht's a noble man, but I have to say that we crossed
swords many times. We had an awful row in Denmark. What do I
care about who was right? – I don't insist that I was. But I have to
repeat, we practically lived next door to each other for many years,
one can't expect such a long-standing friendship to exist without
disagreements. I wouldn't be surprised if... I never wrote that down
except in my letters; you can read it there. There is one letter to
Brecht where I say to him: 'On top of our verbal discussions about
our disagreements or arguments, I don't want to have a written
debate about them as well'.[82] We had a dreadful row in Denmark,
which was resolved in a true Brechtian way. To reconcile me, because
I was angry with him (*really* angry which I very seldom am – in fact
I'm never angry with people) and had lost my temper and expressed
myself in no uncertain terms, he just sent me two simply wonderful
poems. 'Now' he said, 'dear Eisler, here are two poems; maybe you
can do something with them'. And that was the peace settlement in
the true Brechtian way. One continued to work – well, my feelings
were only slightly injured, but I was really annoyed at first.

I'll tell you about it because it's interesting. I was away on
my travels for an awfully long time, and when I returned from
Moscow via Leningrad and Stockholm, I really wanted to work
with Brecht again. After eight days, a telegram arrived telling me to
go to Prague immediately to attend an international music congress
because there were to be negotiations about a merger between the
social democratic and the communist Workers' Choral Unions and
I simply had to be there. It wasn't a party directive but it was on
those lines; a political organization had asked me to intervene.

When I returned from Prague, I immediately left for Paris
because I had already booked my passage on the ship *Lafayette*.
I had to go back to New York because my university lectures
were about to start. Now at that time Brecht was working on *The
Horatians and the Curiatians*, which he was planning to discuss

with me. It was also planned for it to have music. However, I worked out that I wouldn't have enough time – at most two days in Skovsbostrand – and it was just too much for me. I preferred to go to Paris and stay there for two days; my brother was there and I wanted to relax a little. The very idea that I might want to have two days off in Paris rather than rush to Skovsbostrand (no matter the cost) to continue work with all possible effort on *The Horatians and the Curiatians* – well, Brecht thought that was outrageous. That took the biscuit. I am after all...well, it was impossible. 'Understand this, great man – I am a great man too! I won't wear myself out. I need to relax in Paris and have some fun, too!' I said. 'I don't want to work for just two days...it would be quite different if it were four weeks!' And so on: it got very nasty. I became extremely angry and left the house in a great rage. And that evening I went to Prague. Our wonderful comrade Grete Steffin was even sent to negotiate but I couldn't begin to think about peace-talks. As you say in Berlin, I was too hot under the collar. Anyway, I had more than enough to do in Prague.

And then, as I said, this little letter of Brecht's with two poems and two lines arrived. And with that the matter was immediately settled. We never talked about it again; the conflict was still-born. And although I went away feeling upset, when we met up again in New York [in October 1935] everything was hunky-dory.

This honestly was one of the few arguments I ever had with Brecht, and it was because he demanded too much of me. It was impossible. One shouldn't ask too much of someone – if a bridge is overloaded, it collapses. The arch of friendship has a certain strength, and it's the same with bridges: this bridge can take so many carts but you can't suddenly have ten tanks going over it, the bridge will simply collapse. So, our friendship was 'overloaded'.

I only tell that story because it was an oddity. I've had very different arguments with my teacher Schoenberg – compared to the fierce differences I had with my old master, I lived in a paradise of friendship and harmony with Brecht.

I'd like to go back to Laughton's reading of Galileo *when the American version was finished. Do you remember this?*

Yes. It was a fantastic achievement. I believe Brecht worked with Laughton for one-and-a-half years on the English script.[83] It's more than just a translation, because of the work they did on it. Brecht understood an enormous amount of English but, as a German poet, he was reluctant to speak it, even though it was actually very dear to him. Unlike Brecht, I had no such scruples. I spoke a kind of pidgin right from the beginning but Brecht was very particular with the way he used English, even though he could speak it very well. So, it is a magnificent new creation, a new poetic version and so different from the original, too. It is a tremendous achievement of Laughton's, whether he likes to acknowledge it or not.

Did you see both productions of the play in America?

Well, of course. I composed the music for it then.

I know that, but I didn't know whether you saw the plays as well.

I did – the one in California and the one in New York.

You left America later than Brecht?

Yes. That was because I was still under arrest – I couldn't leave. I would have liked to leave even earlier than Brecht, but the Americans wouldn't let me.[84]

The entry on 4 March 1945 tells of a party at your house where Charlie Chaplin did a wonderful impression of Paul Muni in the film about Chopin.[85]

Yes, it was priceless.

But is there nothing more to say about it?

Well, I could add (though it isn't that interesting), that these parties in Hollywood were a real curiosity. It is bound to be a curiosity if you have an evening gathering consisting of Bertolt Brecht, Thomas Mann, Heinrich Mann, Feuchtwanger, Jean Renoir (the film director) and Arnold Schoenberg. You'd have to go a long way to find another dinner party like that wouldn't you?

Certainly. Now, a much later note in the Journal, of 29 December 1948. Brecht talks about your visit to Berlin for four weeks. He describes that you are now ready to sublimate your antipathy to marching songs, which, to you, seem vulgar and primitive by changing the 'United Front Song' symphonically, which means you transformed it to a folk song in formally strict pieces. He tries to persuade you to produce 'new vulgar excesses', by offering you the

'Song of the Future' but you, in turn, give Brecht Mao Tse-tung's 'Ode', written during Mao's first flight over the Great Wall. Brecht thinks it is a wonderful poem and plans to adapt it. Brecht is pleased that his 'expectation of a renaissance of the arts, triggered off by the rising of the far east, seems to be approaching fulfilment earlier than one might have thought'.

That's a very good observation. It was like this. During the exile, we used to hear those terrible Hitler songs over the radio. They were partly nicked from the working class movement. They started putting fascist texts to quite a few of those tunes and when we returned to Berlin I felt such disgust towards the whole business of marching in general (that is a fairly undialectical position, a position of taste), that I preferred to look for things like the 'Ode' by Mao Tse-tung. On the one hand, Brecht understood that, but on the other, he also missed our plebeian vulgarisms, which are so very necessary. Somehow, a shadow hovered over this particular genre because of its misuse by the barbarians and one had to be careful and give it several years to get it out of one's system.

Unfortunately, the time for that was far too short. What I hear nowadays on the radio in the well-meaning compositions of my younger, as well as my older, colleagues often has an embarrassing 'after-taste' that reminds you of this time – this is, of course, also due to the often wretched texts. Neither the 'United Front Song' nor its music, however, nor the marvellous poem by Brecht, the 'Solidarity Song', have anything to do with this genre – definitely not.

They are written in another genre that has both poetic and musical status, in which simplicity has a healthy function without turning its back on artistic principles. And which, unfortunately, has never been imitated. What *was* copied from me was actually what was most compelling, what was in fashion. But it didn't work: the refinements weren't imitated (maybe they were too difficult).

When he wrote these famous poems, Brecht was at the pinnacle of the genre of workers' songs. But no other poet tried to follow his example, which even today is a crying shame. Brecht didn't achieve much more in that field, now I come to think about it, although he did, of course, write other great things.

Also unique in Brecht's work was what we called marches for the working class, most of them written in London. Take, for example, the beautiful 'Song of the Future' with its refrain 'A wonderful flag that's red' – it's a terrific poem, and I prefer the refrain to the verses that come before it (which don't seem to me to be quite up to Brecht's high standards in this genre). The refrain is quite rightly regarded as one of the most beautiful because of its deep simplicity: here you see the flag and the colour red with new eyes – it's wonderful to be presented with such a well-known symbol as the red flag in a new light.[86] What a great poet.

Looking further, we can find lovely children's songs by Brecht and popular rhyming poetry; for example, the great 'Song of Peace' to words by Neruda. On the other hand, there was no longer any reason to write true proletarian marching songs since our workers unfortunately don't sing any more when they're demonstrating, which makes this art-form obsolete. This art-form is also of no use if it's produced just for the desk or for the occasional meeting. I think Marx or Engels mention somewhere that it was the same with the songs of the Chartists. They made sense in their historical context but from a certain point on, they became outdated.

The most enduring songs of this genre to my way of thinking are the 'United Front Song' and 'Solidarity Song', which were never surpassed – neither by me nor by Brecht, nor anyone else. You can only write something like this when you come across a wholly certain, concrete social situation and this was just a lucky coming together – that's all I can say. Unfortunately, I didn't set Mao's 'Ode' to music; I only made a few sketches. But, I'm aiming to set it to music one day because it's a marvellous poem.[87]

It's nice, this exchange of tasks. Brecht gives the 'Song of the Future' to you and you give him Mao Tse-tung; then each of you gets to work.

Each of us gets to work. One thing is clear: here are true artistic interests – not in conflict, but different, both following the same purpose, which is to make socialist art. I like that very much.

Earlier we spoke about your departure from America and your hearing before the House Committee on Un-American Activities. I would like to hear more about that.

Brecht was so smart taking a tape recorder with him.[88] He had a confident approach and he was so clever not to lie – that was punishable as perjury, up to three years. He spoke nothing but the truth, and in such an intelligent, considered manner. And because he wasn't a practising politician or even a conspirator, not even the biggest idiot could catch Brecht out. So, he got away with it.

I have to say straightaway that, like Brecht, I'm no politician or conspirator either. But, as you know, I do have a remarkable brother, and actually I put my head on the block for him, or rather the ideas that he stands for. Had it not been for my brother Gerhart, I would never have had such difficulties – I want to be quite clear about that from the outset so that I don't appear a political martyr, which is something I'm definitely not. These great troubles beset me because I had to defend my brother. *C'est tout.*

Brecht was in an easier position: he only had to defend his friends, for example, me. He quite freely admitted that, in the evenings, we spoke mostly about politics. They thought he would say he was out picking flowers with me or Gerhart, and because he admitted that, they thought he was a truth fanatic and let him go immediately: 'We don't need to hear any more from him'. They also thought he wasn't quite right in the head because, in this dreadful climate of hate, he owned up to his relationship with the Eisler brothers, with me as a friend and my brother as a good acquaintance, and to the fact that our evening talks were, without exception, devoted to politics. That was such a wily Brechtian manoeuvre. The committee didn't know what to make of him and sent him away. On my advice he flew to Zurich the same night. I told him: 'If you get away from there, go to New York and take the first plane out. Don't even wait twenty-four hours'.

Brecht once mentioned the 'lawyers for the nineteen witnesses'. Who were those witnesses?

The nineteen witnesses? I thought there were only ten – are you sure you're not mistaken?[89] These 'witnesses' were very decent, courageous people – screen writers – who were all imprisoned for six months to a year. Some of them (only a few) gave in: two screen writers and directors gave in, a certain Edward Dmytryk and a certain Robert Rossen. One of them flew to Mexico but then 'sang', as they say in the gangster jargon. After this, the unfortunate Dmytryk was imprisoned for six months and told them everything they wanted to know. He wanted to, as it were, regain his status – and he did.

The other eight are still blacklisted today and so have no way of earning a living. They behaved very well, especially towards us – we were in a difficult situation and were all in the same boat – and with the utmost camaraderie. Brecht, of course, had access to all these lawyers who worked *pro bono* – not that he needed them in the end. They did everything to help those two foreign friends and ease their extremely difficult situation.

Your hearing was not in connection with Brecht?

No, I was on my own during my three-day hearing.[90] I was a special case – not, as I said, because of my political merits (unfortunately) but more because of my family connections.

But you took a certain 'guilt' of Brecht's on your head.

Yes, that was quite straightforward; there was nothing else I could have done. Those people wanted to pin something on me. HUAC had had the words to my songs translated; they read them out and attributed them to me. Now well, I couldn't very well say, 'I'm sorry, but I'm just a composer'; such a political position is indecent. It's impossible. I therefore decided to defend those texts as if they were my own. At that time, I didn't know whether Brecht would be interrogated as well and, anyway, I had made a decision: that I would not mention any names – I'd never tell them a single name, ever. Whatever they accused me of, I'd take it on my own head. And that's what I did. Those people probably knew full well that Brecht's name was on the score as well. They did in fact summon him to the hearing later, but they didn't tell me that at the time.

The committee wanted me to appear in the papers as a monster who writes obscenities because they thought some of the texts were 'filthy'; for example, the beautiful 'Ballad of Paragraph 218', which is opposed to the abortion law.[91] One senator called it 'pornography which couldn't even be sent through the mail'. Because, by law, in America you can't send pornography through the mail. I disagreed: 'It's not pornography; I have to tell you, even though I wrote it, that it's magnificent poetry', to which he replied: 'I don't need any lectures from you – I'm an authority on literature'. Again I disagreed: 'Excuse me, Mr Senator, you are not, otherwise you'd see that it's magnificent poetry', whereupon the Senator became extremely angry.[92] And so it continued: 'Your play *The Measures Taken* – what kind of a play is that?'[93] That's how I appropriated to myself the best of Brecht's plays, one of the most successful literary thefts of all time. Brecht, himself an expert in this field – you remember that, somewhere, he borrowed a few lines from a Villon translation[94] – told me that mine was a virtuoso performance and that, compared to me, he was a mere beginner: he had only taken twenty lines, but I had appropriated entire works by him. He was very touched by it all and never forgot what I did for him although it could hardly be called an accomplishment.

It wouldn't have done me any good even if I had brought Brecht's name into it. First of all, it would have been behaving like a crook, and who wants to be a crook? It wouldn't have changed anything anyway, because it was me they wanted to pin something on. It wasn't any special achievement on my part; it was the most natural thing in the world. And besides, Brecht is an old friend of mine. If I'd dragged him into this cesspit as well, it would have been too much.[95]

When we were sitting together in the Berliner Ensemble canteen after the Brecht birthday celebrations,[96] you came out with some anecdotes and I took some notes. So those anecdotes are coming back to haunt you now.

Let's hear them.

I have one note that says: 'You shouldn't speak the truth out loud'.

That refers to an occasion, one of the very few, when I could at last present myself as superior to Brecht in wisdom. I seldom had an opportunity to do this because Brecht was so terribly wise, you could hardly ever lecture him about anything. Furthermore, no matter how genial, he's also incredibly intelligent and astute – even if he hadn't become a poet, he would still have been an astute man. It's not easy to get the better of him.

Once, when I came to see him in Hollywood, he said: 'You know Hanns, it's astonishing. Yesterday evening, a certain Doctor S.' (I won't say his name) 'called round and after an hour, he left the house in high dudgeon, slamming the door behind him. I don't understand him'. Brecht said: 'I only told him the truth'. To which I replied: 'Dear Brecht, how loud?' He said he was going to use this incident in the *Keuner* stories, although he never did.

He must have forgotten about it.

Oh well, it wasn't as important to him as it was to me. It is my big hit. It was one of the few times I could puff myself up like a peacock and say that I got one over on Uncle Brecht.

I've also written down 'Mr Brecht insists on being called "Comrade Brecht"' – it's the anecdote about 'I will not have the Mister'.

There was an exciting discussion at the Academy of Arts between a comrade from the central committee, a cultural functionary, and someone else when they hotly debated the art exhibition in Dresden. That must have been about 1953. It was just before they dissolved the so-called Art Commission (which later became a Ministry) and we'd invited its leading functionaries – the Commission was under fire for being too narrow-minded – to come and debate with us. And Brecht, because he could never let anything go, attacked this particular man, a completely harmless man, for always addressing him as 'Comrade Brecht' and using 'Sie' [formal you]. Brecht was never a member of the party so the informal party 'Du' [you] couldn't be used, just the formal 'Sie' and 'Comrade Brecht'.

So this man, who already felt deeply insulted (he was no angel of wisdom either), then started to call him 'Mr Brecht', which was an insult in those circles – one simply can't switch from 'Comrade' to 'Mister'. We're all members of the socialist movement, whether a card carrier (important!) or not, so we call each other 'Comrade' in these committees. You could address each other as 'Mister' or 'Colleague' but only if you do it right from the beginning and I wouldn't suggest anyone address Brecht as 'Colleague' as that would be going a little too far. But if you begin 'Comrade', then you have to stick to 'Comrade'. I should like to point out that leading comrades called Brecht 'Comrade', naturally. Walter Ulbricht would never have addressed Brecht as 'Mister'; when he wrote to Brecht he didn't begin 'Dear Mr Brecht' – neither did Wilhelm Pieck. Small-time officials in particular, take note! So when the man called Brecht 'Mr Brecht' for the second time, Brecht said, or rather shouted: 'I will *not* be addressed as Mister! You must call me Comrade!' To which the man, now very pale, replied: 'Yes, Sir! Comrade Brecht'. I think that's a story worth preserving.

Then I have noted down: anecdote Kesten.

I don't remember.

There was another story about a meeting between Brecht and Egon Erwin Kisch.

Kisch greatly mistrusted people like Brecht because he didn't understand them. I don't need to heap any more praise on golden-boy Kisch, because he's very popular, and quite rightly so. I have to say his travel books are a better read than many novels from the same time. His writing is fresh, funny and informative, and Brecht thought so too. However, Kisch didn't know what to make of Brecht's theatre. His literary taste was rather conventional (as was common among these highly polished, 'shining boys' of his generation) and he was somewhat uncertain about Brecht. Everything about Brecht was far too earnest for him. In a nutshell, Kisch, a man who embraced life and made great jokes, had nothing much in common with this strange Bavarian puritan.

Brecht really enjoyed being in Kisch's company, or maybe it was the other way round. Kisch showed sufficient respect for Brecht, although he didn't really understand anything about poetry, which did make things difficult between them. Moreover, Brecht – even though he liked Kisch a lot – was relentless. I'll give you an example. I was making a film with Joris Ivens, *New Earth*, about the excavation of the Zuidersee in Holland: once the water is gone, grain is planted on the dry seabed – which is as far as Joris Ivens got with his film. When he showed it to me (I was supposed to compose some music for it), I said:

Here is what you should do. You have to let the grain grow, thresh it nicely, fill up sacks with it and then (and this was during the great economic crisis) you throw the flour back into the sea. This is how the cycle of crisis works: a huge effort to excavate the sea, an abundant new harvest, and then back into the sea because the world market is groaning under the weight of the grain sacks.

Joris Ivens liked this idea very much and that's how we did it, albeit with very modest means. We couldn't find anywhere in Europe where you could throw flour in huge amounts into the sea, as they did with the coffee in Argentina, but we did find a spot on the river Seine. We all pooled our money and Joris Ivens bought three sacks of flour, which were then poured into the water. It was probably only a medium camera shot so it didn't really look that amazing, and at the end they sang my ballad 'The Sack Throwers'.[97] When I told Brecht the story, he cried with laughter. He could be very enthusiastic when something felt right and then he is also generous in his opinions. He knew making films was expensive and this was an avant-garde film for which there was no money. (I made a contribution out of my own pocket, as did a friend from the film industry who gave Ivens money to continue with it.) So, from the outset Brecht liked the idea very much and when Ivens showed the film to Kisch, Brecht and me, Brecht was all smiles and sat there, very happy. But poor Kisch said: 'Listen, that's all very well, but it could be improved a bit. This flour scene is a bit thin'. Whereupon Brecht shouted at Kisch: 'Kisch, this is a classical masterpiece! What are you talking about?' Kisch responded: 'I like it as well – I like it very much, I just think…' Brecht immediately came back: 'You're not supposed to think anything'.

To cut a long story short, poor Kisch was silenced. After that, Kisch wasn't too keen on Brecht any more. But that is an example of how loyal Brecht could be: he could forgive a certain deficiency of artistic means if the piece was truthful. That was the Brechtian principle.

What happened during the production of The Mother *in New York?*

It was a total disaster. The translation was a catastrophe, largely because, at that time, I didn't speak enough English to understand it and neither did Brecht. They…you know…changed it. They made a Gerhart Hauptmann out of it, a naturalistic play. So, instead of Weigel's wonderful monologue where the son drinks tea, you had: 'It's turned out nice again' and so on. What I mean is, the text was converted into naturalistic dialogue. It was terrible – the struggle to make the translation more realistic or even just better, took all the fun out of it. The director was a seventeenth-rate disciple of the great Stanislavski, minus his talent. What happened on the stage was like what happens at the *Tegernseer Bauernfestspiele* [Farmers' Festival at Lake Tegernsee]. It was really awful.

Apart from this, I worked on the score of my version for two pianos; the pianists were magnificent and the chorus was also actually very good. Brecht, who's engaged in an eternal blood feud with players and musicians, mortally offended one of the pianists by swearing at him because he didn't get the hang of something straightaway – okay, that was still all right. But when it came to the song 'The Party is in Danger' and the chorus, instead of singing it to the audience, shouted it into the sick mother's face[98], my patience ran out and so did Brecht's. I'm afraid to say that I told the director the truth, very loudly. His name was Wolfson and since then he's become a fierce enemy of the Communist Party in America (as have nearly all of these people today, with two brilliant and brave exceptions). After a lot of to-ing and fro-ing, a board member of the theatre asked: 'Why are you shouting like that, Mr Eisler?' 'I'm not shouting' I replied, 'I'm simply trying to explain to this director what an abysmal idiot I think he is'.

After that, because this is America, not Germany, we were not actually beaten up, but were both politely but firmly thrown out of the theatre by two people. There we were, standing by the stage door. It was drizzling. We were speechless: God, what's happened? Then we said: 'If they come back for us, we'll beat the living daylights out of them so we don't have to go back into the theatre'. We looked at each other. Where were our hats? Still inside. Then along comes the excellent stage designer Mordecai Gorelik and we asked him: 'Dear Max, can you please get our hats?' He immediately understood what had happened. We weren't allowed to set foot in the theatre anymore and the performance took place without us. It was a disaster, I can tell you, a disaster of gigantic proportions. The press hadn't a single good word to say about us and the audience didn't like watching those strange performances that were a cross between Chekhov and the commonest kind of cliché-ridden slang, without any poetic qualities. That was that.

Brecht stayed on in New York a bit longer before returning, very unhappily, to Copenhagen. We used to go to the cinema, especially to gangster movies, in order, as we kidded each other, to undertake social studies. Brecht lived next door to me. He had a flat on the same floor, and I only had to knock at his door and say: 'Listen, shall we do some social studies?' before we were driving to 42nd Street to watch gangster movies (*Public Enemy Number One* among others) with the wonderful James Cagney. Those were the 'social studies'.

It was a difficult time, and it was winter. I took Brecht to the boat during a snow storm and away he went, back to Denmark,[99] beaten, or as you might say: the war continued but he'd lost a battle.

And what about the whisky bottle in the pocket?

Brecht never drank, you know. He had the odd beer, but that was all. During that period, he carried a small, thin silver flask of whisky and he told me: 'You know very well that I never touch a drop, but from time to time in this city I just have to'. Brecht swigged it as much as... well, hardly at all. I had far larger quantities. Brecht said: 'I can't get by without whisky. Every now and again I need a little snifter'. I keenly observed, however, that this flask lasted for weeks and weeks; he must have sipped at it like a bird, while I drank double scotches openly and shamelessly from tumblers. That was the only time Brecht carried alcohol with him. It was an awful time. Brecht desperately needed his plays to be performed. A terrible time.

You were describing a meeting between Brecht and Stefan Zweig.

Yes, that was wonderful. I lived in London in Abbey Road and Brecht lived opposite.[100] We had just received, I think, the piano scores from *The Round Heads and the Pointed Heads*. I had everything ready and on one occasion somebody brought Stefan Zweig to the house. He's a very elegant man, you know, Stefan Zweig – this famous industrialist, this businessman-publisher. I know what I'm about to say is heresy, because Zweig's supposed to be a humanist (even the stock exchange has a certain kind of humanism), but I can't grant him more than a cold-blooded stock-exchange humanism or stock-exchange pacifism. An unpleasant man – anyway, there he was. This extremely elegant man had a superb apartment on Portland Place. I had, of course, invited Brecht to my flat as well, so there they were: Stefan Zweig, some writer who had brought Zweig, and Brecht, all in my room. And Brecht, who always thought along the lines: 'Ah, here's a rich man... there might be a possibility of some funding for the theatre'. He had never read a word Zweig had written, but Zweig knew Brecht's name from the Weimar Republic days when he was very famous. So, there was a certain friendly interest, although it is likely... well, they were worlds apart. 'You know what, Zweig' Brecht said, 'Eisler ought to play something for you. We have just finished a play'. I asked: 'What shall I play?' and Brecht said: 'Play Mr Zweig "Song of the Invigorating Effect of Money"'. So I played it for him. I just knew things would turn out badly. To play to a man famous for his wealth (inherited wealth) – the man who financed the *Insel* publishing house, financed his whole career – this song! When you read the text of it...Zweig listened to it with a stony face. It was one in the eye for him but he said nothing – a man from polite society. Then I played him the song 'Water Wheel' and by then he'd had enough. He said it would all be very interesting, quite simply 'interesting'. Nothing more came of it.

There was a journalist as well, a very nice guy called...[101] He's now chief editor of *The Manchester Guardian* and was then politically quite left wing. He'd just come back from the Saar area and told us how the vote had gone. To please him, I offered him, Zweig, who was still there, and Brecht a little song about the Saar, which I'd set to music. It is a beautiful text – Germany occupied, governors appointed – wonderful, don't you think? I'd composed a simple melody and we played it; the journalist was beside himself with delight that something so beautiful was even possible (he spoke perfect German). But somehow Zweig...'Well' Brecht said to Zweig, 'that was just a trifle, you know, a by-product, to help the cause' to which came the reply: 'Don't call it a trifle, Mr Brecht; it might be your best!' This is how it goes between writers – one stab in the back after another. Brecht deals Zweig 'Song of the Invigorating Effect of Money' and then a little song about an election becomes possibly the best thing Brecht ever produced. So the two men were equal on points and went out to lunch.

About the miserliness of this lunch – I didn't go with them; the two writers wanted to be by themselves – I have only this to say. When I asked Brecht how much Zweig had paid for the lunch, he said: 'Two and six' (two shillings and sixpence). So he must have led, no, invited, Brecht to one of those awful mediocre London restaurants, this man who usually likes to dine at the Savoy, and paid for a wretched meal. And that was the one and only meeting between Brecht and Zweig. I repeat: *Stefan* Zweig. With Arnold Zweig, Brecht was truly good friends.

And then there is the story about the Bajazzo *movie?*[102]

Yes, that was really a big deal, for which we actually have to thank our mutual friend Kortner. Brecht saw the clouds of war looming and thought to himself that he wouldn't be in the safest of havens in Denmark, thirty kilometres from the German border, and started dreaming of buying a little house, a log cabin, either in Norway or in Sweden. For that he'd need 500 pounds. Now, 500 pounds at that time was about 20,000 gold marks, one pound being worth twenty marks – that was before the devaluation of the pound[103] – all the same, it was a lot of money. First of all, it needed to be earned. So how could we get Brecht the money? I received a telegram asking me to come from New York to be the supervisor for the *Bajazzo* film, a so-called 'Richard-Tauber-Film'. The music for *Bajazzo* was already written, thank God, but they needed a specialist to ensure that everything was professionally recorded – there was some conducting to do as well... and so on. Well, I signed this fat contract with pleasure because I had nothing else to do at all and it left me with lots of time for my composing. Those conditions felt like paradise. I got a lot of money, with weekly expenses on top – it was fabulous. And I thought: 'How can I share my good fortune with Brecht? Something similar ought to be arranged for Brecht as well'. Big meeting with Kortner, I told him about Brecht's financial problems and about his wish to move into a little house far away from the fascists. Kortner was very understanding and said he would put it to the film producers (he wrote the screenplay for *Bajazzo* for similar financial reasons) that he would be in urgent need of some assistance and was thinking of Brecht, this famous playwright. It could well be to the film's advantage to have at least one Tauber-film with a screenplay by Bertolt Brecht. (In terms of entertainment, Tauber is at the bottom of the ladder, you know.)

And although I only floated the idea, Kortner was indeed able to arrange a contract for Brecht. Brecht joyfully arrived in London without a word of notice and with only the clothes he stood up in. A knock at my door – it's Brecht. I had no idea that everything was already settled and asked: 'What's up?' 'I've got a contract. We're making *Bajazzo* together'. 'Are you getting good money?' I asked, and he replied: 'Yes, I have the five hundred pounds which I desperately need'. 'Well' I said, 'that's brilliant'. Whereupon Brecht got down to work. But Brecht is a different man from me. My contribution to the *Bajazzo* arrangement was zero. I travelled to Paris on Saturday and came back to London on Monday morning. At that time, I was composing what will, I hope, be premiered this year: a large full-length work called *German Symphony*. I wrote this symphony paid for by the *Bajazzo*-production company.

Brecht really engaged with *Bajazzo* – and that was his downfall. He was a hard-working man and wanted to achieve something too. In his hands, the *Bajazzo* script took on the strangest forms; great poetic beauty was appearing that the producers found unbearable, especially Tauber. And what's this – interesting dialogue? No, totally unbearable. In a nutshell, things developed to the point where they said: 'That's gone too far, Mr Brecht. After that last draft ... Here's the rest of the money. Goodbye, sir – and don't come back'. Brecht was deeply hurt – what, they didn't even need him in this shithouse? He'd really enjoyed doing the work and went away truly sad. The fact that Kortner stayed gave rise for several months to a certain discontent. Brecht accused Kortner of disloyalty; he thought he should have left immediately as well. The movie was a catastrophe, it was absolutely terrible. The company went bust after the movie because it cost a fortune. So Brecht was bloodily avenged.

Among my letters there's one to Brecht: 'After this awful time in London you will have recovered at last with the production of *Pointed Heads* in Copenhagen', which was a reference to this dreadful defeat, where the lowest scum of the film world preferred to pay Brecht his money rather than listen to a single one of his ideas. You should be able to find something in Brecht's notes about *Bajazzo*.

Perhaps we'll find it.[104]

It would certainly be very interesting; it would definitely enrich the literature on opera.

There is also a draft by Brecht for Tales of Hoffmann?

A brilliant, marvellous draft.

I should ask you in particular about Brecht's early career, and about the beginning of your collaboration. Hardly any material exists. Also, Brecht wasn't keeping a Journal then as he did during his time in exile.

I'd like to meet up with Elisabeth Hauptmann, Brecht's secretary at that time, to talk about that period. She could correct me although I wouldn't be able to correct her, because she was with Brecht so often. Brecht and I were together working on *The Measures Taken* and *The Mother* every morning in his apartment on *Am Knie*, usually between nine and one – those were long sessions, every morning. Hauptmann will be an invaluable help with this. Her knowledge of those early days is very comprehensive. For the time even before that there is, of course, Weigel and also Arnold Bronnen. I only started working with Brecht in…We had already known each other for some time, but the collaboration only started in, I think, 1929 – 1928 or 1929[105] – I don't know the dates. Hauptmann will know. I would suggest a next meeting about the early days with Hauptmann.

From the later time, could you perhaps say a bit more about the collaboration on Galileo *and* Schweyk?

Galileo was hardly a collaboration at all. Brecht really did everything with Laughton.[106] I barely contributed anything constructive, just a few suggestions.

With *Schweyk* I also contributed very little. I once suggested to him that he tone down some sentences of this storm trooper, I think his name was Bullinger. (By the way, there is a make of champagne in France, a very famous one, called *Bollinger*, not that it has anything to do with this: I'm only saying it here to contribute something to your education.) I merely suggested only one or two things. Brecht did it all by himself. He was also very tactful. Since he wrote this drama for Weill, he didn't want me to spend time on it; despite the fact that I was a friend, he felt I shouldn't get involved. Quite the opposite: when he asked me something relating to *Schweyk* he felt embarrassed for pestering me with it on top of everything else. It wasn't my project.

Do you still remember any details from the time when Brecht worked on the Communist Manifesto?

He was always reading us extracts from it and…Unfortunately we, that is Feuchtwanger as well as me, behaved really badly.

You were against this project?

Yes, Feuchtwanger was against it because of issues of style. And I told Brecht:

I'm happy if they can read and understand it in prose. But you're making it even harder. The style of an epic poem in hexameters isn't popular any more. Hexameters are a high art form which hasn't been popular since Goethe's *Reynard the Fox* etc. Gerhart Hauptmann has made a few attempts but the days of the hexameter are over. You've taken a high art form and then you reshape it…

I'm ashamed to say that I spoke like an oaf because, if you disregard the propagandistic effect, the *Manifesto* is marvellous! If only we had an art form for it...

I maintain that in fifty years' time, Homer will be read like the Berlin Evening Newspaper, and when this happens, everyone will be mad about the *Manifesto* in Brecht's art form as well. It's a real shame, but I have to own up to this: Feuchtwanger and I were guilty of spoiling Brecht's good mood with regard to this work.

You didn't work together on it?

No, I couldn't do that – there wasn't any room for collaboration. Brecht sat surrounded by the *Manifesto* writing hexameters.

There are letters, for example from Karl Korsch, who suggested quite a few amendments which Brecht took on board.

Unfortunately, I didn't do anything like that. I didn't take any part in it, quite the opposite. As I said, to a certain extent I actually stopped it happening.

And what about Brecht's collaboration with Feuchtwanger?

I can't say anything about it because I was never there with them. Brecht often came to my house before he drove on to Feuchtwanger's (he lived close by) or on his way back. I would ask: 'What did you do?' and he would reply: 'We worked on *Simone*... Feuchtwanger's a very good man only it's rather difficult to teach him; he has no sense of the gestus'. But he admired his clarity, rationality and logic.

And Fritz Lang?

Oh, that was terrible, just dreadful. They didn't understand each other at all. Lang's a very skilful director visually, but a complete illiterate and a bad UFA-hack who was able also to flourish in America. Brecht and I loved his movie *Fury*. But the collaboration with Brecht[107] led to terrible disagreements that hurt Brecht's feelings. Brecht is a hard-working man and he's a moral human being, who doesn't want... Lang didn't involve him at all during the last ten days of working on the script, which hurt Brecht's feeling tremendously. You can't cast aside someone like Brecht for being a nuisance.

Lang was an emigrant in America too.

Yes. He used to work for the UFA. He did those terrible epics: *Metropolis, The Nibelungen* and *Doctor Marbuse* – he was a cheapjack moviemaker, but also made quite an interesting film, *M.* You could say he was an admirer of Brecht in theory until they worked together in practice. He was a true ideologue. You can admire Brecht in an abstract way, but this admiration only makes sense when you are also able to work together. It wasn't good.

Do you know anything about Karl Korsch?

Only a little. I once met him at Brecht's in Denmark. He was formerly a law professor at the University of Halle then, for a short time, Minister of Justice in Thuringia, also a member of the Central Committee or of the Politburo of the KPD. In 1924 (or '23 or '25 – you'll have to look that up in the party history), he left the party and has since worked as a freelance academic. He mostly published theoretical papers and, as far as I know, doesn't do battle against his old party by which I mean the KPD. He's an opponent, but of the rather genteel sort. For some reason or other he still wants to … he sees it as his main task, and I quote: 'to expose dialectics to be a swindle'. In him Brecht acquired a comrade who was just about his complete opposite, but Korsch is a very intelligent, educated man and that must have attracted him to Brecht.

They were writing to each other until the time in America ended and Brecht had, as one can see, acquired a lot of knowledge about Marxism from him.

Brecht had a brilliant quality, which was that where there was something to learn, he was able to learn it critically. He didn't become a 'Korschist' – Korsch opposed dialectics. He thought dialectical materialism was an invention, a phantasmagoria.

A few times I found the names Albert Schreiner, Hermann Duncker and Jacob Walcher in his Journal.

Our old Hermann Duncker is magnificent … As you know, he was a leader and one of the great teachers of the working class movement and a great friend and admirer of Brecht. Walcher, a splendid working class functionary and union specialist of the KPD, resigned from the party for two years, but has now rejoined. He's a great chap, first class. He is a worker from Swabia, who combines practical skills with a theoretical instinct – very valuable! Schreiner is a historian. I know him, but maybe Weigel can say more about him.

And then I found the name, Ben Hecht.

He's a famous journalist from Chicago. He wrote one of the most frequently performed American plays, *Front Page*. Ben Hecht didn't have a clue who Brecht was. I had a cursory acquaintance with him through my friend Odets and the pianist Levant and I met him a few times. He's a clever hack, a soap opera writer – had no idea who Brecht was! He must have met Brecht somewhere, maybe even at my place, but I can't be sure about that any more.

And Dieterle?

William Dieterle, a former actor under Reinhardt, then a director and one of the few Germans who achieved success as a film director in America. Oh well, he was a great admirer of Brecht and helped him a lot, especially at the beginning. His conduct towards Brecht was so exemplary that I won't criticise his artistic work; out of respect for Brecht I'll say as little as possible about Dieterle's talents, that is – nothing.

Were you there when Brecht and Reinhardt met?

Yes, we met at Reinhardt's.[108] Reinhardt had just read *Fears and Misery of the Third Reich* and said to Brecht: 'This is surely the best since Büchner'. Brecht was delighted with this praise. Reinhardt, at that time, was very ill and virtually out of money but he still had some of the glitter of the old times about him – a butler, a villa by the sea and all that. It was pathetic.

Brecht mentions a Robert Thören.

A cheapjack writer, a former actor under Reinhardt who was quite successful in America and died about nine months ago in Munich.

And Czinner?

Paul Czinner, Elisabeth Bergner's husband, did some film business in the shadow of that great actress – an unpleasant figure, but an admirer of Brecht.

Brecht also met Alexander Granach and Oskar Homolka.

Alexander Granach was a splendid actor. And the infamous Homolka was a type of Viennese Apache, hugely talented, very amusing, funny, fresh, unbelievably talented, who, as I've already told you, never wrote to us and was never to be seen again after the HUAC scandal[109] Brecht and I (Homolka also used to be my friend) were involved in. Brecht's feelings were very hurt by that.

At the back of my mind I have the idea that Brecht imagined Homolka playing Galileo.

That would have been extremely interesting, too – Homolka as Schweyk was fantastic also as Azdak, alternating with Ernst Busch. But this guy was too rich; he inherited money and now he's a millionaire and drives around in a Rolls Royce. He doesn't give a damn about his old socialist friends.

Then you mentioned Mordecai Gorelik when you talked about the New York Mother *affair.*

He's an excellent stage designer and a very good friend of Brecht's and mine. His book about theatre, a history of stage design, is a very valuable contribution. I have it here, by the way.[110]

Somewhere I read about someone called Steinbeck.

Do you mean John Steinbeck, the writer?

I don't know. I only remember the entry vaguely.

Brecht never got to know him, maybe he writes about him, possibly about his book *The Grapes of Wrath*, which Brecht admired very much.

Then I would like to hear something about Brecht's collaboration with Grete Steffin.

Well, Grete Steffin was a great kid! She was a working class girl from Berlin (relatives of hers are still alive today and I see them here and there), astonishingly gifted – with brilliant taste in the most sophisticated literary matters, although she was self-taught. Sadly, she was severely tubercular and died of TB. She was Brecht's most valuable assistant and I have to say that the description of the working class milieu in *Fears and Misery* could never have been written without her. Steffin helped to convey to Brecht a knowledge of the Berlin workers in their kitchen living rooms – Brecht desperately needed that. He became very attached to her and was still shaken by her death from this severe tuberculosis when he was in America. She was a courageous, highly talented woman whom I admire very much. I even dedicated a musical composition to her.[111]

What did Brecht think of Bloch?

Well, since Bloch is under attack at the moment, I wouldn't want to say anything about him, not even for your archive. I refuse to comment.[112]

And what about Brecht's collaboration with Herzfelde and Heartfield?[113]

You can only say that Brecht was infatuated with John Heartfield. He totally admired this wonderful man and did everything he could to help him. His constant concern was: what do we do about Heartfield and when will there be a major exhibition of his work? This only happened after Brecht's death. As you may know, initially there were problems with Heartfield's montages being accepted in our GDR (they had a different understanding of art in those days) but now, at this moment, he's … well, he went far beyond mere 'rehabilitation'; there's no comparison – *Nationalpreis*,[114] a huge exhibition – now he's the role model for all GDR artists. For many years that's what Brecht fought for but unfortunately he didn't live long enough to see it happen.

He put Heartfield's name forward very early for the Nationalpreis.

Again and again – and when he was a member of the Academy of Arts. When he thought really highly of you, Brecht was your best friend; then he spared no effort. He regarded Wieland Herzfelde highly as a brilliant publisher and as a man of great literary taste.

Were you aware that Brecht wasn't so happy with the edition of the 100 Poems?[115]

I made him aware of how scandalous I found what had been done to the punctuation, for instance, in the poem 'The Jewish Whore Marie Sanders' to mention just one example. Whatever did

Herzfelde do there, for God's sake? Or, to give another example, the last four lines were left out of 'Song of the Cranes'.[116] I called Brecht up all the time in Buckow. I was in the final stage of editing my first volume[117] and, comparing the texts from the published edition with my manuscript again, found these discrepancies. For example:
'One morning, early at nine
She went through the city in just a shirt'.

This is Brecht's version, as I have it in my manuscript. In the book, however, my friend Wieland (whom I otherwise like a lot) had printed:
'One morning, early at nine o'clock
She went through the city in just a shirt'.[118]

Even after I pointed out ten of these errors to Brecht, he was still reluctant to look into Wieland's mistakes. On one occasion, I called him and said: 'But Bert, don't you see! What he's done is just impossible! You have to admit that!' 'Yeeesss', he responded. And Helli said to me: 'You know, he's such a loyal friend'. All that aside, one has to say that Wieland Herzfelde made some enormous contributions to German literature; his publishing house, the Malik-Verlag, is a classic publishing house and his knowledge of certain literary genres is astonishing. But even an important man like Herzfelde can make careless mistakes – to improve Brecht perhaps? You can't improve Brecht.

Then there is the name Budzislawski in the Journal.

Our Hermann Budzislawski – he's a great chap.

Do you know if they worked together on a production?

No, but whenever Brecht met Budzislawski, he liked to get the latest political news from him; he was one of his sources of information. Budzislawski read all the newspapers: he always needed to be very well informed, on a daily basis, about what was going on. Budzislawski could give you, intelligently and humorously, a summary of the international political events of the past eight days – it was simply a pleasure listening. Whenever Brecht went to Leipzig, he always visited the Budzislawskis where he had this superb Chinese food, which Brecht liked so much and where he was always made wonderfully welcome as a guest. The Budzislawskis were, in turn, great admirers of Brecht, as is every reasonable human being today.[119]

Then there is Brecht's translator, W. H. Auden.

For God's sake don't call Auden a translator. He is not. Auden is the greatest poet in the English language. Brecht admired him very much.

What I meant was, he translated Brecht, for example the lyrics in Chalk Circle.

Sadly, he didn't do any more than those, because when it comes to language he's a fantastic virtuoso. Regrettably, he has become a Catholic – his political views were left-wing and were influenced by Brecht. Unfortunately, you don't speak enough English otherwise I would lend you Auden's collected poems; in them you'll find certain verse forms and street ballads that show Brecht's influence, although Auden is an original talent. Brecht thought very, very highly of him. The last time they worked together was on Webster's *The Duchess of Malfi*, for Elisabeth Bergner. Brecht always got on with Auden although the Catholic Auden had a certain mistrust for the Marxist Brecht. But the English are civilised people, you know; they won't bring up certain matters.

I think that is enough for today. I suggest closing this meeting.

But you should also mention the name Isherwood – Christopher Isherwood, with whom, especially to make Brecht happy, I always discussed Buddhism. That was how we joked in the evenings. Isherwood discussed it with stony seriousness and I was very serious too. Those conversations... Since a Buddhist is not only *not* allowed to stamp on a fly, he can't insult a composer either, so therefore he had to endure everything I threw at him, and I exploited that ruthlessly. Anything else you want to know, dear Doctor?

No, not for the moment.

Very good. We've covered a lot of ground in this recording. In case I have said something not quite proper about people, I would kindly ask you either to erase it or bury it so deep that it won't be found for the next twenty years.

Yes. But you've hardly ever done that about anyone, except for your enemies.

Well, there are...I don't want to repeat the names, but this passage with Erpenbeck you'll have to...He's an old communist, after all; one has to recognize that – he's not just a rascal. If he behaved badly towards Brecht, intellectually, I mean, oh well, it's not so important any more.

So, we'll plan to have a meeting with Elisabeth Hauptmann.

Any time. Maybe we could talk about the years...Elisabeth will have to tell us – was it in 1928 when she started her work with Brecht? You could ask Weigel. I remember that after the morning's work, about twelve thirty, Brecht often invited me over to Weigel's apartment in *Hohenstaufendamm* to have lunch with them. (After lunch I went home and he had a nap.) Surely, Weigel will remember exactly when those lunches started. I'd known Weigel since 1919, long before I met Brecht but I got to know Hauptmann only through Brecht. I can't very well speak about her enormous talents in front of her, but I just want to say that she was, and still is, a hugely talented girl – astonishingly gifted. In particular she's truly cultured, which is so rare. I'm bound to say that. I'm telling you this before you bring her here.[120]

Erik Wirt, Bertolt Brecht and Hanns Eisler at a Recording Session in Berlin in February 1931.

Conversation 5
13 July 1961

Brecht's Hexameters for the *Communist Manifesto* – Was Brecht a Marxist? – Brecht's Method of *Verfremdung*

After the fourth conversation Bunge and Eisler had to take a break in their work of about three years. Eisler had gone to Vienna and became very ill there. The conversations were continued on 13 July 1961. Bunge raised the topic of Brecht's attempt to turn the Communist Manifesto[121] into verse.

I remember that I was a bit surprised, and I mean surprised in a negative way, that Brecht suddenly started to work on this project, because it was a time when even German-speaking workers weren't aware of this crucial document. I said to myself, 'When we go back it will be so difficult to re-explain and reinterpret the *Manifesto*.' As you know, the *Manifesto*, although it's written in a wonderful language, isn't easy to understand if certain conditions are missing. The most fundamental condition to the understanding of it is the class struggle in practice and, if you leave out the illegal resistance, this was non-existent in Hitler's Germany. That's why I was a bit unenthusiastic about our dear Brecht now complicating the *Manifesto* by putting it into a not very successful form of German poetry, namely the epic hexameter.

I had a certain distrust of the form, that is the epic in hexameters, when I remembered the sad fate of one of Goethe's most brilliant works, *Hermann and Dorothea* which, along with *Reynard the Fox*, ended up in the hands of German grammar school teachers who made it (as far as German lessons are concerned) terribly boring for our young people and left us deeply depressed. When I read

Hermann and Dorothea today, I look at this 'misery' (which also brought the great Goethe down) with great admiration.

When we think of the end of *Hermann and Dorothea*, especially the passage where he talks about peace, we see Goethe in the light of our experiences of the last fifty years and discover a new side to him. But his miserable… let's say, his attitude towards the French Revolution, which is the main topic of *Hermann and Dorothea* (it's about fugitives from the French Revolution who flee over the Rhine), is very strange to us. Just remember that Goethe, who was then accompanying the Duke of Weimar, followed the idiotic call of the Duke of Braunschweig and went as far as Valmy in Champagne in France! Although he didn't see the Jacobins, he heard the whistle of their bullets and the retreat made a tremendous impression on him. But the description of the suffering émigrés from Lotharingia and from Alsace – so undialectically (and so beautifully!), is a part of our German misery, which, frankly, I wouldn't want to do without.

With those experiences in my mind, I knew, of course, that Brecht could deliver something exceptional. What it showed mainly was that the *Communist Manifesto* is even more complicated to understand in hexameters than it is in prose – which is already hard enough. And that's why I was concerned that my friend the genius was devoting himself to this most complicated task, which would, in the long run, have been neither practically nor politically useful to us.

If you're reading Hermann and Dorothea *now with such pleasure, is it because of the content about which you've just spoken or is it also because you enjoy the form?*

The form is… Goethe is Goethe, although in his poetry I see patchwork too; in other words, it doesn't have the unity that you usually find in Goethe. The demands of the classical metre force Goethe to go through certain contortions, contortions of the highest possible order, and this linguistic virtuosity, even in *Hermann and Dorothea*, is something I can get really enthusiastic about, without being a know-all.

Today, however, I read through the lenses of experience. You know we read the classics five times; we read and re-read them – as we do with texts by Brecht, by the way. After significant events I always listen differently to Beethoven, or even to this awful Wagner who was, I suppose, a great master. I read Goethe in different ways before and after the Great War. After the great revolutionary events in Germany, and after the workers seized power in the Soviet Union, I read him differently again. During the great crisis of capitalism before fascism took over, I read him differently once more. And in the emigration, I re-read Goethe with the greatest passion, because then I saw a completely new element of humanity that I'd never observed before because I'd been interested in other qualities in the classics. After my return to Germany in 1948, I read Goethe for the fifth time, once more making fresh discoveries because, again, I was seeing things in a different light – not my personal light but the light of historical development.

This is why, nowadays, I read *Hermann and Dorothea* with great pleasure. First because it's beautiful (as a Marxist, I could defend this) owing to its perfectly executed form. Don't forget that we, especially we Marxists, often behave like barbarians when it comes to aesthetics – a bit like our forefathers, the Jacobins. And second, because of the strange contradictions inherent in the work arising from Goethe's petit bourgeois views, or rather than petit bourgeois, perhaps I should say Goethe's limited German and parochial views. When, for example, Dorothea explains why her fiancé left Verdun for revolutionary Paris and, during the September terror, became a victim, we can see certain contemporary parallels: a young man leaves Verdun to go and fight for what he believes is right and falls victim to those who are fighting each other for what *they* believe is right. That rings a bell and we are able to make connections – but a different generation would find this impossible. You have to have been through a lot to understand this.

It's probably not as complicated with the Manifesto *as it is with* Hermann and Dorothea. *In this case, you couldn't foresee the way that certain current events would suddenly create new ways of looking at it. But the* Communist Manifesto *never lost its currency, even if, for different reasons from* Hermann and Dorothea, *it fell temporarily into oblivion. The subject matter should have lost nothing because of Brecht's adaptation. What it's all about is whether it's possible to enhance interest in the subject matter through the transformation.*

Yes, and here's an insufficiently thought-through contradiction that I entertained at that time. I didn't want my friend – and again, I must repeat that this was my private opinion – to get involved with work that I thought unnecessary. In 1945, the concept of doing what was necessary, and that included our artistic work, was very important for all of us.

The intellectual content of the *Manifesto* stands in stark contrast to the quiet flow of hexameters, although the hexameters of Homer do have a truly great descriptive power. The *Manifesto* describes entire conditions and whole developments and, for the first time, delivers a historical perspective, which goes far beyond Hegel and which puts him in his proper place. But, the hexameters form seemed contradictory to me, especially because of the modernity of the *Manifesto*. There was a risk of true formalism. This isn't just the view of 'malicious Marxists'. You'll find that both Goethe and Hegel disapproved of formalism too; of course they did.

So, I asked myself: 'Why?' Wouldn't it sound hilarious if you said: 'Then the bourgeoisie seizes with iron hand ... '? Wouldn't the word 'bourgeoisie' be completely anachronistic in a hexameter? Things that were already difficult for Goethe to achieve consistently – can hexameters really be compatible with the modern language of communism? These were my initial reservations.

And then I immediately noticed something that is easy to see because every schoolboy can do it for the reason that his father forced him to learn how, that Brecht actually couldn't write in hexameters. I wouldn't have given it a second thought if Brecht hadn't stubbornly insisted that they *were* hexameters. I don't care which verse form he wrote in – one thing is certain: it wasn't hexameters. And so I was deflected. I now had to defend the hexameter. I said to Brecht: 'I truly admire what you're writing but you're not writing what you think you are. You're writing a kind of jazzed-up hexameter, sometimes they're pentameters, sometimes they're iambic forms, kind of hypertrophic iambic forms, in a nutshell, the strict form, *you ain't got it*'.

Unsurprisingly, Brecht was deeply irritated. He really wanted to master this form, and consulted the even more highly educated Feuchtwanger, who also told him: 'They're not hexameters'. Whereupon Feuchtwanger and I started to declaim hexameters to Brecht in Greek (Brecht hadn't learnt Greek) showing him where the caesura, the hiatus, occurs and how it is augmented. [Eisler quotes the first two verses from Homer's *Iliad* in Greek.] Having been fortunate enough not to have been tortured by an old Greek professor for six years as I was, Brecht, in short, could only copy by ear.

Not that it wouldn't have made a great difference then anyway – but so what? I asked myself what level of cultural appreciation would readers of the *Manifesto* have to attain in order to be able to enjoy it as poetry? We would have to assume a stage of social development where the *Manifesto* was as familiar to everyone as the Bible, and where a poetic version would bring to it a new interest, an aesthetic interest, like the great religious epics, which assume a common knowledge of the Christian religion. Take Klopstock's *Messiah*, or any of the great passages from the Bible that are continually being adapted – or indeed music, which is the same. I'm afraid I wasn't able to envisage a time when the *Manifesto* became so well known that a poeticized version would give it a new social meaning. I tell you straight: the moment has not yet arrived, although I certainly think that the day will come – I'm arguing against myself now.

I beg your pardon! We're not used to learning prose by heart, only in school you learn poems by heart. Could it be that Brecht believed that the reader really could become more involved in the Manifesto *if it was in verse? I assume that, ultimately, he would have gone along with his hexameters, despite also being very critical of them. Recited, spoken hexameters do have a different effect from a read prose text. I think the flow of hexameters goes well with the material of the* Manifesto. *And you yourself pointed out the description of historical periods and occurrences. When you read Brecht's poems aloud, you feel the power of the language. That has great strength.*

That's right. Besides, we're not such traditionalists that we say the hexameter is weak! Brecht is strong and to hell with the hexameters! It's pointless to demand today that this man should write Latin hexameters like a minor seventeenth-century Latin poet – and then be awarded a certificate from the monastery school. That's not what I meant. But I tell myself, the hexameter didn't extend further than a certain so-called educated circle (despite Goethe or Voss' magnificent translation of Homer). And even that dries up roughly in the middle of the nineteenth century. While at the end of the eighteenth century an educated person would still know his Homer (partly by heart, too), in the nineteenth century he (Homer) became more trivialized and sank into oblivion, although in my day, we still learnt the famous 100 verses from the *Iliad* by heart. It was a certain responsibility we had towards culture. Homer was 'alive' only in the classical period. During the romantic period of German literature, he slowly died and became an abstract shell and since then, even though he was such a rich source and artistic beacon for the great masters of the classical and the pre-classical periods, his fame has been merely regurgitated.

'Good Heavens!' I say to myself, 'The very Devil! Homer isn't popular in Germany, neither read nor recited.' He still isn't popular today and neither are Goethe's epics or even Voss' idylls, like *Luise*. The magnificent Dante can't be hammered into German heads, although that's probably partly due to the mediocre translation, nor even into the heads of the intelligentsia. How are our industrial workers (they, apart from the intelligentsia, are our audience after all) suddenly supposed to digest something in verse which they don't understand in prose, not even if it's read aloud to them? Because reading the *Communist Manifesto* aloud can only happen in groups where it can be analysed sentence by sentence.

Reading Marx is not about private diligence any more – he can only be dealt with collectively, an experience gained by the working class in their educational associations since 1860. The individual – neither the progressive worker nor a member of the intelligentsia – can't digest the classics of Marxism any more, except for a few who, while versed in philosophy and economics, tend to be politically weak. So, even politically interested people have to take laboriously small steps in order to understand something. The enjoyment of hexameters doesn't clarify the matter; it merely poeticizes it and poeticizing something doesn't always mean that it becomes clearer … I can't remember Brecht's verses any more. But in those days I asked myself, 'What's it for?'

Well, and here comes a big slice of self-criticism, I took a far too practical view. I thought: 'What baggage do we bring back with us when we return to our destroyed Germany? What can we rebuild it with? We won't achieve a lot with the *Manifesto* in hexameters.' Today, in 1961, I regret having discouraged a great master like Brecht from this project rather than having encouraged him.

Don't get me wrong, if Brecht wanted to do something, nobody could restrain him – nobody, regardless of who or what he was. So I wasn't really the one who held him back. But if, in the isolation of the emigration, a man hears every day from his best friends: 'What on earth are you doing? And anyway, the hexameters are wrong!' … after a few weeks, he'll simply lose his enthusiasm. Both

Feuchtwanger and I discouraged him, and we were both completely in the wrong. We had completely forgotten that Marxism and the struggle of the working class take place to varying extents, and in many different ways and arenas, regardless of any considerations of practicability. Were we to have the *Communist Manifesto* in epic form by Brecht, it would have gone down in history as a unique work of art – it would have been magnificent for the finest literary minds to have had access to it.

I couldn't see this at the time, neither could I foresee that our young working class students would already be there to consume Brecht's poetry like hot cakes. This is a major warning: one must think about the current questions of the day, one must weigh them up, but must not squat on them like a frog in his pond. We should think more about the future, that's what we should do. This was my big mistake – but not Brecht's.

Well, Brecht not only had friends who tried to talk him out of it. On one of his trips to New York, he took the manuscript with him and read it to Walcher, Duncker and Schreiner.

What did they say?

They liked it and encouraged Brecht to continue with the work. On top of that, Brecht was in constant communication with Karl Korsch. Korsch read the manuscript very carefully and made lots of suggestions. So, Brecht also had people encouraging him.

That's right – good, you've just taken a weight off my mind. It must be that, after some time, Brecht simply lost the joy in it, and I was, certainly, only a detractor (he had supporters and detractors). And because Brecht always decided for himself, he took the difficulty of this enterprise into account and just dropped it before his hasty return to Germany in 1947. Nevertheless, I can't talk myself out of a little responsibility. Had there been somebody to encourage him in Hollywood, and not only in Boston where Korsch lived, maybe he would have finished it. In brief, this is, in any case, a story you can learn from.

You said, that you think the Manifesto *can be seen today as a work of genius. Is that because Brecht might have foreseen that there are young people who engage with the* Manifesto? *Or with hexameters? Or is it because, today, you now like the* Manifesto *in verse because of its technical form?*

I don't think that our young people are engaged with hexameters, but they could have got to know some through Brecht – and only Brecht, because no one else is acceptable. Those who don't think highly of the *Manifesto*, and there are quite a few among our own youth, might perhaps have tried reading it in prose had they discovered Brecht's poetic version. They have no idea how difficult it is. I'm referring to a certain section of our youth, not all of them. I know brilliant, and not so brilliant, young people who can't cope with the *Manifesto* and it would have been worth trying to bring it close to them via a detour through Brecht's poetry.

It is strange that people who want nothing to do with Marxism consume Brecht like hot cakes. The same would probably have happened with the *Manifesto* in verse. It's no exaggeration if I say that, when you have a genius with Brecht's brilliance and magnetism (he is such a historic figure), many things become much more attractive to an audience when expressed in verse. It's the same with his plays – so unlike what's thought of as boring and grey in the shallow prose of everyday life or in the complexities of the class struggle, or in the faculties of the *Gewi* (as we rather oddly abbreviate our *Gesellschaftswissenschaften* [Social Sciences]).

Because of Brecht the *Manifesto* acquires a golden patina. It was impossible for me to foresee that. If Brecht were still alive today, I'd say to him: 'Please finish the project immediately so that our young people get to know it, at least in your version.'

Brecht wanted to continue with it in Berlin. He probably didn't get round to it because of all his other work.

Yes, in order to undertake such a task you'd either have to be on holiday, in hospital or in the emigration – but not in the middle of your day-to-day work.

In the manuscript of one of the versions, there are symbols that I haven't been able to identify up to now. After many of the verses, for example, there's the letter 'g'. Is it possible that you put these notes there?

[Looks at the manuscript.] Yes, that's quite possible. 'National interest, one law and one government...' – I put a question mark there because it seemed to me that the verse jarred; 'will be brought together in one nation with the one and only national interest, one law and one government'. The metre's wrong – these are formal things that every high-school teacher would be able to explain better than me! But what an absolutely idiotic criticism! I herewith solemnly withdraw it!

I'm interested to know if you had the manuscript in your hands then.

Yes. Brecht often showed it to me, but I didn't correct anything, just made him aware of some things.

Please, here is a verse: 'not as purpose for living is this house, the cloth not for clothing' and in the margin in pencil is a 'g'. What could it mean?

It could stand for *gut* [good] – but it's more likely to be *geht* [this works]; we wouldn't have used a term like 'good'.

Is it safe to say that the note was made by you? It would be important to know for the annotated critical edition of Brecht's works.

It's most likely made by me. It could be my handwriting; I can't remember exactly but I'm pretty certain. That was Brecht's method. He'd say: 'Make a note in the margin.' He didn't say that just to me but to all his friends and pupils: 'When something occurs to you, make a note in the margin. Write it down!' He immediately wanted everything in black and white.

I'd like to change the subject. Was Brecht a Marxist? Does this label accurately define him?

This is an academic question – and it's a difficult one to answer. Everybody will be surprised at that because, of course, in common parlance Brecht is a Marxist, although I'd prefer to call him a Leninist because he learnt more from Lenin than is commonly known. None of his biographers, I can't remember your book about Brecht,[122] has traced Lenin's tremendous influence on Brecht. Lenin was probably Marx's best pupil but with the advantage of reading Marx through the lens of Hegel, something that none of the great reformists, such as Bernstein, Kautsky, not even the great Franz Mehring (whom we all admire very much), did. That's why Lenin's Marxism contains something that is pulsating, dialectical, moveable and contradictory in a new way – something that stimulated Brecht enormously, and which I've been aware of since I was young.

Brecht's favourite essay was Lenin's 'On Climbing High Mountains', which he thought was one of the great masterpieces of international literature. He read Lenin thoroughly and what he especially liked in Lenin was his cleverness in adhering to his principles. This cleverness, this cunning, Lenin's cunning – the cunning of smuggling in rationality where it doesn't have a place, or of rescuing it from the quagmire the instant it's about to disappear – you can make progress through force, but also through cleverness, through adherence to principles and through tactical manoeuvrability. Yes, that's what filled Brecht with tremendous enthusiasm.

I remember a little incident that happened in Hamburg. I had a discussion with friends, very clever friends, who are, what they call in West Germany, savants. They consistently and outstandingly argued that Brecht is a Marxist – during the course of which discussion the name Brecht was soon dropped, and my three friends went on to talk with characteristic brilliance about Marxism. This was interesting for the students although not all of them. Finally, however, I protested: 'You know', I said to the students (and this was something really rudimentary), 'In contrast to my friends I don't read Brecht because he's a Marxist – it doesn't even cross my mind. If I want to know about Marx, I read Marx. Don't be surprised by this original viewpoint' I said. 'I read Brecht because he's beautiful.'

This shows how far the doctrine of making a Marxist out of Brecht had gone. I've already said if he was a Leninist, then he was a Marxist too. Do you want to dispute that?

The fundamental thing about Brecht is that he consciously applied the methodology of Marx and Engels – that is dialectical materialism – to a field to which it had never been previously applied, namely to theatre and poetry. We're talking here not only of dialectics but of materialistic dialectics. Brecht, in common with each of the great realists (Flaubert, if you like, Diderot and from Voltaire to Chekhov or Tolstoy), applied dialectics at first instinctively; dialectics are among the tools of a great poet. In Baudelaire, and also in Rimbaud, you'll find traces of great dialectics, the ability to reason into contradictions – in Apollinaire too (such an outlandish poet). Brecht had already used it in his early works but his developing it consciously into a method and also into theatrical theory is an enormous contribution in the theoretical field.

If we label Brecht only as a Marxist then we're calling him a Marxist to people who don't have a clue about Marx. If we want to avoid this kind of monkish argument, I suggest we describe him to non-Marxists the way he is. Put simply, what people in capitalist countries (and unfortunately also in our own country) associate today with the word 'Marx' is not Marx the critical philosopher – (take for example, Marx's important work, *Critique of Hegel's Philosophy of Right* or an early work by Marx and Engels, *The German Ideology*) – but the great economic theories that Marx bequeathed to human history.

If we disregard the Mother's little lecture on the subject of political economy in the second or third scene of *The Mother*,[123] Brecht was able to use very little from the economic works. But the social conditions in Brecht's parables are certainly presented from the Marxist point of view. The social conditions which develop between the poor and the rich, the oppressed and the oppressors are, in a way, if we just look at the theory, the ABC of Marxism. It goes without saying that the theory of surplus value is far more complicated than as it is presented in Brecht's plays, but unless we take pains to popularize this theory it won't go down as well as it does in *The Good Person of Szechuan* where the term 'goodness' is investigated in a very thorough German way, which is just enchanting.

Let us not simplify the phenomenon of Brecht by tying him down to a man like Marx whose significance to us is mainly because of his economic theories. I would suggest that Brecht learnt the theory of dialectical materialism from Marx and Lenin and that he applied it, in his own way, to his poetry, plays and prose writings. We would then have everything in one: dialectical materialism, Marx and, in particular, Lenin, who shouldn't be omitted. Many people call themselves Marxists but today that doesn't mean anything.

When we talk about Brecht, we're in a situation of conflict, especially in the capitalist countries. We fight for Brecht. *They* have to swallow Brecht. But *we* will only allow Brecht to be swallowed with all the spikes sticking out. If we say simply 'Marxist', this leads to tedious arguments because most people reflect only on Marx's economics. So, is *St Joan*[124] a Marxist play? Yes – although it's largely a Leninist play. It can't work without violence. Of course Marx has said that violence was necessary, although the counterfeiters, which are the reformists, were bent on concealing violence under the guise of evolution. Lenin brought in a whole new idea that shouldn't be overlooked. I'm horrified to observe that my young friends don't concern themselves sufficiently with the phenomenon of how Lenin established Marxism in its proper position, something which he did in the crucial years of Brecht's development. That's why Brecht has to be described as a pupil of two great masters who applied their methods to a new field.

In West Germany, Brecht is only 'swallowed' – that's true. If you call Brecht a Marxist in West Germany and you explain what you mean by it, then the best that can happen is that people will start thinking about Marxism, and that prejudices can be cleared up. Maybe that's better than trying to explain him through his work. Being mindful of this, I think the detour via Brecht to popularize Marxism is legitimate.

You're right – and I'm not against it. I am only saying that if you open up a page in one of Marx's books, one like *Capital*, which has made world history, then you won't find Brecht there. You could find him, though only rarely, because it's too complicated, in *Critique of Hegel's Philosophy of Right* or in *Anti-Dühring*, or in the *Political Economy*. I'm sure you'd find him somewhere, but it would be difficult. Where you would find him least is in historical materialism, one of the most beloved, vulgar parts of Marxism – not that I mean that historical materialism is vulgar; it's just the way it's handled is often absolutely horrific.

Take, for example, Brecht's *The Business Affairs of Mr Julius Caesar* – the most un-Marxist book imaginable and also un-Hegelian but un-Hegelian in a marvellous way. (Hegel makes fun of the way people believe that history is driven by private virtues, sins or vices of individuals; he also believes in the spirit of history – a pointless, Prussian view of history – but Marx put that right.) Marx wouldn't have agreed with Brecht's description of Caesar (his whole critique of Caesar is very funny) and what Caesar did as a private person is of no interest; Caesar's historic function is much more important than a portrayal of his private behaviour. However, the poet, Brecht, by making great use of private behaviour and presenting it as a splendid parable against dictators like Messrs Hitler and Mussolini who were in power at that time, is able to dismantle this 'great' personality Caesar. Bernard Shaw did the same thing, but differently.

While I might agree to the idea that Brecht is a Marxist, I don't know where this leaves my listeners. The statement 'Brecht was Marxist' reminds me of social democratic workers' youth educational evenings in 1913 – but that's just me. On the other hand, if I can explain it how I've just explained it to you (forgive my superficiality) then we'll get into much more fruitful territory. You have to get deep into Marx and Lenin, you have to consider high politics and battles in philosophy as well as Marx's economic discoveries, and then suddenly a completely fresh wind starts to blow.

Good, we're drawing to a conclusion. Let's just agree that Brecht *was* a Marxist and then, like Leninists rather than social democrats (by which I mean the old-style social democrats, not today's mouldy ones), we can really start examining what *kind* of Marxist he was.

Recently you said Brecht was mainly a writer who wrote from a plebeian point of view, someone who looks at society from below.

Yes, that was his main virtue. It's clear that nearly all of his characters are portrayed from this plebeian point of view, including the ruling class – a 'foreshortened' view, one might say. (I think my friend Hans Mayer wrote something significant about this in the first special edition of the journal *Sinn und Form* which was on Brecht and which I should look at again.) Brecht's plebeian attitude extended to his poetry as well. The term 'plebeian' needs to be re-defined. I had to explain it to students in Hamburg because they had no idea what it meant. In bourgeois terminology, to describe somebody as 'plebeian' is contemptuous. It means uneducated, rough, but to Marx, being plebeian is a great virtue. To act as a plebeian means to act un-ideologically, that's if we use the word 'ideology' in the Marxist sense and not as it is commonly used by our friends today to refer to the blurring of social conditions or 'the murky superstructure'. Let us accept Marx's definition of ideology and avoid modifying (as Don Quixote did) the vocabulary of our period whenever we have a private conversation.

The portrayal of the customs officer in the wonderful poem 'Legend of the Origin of the Book Tao-Te-Ching' is an example of Brecht's plebeian writing. When the customs officer enquires: 'Did he get *sumfin'* back?' – 'sumfin'' that's Brecht using slang; the plebeian sentence emerges and becomes delicious poetry. Other examples are the way the ruling class is looked at from a truly plebeian standpoint in *Chalk Circle*, or how the gods (yes, even the gods) are viewed in *The Good Person of Szechuan*, where Brecht's instructions read: 'The more rotten they get, the more they shine like gold' (so that, at the end when they are most rotten, they appear in glittering gold).[125] And I don't need to tell you about *The Mother* or *St Joan of the Stockyards* (one of my most favourite plays), *The Round Heads and the Pointed Heads* – three masterpieces where you have true plebeianism in its noblest sense.

You can't describe Brecht as a Marxist in an abstract sense. The plebeian in Marxism and how it was transposed into art created a new plebeian realism that had never existed in German literature – let's be quite honest about that! Discounting Gerhart Hauptmann's *The Weavers*, which was actually based on documents from the weavers' rebellion, and discounting the character of Mother Wolfen[126] (the best comedy we've ever had), can you tell me where we can find the plebeian in German literature? In Thomas Mann's *Buddenbrooks*, you'll find the plebeian in three lines, as a joke, while in *Magic Mountain* and *Doctor Faustus* there's nothing – the worker doesn't exist, neither does the plebeian perspective. With Thomas Mann everything becomes virtuoso 'literature' and not always in the best sense. But in Brecht nothing becomes 'literature', which is why he retains his distinctive common touch.

The strange thing is that a work of art that exists at a high artistic level can also possess a common touch, which makes it (ironically speaking) 'low'. It's not intended to deceive and no-one will be fooled – indeed anybody, whatever their level of education, will be able to understand it. This is as true for bankers, who surely are among the worst educated (one of Proust's ideas,[127] not mine), as it is for the ruling class who are not only uneducated but have no feeling or outlet for art. And the workers? Well, it's their literature. Brecht said and wrote in his Journal: 'The working class will always be able to associate my name with the plays I wrote for them.'[128]

To be plebeian, an artist should not only have the intention of writing *for* somebody, but also be able to represent that somebody's point of view. These are the building blocks of Brecht's art, from his most delicate poetry to his great plays – I leave literary experts to give explicit examples. My job is simply to make this point. In any description of Brecht, the plebeian has to be present, otherwise the description is inaccurate in the same way it would be were you to say Brecht was a Marxist and leave out Lenin.

There are plays, poems and also prose by Brecht in which the plebeian is indirectly presented.

Yes, that's the usual way!

It's different in The Business Affairs of Mr Julius Caesar. *Here the plebeian point of view is demonstrated by reciting Rarus' diary.*[129]

Yes, from the plebeian perspective.

But you still have objections to this book?

No, I don't have any objections! I'm only saying that Hegel or Marx wouldn't have agreed with it. They couldn't have foreseen that the book would be written in a time of great dictators like Hitler and Mussolini and that it would be a plebeian necessity for Brecht to take such a dictator apart. Read, for example, what Hegel writes about Caesar in his *Lectures on the Philosophy*.[130] That Brecht, who knew the book as well as I did, ignored it shows his audacity with regard to the classics.[131] (Marx's or rather Hegel's, statement that 'For a valet there is no hero'[132] meant that people wouldn't want a job as a valet, which involved seeing the master, a great player on the stage of world theatre, in his underwear.) In a way, Brecht overstepped a taboo for Marxists (a Hegelian taboo, since Marxists are actually Hegelians) and had to face the objection 'But Brecht, that won't work. You can't take Caesar apart – the progressive creator of Rome's central power (just like Elizabeth in England) – and portray him as a corrupt windbag.' But Brecht didn't just portray him like this. He wrote a parable[133] demonstrating how, as always, the Stock Exchange and the wheat speculators turn him into Caesar, and how his debts in particular compel him to become Caesar – in such delicious German that I was ready to throw any objections of Hegel or Marx overboard and to accept this little book completely. Here I have a clear conscience. While Korsch, Benjamin and other friends strenuously advised him not to continue writing it[134] because it would (a) not be novel and (b) be impossible in respect of Hegel and Marx, I said to Brecht: 'You're absolutely right, continue with it.' Alas, he didn't, but at least this time (thank God) I didn't say anything stupid.

In Brecht's works concerning historical characters, there is always the danger that people think he mainly wanted to portray their stories – in Life of Galileo *the story of the historical Galileo and in* The Business Affairs of Mr Julius Caesar *the story of the historical Caesar.*

In *Julius Caesar* it didn't portray the historical Caesar, rather the composite figure of a dictator.

The same with Galileo.

Yes, although in this he draws on history at a richer level.

He takes from history only what serves his fable, which he also does for Julius Caesar: *Brecht studied the literature and, in my opinion, used for his story only what seemed useful to him of the historical Caesar, and especially what we understand of him today. He describes the economic circumstances in such a way that anyone can understand them without studying the sources.*

Speaking as a Marxist (and a Leninist too), we have to be careful that we don't become barbarians in aesthetic matters. The great danger for a young movement such as the working class movement (it's historically young when compared with other classes) is that, in aesthetic matters, it becomes intolerant in a way that we associate with our forefathers, the Jacobins. Think of the Jacobins (this is rather a poor comparison because Brecht is a completely different kettle of fish) and of the daggers they drew to hunt down Watteau and Fragonard whose work represented the scum of all painting. In their paintings, aristocratic ladies were depicted as whores and whores as ladies. This was art as absolute luxury, art as pure entertainment and it was banned because it seemed to endanger the state!

With the historical emergence, and functioning, of a class that doesn't know how to deal with its recent past, you'll always find this kind of intolerance, an intolerance that sometimes leads to barbarism. Unfortunately, my friends also exhibited this intolerance towards *Julius Caesar* by throwing the aesthetics, which play a huge role in art, overboard. Whether historical or not, Brecht's way of taking apart a dictator who was determined to stamp his boot on Europe's neck, was profound and brilliant and absolutely commendable. It's still utterly magnificent to read today. What I particularly like in it is what I call its 'lower materialism'. And this is a great method. You know how they always go into raptures about how big business stands either before or behind the great bourgeois ideas. In *Julius Caesar* big business comes before Caesar's great ideas, or after, or they produce each other mutually. Even we Marxists can derive pleasure from that.

Brecht used current affairs: like France's downfall, the behaviour of the ruling class in France and so on.

Yes, that was one of Brecht's parables and it's a pity that he didn't finish writing it – and all the other things that he didn't finish, or wasn't able to write. I'm speaking here as a pure Brechtian and I suspend my judgement here. His friends (and I count myself as one of them) should have done everything to support him in his work; because during the emigration you have to depend on the voices of four or five people who happen to be around at the time. It takes a lot of courage to start and finish great works, and a great master shouldn't be disturbed while working – that, I think, is a simple statement of true, healthy obviousness. If the work wasn't any good, well, with Brecht's status you need more than a simple 'wrong' or 'right' in aesthetic matters.

People who met Brecht only in the last years knew that he actually didn't waste a single minute of his working time. Was that the same during the emigration?

It was the same.

Considering the enormous difficulties during the time in exile, weren't there any doldrums?

I wasn't aware of any. If Brecht wasn't working directly on something, he was full of plans and sketches; and then there were the poems. No, there weren't any doldrums, at least not like Beethoven, for example, who didn't compose anything for seven or eight years. Goethe didn't produce anything for more than ten years, I think, until Schiller got him going again. Brecht never experienced that. He was always a very active spirit for the simple reason that he was tormented by boredom. He had to be active simply to be able to walk on the earth, otherwise life wouldn't have been any fun for him. If he wasn't writing a play, he'd start on something else and three or four people would be called in to hear his plans. Experiments and beginnings would be made and nothing would come of them and then something else would be started and carried through to the end. This kind of fluid productivity had really existed since 1928, for more or less all the time I collaborated with Brecht. There were no doldrums.

Could you tell me something about Brecht's reading?

That's difficult to say, because I didn't control Brecht's reading. I can only tell you something 'negative', which is that, except for crime stories, he didn't read novels. Even when I pleaded with him to read Proust, he wanted Proust reported to him. He did look at Joyce's *Ulysses*, because of the technique and every now and then he read Feuchtwanger. I know nothing about his readings of philosophy.

To what extent did Brecht study Hegel? You must have had conversations with him about this?

I certainly did. Brecht had a marvellous talent for reading only what he could use; from a heavy tome of Hegel he was astute enough to select only what he could use – I've no idea how he did this. In the bourgeois and indeed in the Marxist sense, he was a very educated person, with gaps as we all have (it's impossible to be an encyclopaedist these days). I can't really go into detail about Brecht's reading because I don't know what he read in the evenings after I'd left. He had very good knowledge of Marx (including Marxist economics) and of Lenin, and a certain knowledge of Hegel – but to what extent I don't know. When you're friends, you don't sit down and test each other.

It was more a question of what you know.

He gave me Me-ti[135] to read, for example, and I told him that he really had to read Hegel's *Aesthetics*, which he did – although we struggled with Hegel's foreword where the objective spirit makes strange leaps. But when it comes to pure facts, to real descriptions of art, Hegel is peerless. He made a big impression on Brecht. I drew Brecht's attention to the way Hegel writes about Shakespeare, about how the aesthetic of 'ugliness' emerges from the traditional depiction of thieves (always portrayed as ugly) of the early Middle

Ages and to much more, whereupon he avidly read the *Aesthetics* much more critically than I. In this respect, Brecht was ahead of me. He also criticized Hegel even more than I did. He had no time for Immanuel Kant. We had a huge argument on the occasion of the performance of *The Tutor*.[136] Kant's definition of marriage is well known: a contract undertaken for the mutual use of genital organs. Brecht found this tremendously funny, recognizing it as the cause of the misery of the German schoolmaster. I didn't find it funny at all; on the contrary, I thought it enormously progressive that a relationship designated by the church as holy could become statutory law and be described by Kant so dryly and soberly. 'Unfortunately,' I said to Brecht when he made fun, a lot of fun, of Kant, 'this shows that the young revolutionary bourgeoisie is only in our heads; for us it's only attainable as an idea. The bourgeoisie in France cut off the aristocrats' heads' – that's as far as revolution went with the Jacobins, Robespierre wasn't any more revolutionary in his *Triumph of Reason*. I didn't win the argument over my objection to Brecht's passage in the *Tutor*. The performance was a huge success among the young people and was received with gales of laughter. I laughed with them as well every now and then because I am, after all, a dialectician. I do enjoy a joke, even if it's a joke in error. Anyway, it's not the job of Lenz' play to point out the role of Kant's description of statutory laws, or his ethics, which are somehow very strange and contradictory. In the end a play isn't a philosophical excursion.

Brecht gave you Me-ti. Do you know which other Chinese philosophers he was interested in?

He was very much impressed by Confucius and especially by *Tao-Te-Ching*.[137]

Did you get to know Brecht's Me-ti?

He used the form of Me-ti. *Keuner*[138] is actually a Chinese character, meaning 'Nobody'. Chinese philosophy greatly influenced Brecht, as a stimulus to his thinking, especially in 1929/1930. He gave me Me-ti in 1930, or was it 1931? There was at that time a splendid Sinological Society in Wiesbaden, I think, and they published philosophical works, which Brecht was given by his friends. That was a great discovery for us.

How far would you say is Brecht's work autobiographical? When Refugee Conversations *was published, there were speculations as to whether 'Ziffel' or 'Kalle' were modelled on Brecht, in the same way that Brecht was previously identified with 'Keuner'.*

That's nonsense. Brecht never expressed himself 'biographically'. He was an absolute non-romantic. Brecht did everything possible to wipe out any of his history: 'Obliterate the Traces!'[139] He never provided any information about his past; his youth is not well known, nor is his development.[140] I knew his house in Bleichstrasse, in Augsburg; he invited me there once. I was with him in Augsburg in 1929 or 1930. I know the friends from his youth, his father, and his brother. I've known them since I was thirty. It must have been a strange youth. He never said anything about his mother.[141] Brecht's father was a very reserved type, a self-made paper worker who later became director of the mill, but Brecht never spoke about this.

Which of his friends did you get to know?

Georg Pfanzelt, Müllereisert, Hartmann and Caspar Neher. We all know Caspar Neher very well. He's still alive today, thank God. Pfanzelt was a small-time civil servant in Augsburg. I didn't see anything interesting in him. I got to know him only through some beautiful poems; it was a sort of high-school friendship. Hartmann, who unfortunately is already dead, was a judge, a nice man although I couldn't see anything interesting at all in him either. Müllereisert was a very good sports doctor who later lived in Berlin. You probably know of him. Unfortunately, he is dead too. He always took care of Brecht.

When I was in Augsburg with Brecht in the evenings, we usually played cards with these people. We played for pennies. It was a game I didn't know, where I got advice from the clever Pfanzelt and Hartmann, and when I lost two or three marks, there was a huge 'Hooray' from the gangsters who had rooked me, to which Brecht responded with a certain abashed smile. Coming from Berlin, he was actually embarrassed to have such friends. He didn't want to keep his friends from me but he took great care that they didn't do anything stupid – especially politically. It was very touching, considerate even. And there really was a green table cloth, beer, cards and this idiotic card game, which I can't remember any more, that they obviously played when Brecht came to visit; a completely harmless, childish game from his youth. Brecht joined in the game because the judge pestered him but actually he didn't want to play cards in front of me. (By the way, during the emigration we also played some kind of card game, 'Sixty-six' I think, or we played chess.) It greatly embarrassed Brecht that this circle of people suddenly started to pester him wildly in order to rook an outsider like me from Berlin, for one mark fifty, although everything of course was within the limitations of the petit bourgeois.

I'm a little surprised that there is nothing within these friends from Brecht's youth that points to Brecht – they were all pretty mediocre with one exception: Caspar Neher who really is a stage designer of genius.

But still, there is something astonishing. I met Georg Pfanzelt a few times, who was then probably one of Brecht's best friends...

Yes, he obviously must have had something special about him.

... he was a bit older than Brecht and inspired Brecht greatly. I think he was very critical. I was surprised by how well informed Pfanzelt was about Brecht, even though they had hardly any contact afterwards. As far as I know he visited Brecht once sometime after 1933 in Denmark and only met him again twenty years later, when Brecht directed Mother Courage *at the Münchner Kammerspiele and went to Augsburg for a few hours.*

Well, you see, when you're sixteen you're all equal but at eighteen, the talented separate from the mediocre. By the time he was thirty, Brecht was a famous German poet while Pfanzelt was a little civil servant who wasn't able to make anything of his critical talent, in spite of the fact that he was stimulating. Brecht had greatly outgrown him.

That might be so but I wanted to suggest something different. Pfanzelt had no intention of claiming anything. He recollected the old friendship warmly, but he talked about it dispassionately and didn't think of claiming this friendship as being important for Brecht. He didn't know much about the later Brecht and expressed surprise at how famous Brecht had become. He just spoke about 'how Brecht was then', about the discussions they had and how Brecht reacted, about how he formulated arguments and how he included his friends in his productions. Pfanzelt talked about all that without pretention – he was more afraid of saying too much than too little. What I found surprising was that what I had thought were the results of later experiences I now recognized as the opinions of the young Brecht; I recognized his Augsburg roots.

It's a pity that Feuchtwanger is also dead. He got to know Brecht at a very good time, in about 1919/1920, when he was a young poet in Munich. Strangely enough, Feuchtwanger never talked much about Brecht except to say that one of the most enormous impressions of his life was when this young man from Augsburg came into his room. As soon as Feuchtwanger read the first page of what Brecht had written, he thought of Brecht as an astonishing phenomenon and from that moment Feuchtwanger became a devoted friend and fan, sometimes mixed with a little jealousy.

Epic theatre didn't mean anything to Feuchtwanger, however; he was appalled by it. Once, in Hollywood on the occasion of the production of *Simone Machard*, which they had written together, Brecht walked around with Feuchtwanger, cigar in his mouth, trying to explain the principles of epic theatre. But Feuchtwanger said to him: 'You know, Brecht, you can kiss my arse with your epic theatre. I can't listen to this any longer. Let's keep walking!' Feuchtwanger understood absolutely nothing.

Brecht couldn't always express himself clearly at first. In discussions with Brecht, I often noticed that the first hour was a back and forth, a tough back and forth, with seemingly completely unconnected excursions into related, or unrelated, ideas. Then, after an hour and a half or two hours, suddenly something crystallized. The persistence of Brecht's thought processes and their complexity, the detours, are of particular importance, and from these detours astonishing things emerged, often extremely simple things. The simplest statements were written down after two hours of bitter discussion, discussion that stretched from the theory of relativity to, I don't know, day-to-day politics. And the result was: 'Hello, my friend!' Although I say that now as caricature, it really was like that. Brecht never lost the thread in these two hours, while I was already completely exhausted – not just me, but everyone else, Elisabeth Hauptmann, or whoever happened to be there at the time. That was astonishing, an intellectual strength that I haven't often come across in my life.

In connection with that I'd like to talk to you about the philosophical foundations of Brecht's method of Verfremdung[142] *and the abilities he developed when he was reading in order to find just what was useful for him ... he must have read Marx's* Capital?

The first volume at least.

No more?

That would have been enough for Brecht.

Would you confirm that Brecht, and this is an approximate quotation of his, came across concepts that he himself had started thinking about or had partly thought through already? And that suddenly he found a method of arranging the questions in order to gain an overview.

He found the historical view, which is what's crucial to Marx.

Would it be right to say that Brecht's ability always to take a critical position is the origin of Verfremdung?

Verfremdung and criticism are not the same, although *Verfremdung* can lead to criticism. Let's start with an analysis of our own and of other people's performances. We need to find out where (to use Brecht's excellent term) the *Rabitz*-wall[143] is, the false wall; and where those stage effects are, which are useless and meaningless. The so-called criticism of a poetical realist has to begin here. *Verfremdung* starts at a later point. The term *Verfremdung* was in Brecht's blood from the beginning. The great *Verfremdung* is in the Mr Punch-figure, the *Hanswurst* theatre, in popular art. Brecht didn't invent *Verfremdung*; he simply elevated the term enormously and used it in a new way, in a high, classical form. He brought it out from the fairground and onto the stage of the German theatre, and used it to do battle against naturalism and culinary theatre.[144] That shouldn't be forgotten.

You're talking about the application of this method for the theatre...

That's right, because that's what Brecht is all about.

Where, consistent with his talents, he used it skilfully...

... and also where it had its greatest impact on contemporary art and on the theoretical consciousness of our time. In Paris, every second intellectual you met would say immediately: *Je suis un Brechtien*, [I'm a Brechtian] and would say the word *Verfremdung* in German.

But the method is not limited to plays and performances. It's about a philosophical method. It's dialectics in action.

Of course. I could give you this as an example:

I saw thousands of people stand opposite thousands of other people (for a reason unknown to me, or for whatever reason) and they had a strange piece of iron in their hands with some wood glued underneath it. With this piece of iron and the wood underneath they started to shoot at each other although it was unclear what was actually happening.

(I'm improvising here and using a banal example.) You can find *Verfremdung* in Voltaire and also in Diderot, or you can go back to the great pre-classics – but what you won't find is *Verfremdung* used in such a conscious and systematic way as Brecht used it. Voltaire and Diderot accomplished single achievements of genius and influenced Brecht enormously, especially Diderot, whose works about the theatre exactly expresses Brecht's theories. Brecht always wanted to establish a Diderot Society.[145] You should read Diderot's essays. What he writes is often completely astonishing. It will, how do you say, take your breath away. Diderot wrote for a feudal audience who didn't want to be stimulated but simply wanted to watch a game where everything is in the open and where the rules are known. Unfortunately, I don't recall the title of this one particular essay but you should get hold of it.[146]

But to use this method of *Verfremdung* at such a high level and consciously and with such poetic power! Without Brecht's poetic strength, the theory wouldn't have any value. Brecht and poetry is one and the same thing. Otherwise, what use is *Verfremdung* to me or for that matter Marxism and Leninism in the arts – unless of course I'm a politician because then it becomes an entirely different matter. Brecht is just nature's unique stroke of luck; that this theory came into the hands of one of the greatest poets of German

literature. I was quoting Goethe: 'genius is nature's stroke of luck'.
Yes, then the theory adds up to something! Forget that, it's of no
interest.

*But where is the source? What has been stimulated as a result of
what?*

Brecht had at his disposal an enormous poetic power as well as
a realistic insight into things. To possess this enormous talent and
what's more to apply it consciously ... well, that was just Brecht.

A conscious application of this method of Verfremdung *is first
recognizable from about the mid-1920s. What makes you say that
Brecht was born with* Verfremdung?

Dialectics is not a method of thought invented by philosophers –
I'm speaking here of classical dialectics. I'd like to remind you of
the conversation between Hegel and Goethe. Goethe was highly
suspicious of Hegelianism. His pantheism, his whole way of looking
at nature, also his idealism ... the *ur*-plant (by which I mean the un-
historical views which he still held), all this meant that he could
only be wildly suspicious of Hegel, especially because the young
people were so enthusiastic about him. That usually makes an old
man suspicious. Now Hegel came to dinner at Goethe's at Weimar
with the idea of seducing him, and said to Goethe: 'We have been
talking such a lot about dialectics, Mister Privy Councillor. So what
is dialectics? It's just common sense, it's the spirit of contradiction
which lives in every person who views a thing from two different
sides.' And that's how Goethe came to understand the concept.

Dialectics is the most popular thing that ever existed. It's not
something invented by philosophers, it is part of human behaviour.
You can trace it from Aristotle to Hegel and then finally to Marx and
Lenin – except that it takes on different forms. Idealistic dialectics
turns into materialistic dialectics. In the hands of a physicist with
no idea whatsoever about dialectics, it takes on the most outlandish
forms. You can see this in Einstein, and certainly in Heisenberg,
whose famous 'uncertainty principle' theory is like a favourite dish
to us. When Heisenberg says that an object to be observed changes
as a result of the process of observation so that we can no longer
be certain about it (that's almost the exact description), that simply
becomes a playground for us. A farmer might be able to say the

same for his sphere of interest. One should add, however, that if the method changes we can now recognize the modified object as well, thanks to the historical development of physics.

Dialectics is not simply innate in a human being; it belongs to nature in the same way that natural activities of everyday life are subject to nature's dialectics, in the sciences and in ordinary everyday life as well. And if it was your misfortune not to become a priest and practise religion badly (the church fathers are great dialecticians), then this is as it should be, except that the people are unaware of this. They boil an egg, but they've never investigated why the egg turns out the way it does.

Brecht was a very thorough thinker and his great stimulus was folk wisdom. This has something to do with the geography of Augsburg, with the way he grew up, and also with the relatively early death of his mother. All of which would have been of absolutely no relevance had he not possessed original poetic genius (discernible from very early on) in the first place. I know that what I've just said sounds like shallow idealism but believe me, it's the truth – otherwise we'll make a Marxist bogey man out of Brecht and that would be of absolutely no interest. In that case we might just as well ask, as someone once asked me, why Marx didn't write great plays. This idiot didn't even know that Marx wasn't interested in writing plays. He should have read a bit more. If everyone could do everything, we could all call ourselves geniuses.

I can describe Brecht's plays in purely theoretical terms, for example the plot of *Chalk Circle*, in two minutes; every six-year-old child can understand it if you strip it of its poetry. The same is true of *The Good Person of Szechuan* although not of *The Mother*, because this play is about a political development. *St Joan* is even more complicated because economics has a part to play as well. But in the plays about the behaviour of human beings (as in *Chalk Circle* or *The Good Person of Szechuan*) you have the whole truth in a nutshell; anyone can bring a plot to the table, it's not difficult. But then, *then*, we're put in our place. I'm saying this to contradict my friends who try to turn Brecht into the theoretical showpiece of Marxism (which is true), forgetting that it is his poetic brilliance that attracts our young people. I'm repeating Brecht here. He was always complaining about the decline of aesthetic categories.

I complain too when someone publishes an article about me. My music isn't discussed anymore. I'm referred to as nothing more than a propagandist, a collaborator with the working class, a communist – but not a word about my music. It's the same for Brecht. Suddenly all Brecht's aesthetics (which the older Brecht especially valued most) are forgotten. He complained bitterly about being used so one-sidedly. Shallow idealism, as in 'a genius is just genius', doesn't cut much ice and I would certainly reject that too.

The one-sidedness has its causes and maybe has to be explained by our situation. In West Germany they try to divide Brecht, on one hand into a political fool who's no longer of any interest and, on the other hand, into a great poet who can be accepted. We feel ambushed and we react to that. And since, in this context, Brecht's political viewpoint is of interest, the discussion becomes mainly political. We defend Brecht's work against erroneous political interpretation. And a concomitant is often that aesthetics not only takes second place, but that a certain mistrust arises against it, especially because the enemy uses it as a weapon.

That's right. And then we often push it too far, whereupon young people, including those in the West, begin to flounder because they don't know where to go with the argument. They want to accept Brecht as a theorist, but if Marxism-Leninism is only explained to them in an abstract and superficial way, it's hollow, a dead doctrine. They have to be shown where Marxism-Leninism really pulsates, how it functions in Brecht's work. And only then can Brecht be truly described as a Marxist-Leninist. But such generalizations... for heaven's sake! Is Friedrich Wolf a Marxist? Of course he is even though some of his plays could be seen as idealistic. But you see, that works too.

'Functioning' is a term that Brecht used. Brecht says about Lenin: 'he was mainly a functionary whose greatest achievement was to function.'[147]

That's how he should be described, by describing the way he functioned. But this quotation also shows how enthusiastic Brecht was about Lenin – you have no idea how enthusiastic. Young people don't realize this because, strangely enough, Lenin is not widely read any more (such a loss for our young people's theoretical thinking) whereas we grew up with him. I can remember, for example, in 1922 glad tidings came that Lenin's *Empiriocriticism* has just been translated. We'd been waiting for this book, Lenin was still alive, and we heard that it was just in the process of being translated. Those were sensational times! We'd also been waiting for *Left Wing Communism: An Infantile Disorder* ever since it was advertised. These were really new ideas. That's when we started to think in a different way. After the Great War, we had Social Democracy in our heads, or rather some sort of foggy utopianism. This was the 'first course' so to speak, after which we started to read Marx anew.

You said that you wanted to talk about a certain characteristic of Brecht's – his modesty.

Yes, his modesty was genuine. When he was in doubt, he would accept praise only from a few friends but if his mind was made up, he politely ignored the praise. In 1934 he told me: 'I'm famous enough. I don't need any more. I have my share of fame and I'm no longer interested in it.'

You mentioned an example: in 1938 you came to Denmark and Brecht showed you the poem 'To Those Born Later'.

It was already earlier – in 1934 or 1935. He didn't give me this poem – no, he gave me an envelope containing about thirty poems and said: 'Have a look; maybe there is something useful for you' by which he meant ideas that I might set to music. I looked through these yellow typewritten pieces of paper, found this poem and went straight to Brecht and said: 'Brecht, this is magnificent!' 'Really?' he replied. 'Do you think it's useful?' He never said any more than that: 'useful' – that was the word. 'It's magnificent!' I said and set it immediately.[148] I played it for him and he approved of it. His attitude towards his poems was: 'if it's good, then it's useful'. He didn't ask 'is it beautiful?' but only 'is there a point to it?'

Now I want to try an experiment with you: don't you think it's important for you to play some, or, what I'd like best, all of your songs and sing them for the tape recorder?

Yes, but it would be too much of a strain on me now, think of my bad heart. I've got some songs from *Schweyk* and quite a few others, but it would exhaust me too much. We'll have to try to do it at a different time, maybe do half an hour here, one or two songs there.

I suggest recording one song in each of our conversations.

Yes, but I'm too exhausted at the moment.

I'll come back to this next time if you don't mind.

That is a good idea – much better! Then we can look for something sophisticated that nobody knows, and record it.

But also 'To Those Born Later' please.

That goes without saying. It's hardly ever sung because it's so difficult, for singers as well as for the listeners – difficult for the time being, that is. But those difficulties will be overcome in a few years' time. Ten, twenty years are nothing in music.

As with the use of hexameters.

As with the use of hexameters, that's right.

Conversation 6
18 July 1961

'To Those Born Later' – Boogie-Woogie – Eisler on Religion – *Galileo*

You wanted to sing Brecht's poem 'To Those Born Later' in the published version, which is different from the one written for Ernst Busch. What is important is that we show the gestus of the song.[149]

[Eisler sings. After listening to the recording] –
That wasn't good. We'll try it again.

I think it would be good if we had both attempts side by side. You criticize the first performance; when you sing it again we shall know what changes you want to make.

All right. That was dreadful. I sang really badly because I can't read the notes any more. I haven't had them in my hands for twenty years and I simply couldn't cope with the technical difficulties. When I became expressive, that is when I sang with great emotion, it was because I couldn't get the notes. It's terrible. The song is, I think, much better than my interpretation of it. Do give me a chance to repeat it, dear, cherished comrade Bunge. Now that I've played the notes again after twenty years (I'm not exaggerating), I think I can perform it better, that is to say in a calm and friendly manner. Friendliness – that's what's missing in my performance; it has to be sung in a friendly way, not barked out like an offended dachshund.

And anyway, our technical set-up is totally inadequate. The piano is far too loud.

Right. I'll play the piano very softly now. The stupid thing with me is that I can neither play the piano nor can I sing. I'm a true composer: I have the music in my head, which makes it unquestionably difficult when it comes to performing it. I think, however, in the interests of our friend Brecht, it would be worthwhile to preserve even these recordings somehow before they blow away on the wind.

You told me recently that Brecht, with great enthusiasm, said of your composition: 'That is very epic'.

You know, we didn't use terms like 'great enthusiasm' – we found things 'useful'. When Brecht gave me the poem to see whether I found it 'useful', I *did* find it useful. What I composed the next day, Brecht found useful too. We didn't say any more about it, either at the time or since; once it was agreed, that was it. It was a small matter. Poetically, it is one of Brecht's greatest poems and the music is (I hope) not so bad either. I even set it twice. There is nothing more to add. The difficulties of writing something like that during the emigration and setting it to music we might understand better in fifty years.

Anyway, I'm very embarrassed that I sang so badly, even though I'm not a singer. I suggest that I play it again, with the piano softer. And I hope I'll find the gestus of the music that Brecht found so epic…I can still picture the scene – him listening, smoking a cigar and saying: 'Ah, is that epic!' with real relish. Maybe that's a memory that should be preserved. Can we record the song again?

[After a repeat of the recording:] –

Let's talk about it again. I think both performances of that same song are impossible, I'm just not relaxed enough. I'd like to ask you to delete these two recordings and absolutely not to give them to anyone else. They are simply bad. First, I can't sing, and on top of that I have an especially hoarse voice today. It should be sung very lightly. I think it was a terribly weak, almost demonic, performance; also it contains a, you can only call it, self-satisfaction with one's own despair and downfall, which I find distasteful. This is not the way to sing it at all. One should sing it very lightly, relaxed and cheerful. At this moment I can't do it.

If you analyse the poem's content thoroughly, there is also a certain coquettishness: 'although we are very great people, we ask your forgiveness'. This coquettishness is not shared by Brecht, but unfortunately you'll find it in my performance. I'm glad that these songs haven't yet been performed in this way and I hope that in twenty years' time a reasonable person will sing them...and in a light, radiant, almost humorous way, which is how I want them to be performed. What I did was completely wrong and doesn't do justice to Brecht's brilliant poem – which by the way has its vagaries. It also didn't help my performance that at five o'clock in the afternoon, instead of resting, I have to answer my friend Doctor Bunge's questions about what we thought back then in 1935.

Why did you write another setting of this poem, in a more popular style, for Ernst Busch?

The original song was technically too difficult for him. The popular version is, of course, also very funny and Busch interprets it magnificently, although other people than I have to be the judge of that. All I can do is write two, or maybe three, versions of songs. Other people have to decide which is the more useful and I don't mean better. I'm bored when people discuss my music, especially when I want to talk about a true poet.

I don't think the popular version is any more popular than the other version; it's just that it's easier to sing. I gave Busch the chance to mould the song into a popular musical form, which in turn is also a strange contradiction between Brecht's lofty verses and a very simple melody.

Does the gestus stay the same?

Yes, the gestus stays the same, but that doesn't always happen automatically. The gestus is not the same, for instance, when the artistic material changes. But in this case I think it's the same – well, it may be a bit simpler. It's very complicated to sing unless you understand high-art music, but if you do, it's not so complicated. In any case, this is one of my many works that has yet to become popular.

Who actually interprets your songs 'well'?

We have to talk about different genres. In vocal music, you have many genres, kinds of music. For example, no one sings Mayakovsky's poems I set to music better than Busch; there is no one in the world who sings them better. He sings them well because he *understands* them. The person who interprets the text well and manages to avoid sentimentality, bombast, pathos and stupidity in all its forms is the person who'll sing it well. Such talents do exist although it's pointless to mention names.

I have to tell you that this is all quite difficult for me. Nearly every year, one or two volumes of my *Songs and Cantatas* are published and I can't see any sign yet of the singers who will interpret them well…But what can I do? Even Schubert is terribly badly interpreted too.

First, one must have a very good voice, great musicality and something that I call 'musical intelligence', which means being able to sing against the text. For example, when the word 'spring' occurs, the singer shouldn't imply spring by a melting of his voice. These are very complicated matters that you can read about in my theoretical works,[150] but which take time to explain. In any event, it will take an intelligent person to sing it well – maybe even without a good singing voice.

Besides the publication of your Songs and Cantatas, *there are also the recordings. When you agree to the production of these records, do you then also agree to the interpretation?*

No, not at all. There are records produced by many different singers. I listen to them once. Some I find dreadful and others brilliant but I'm too tired to concern myself with every bit of nonsense. If record producers contract some female singer to sing a song by me, which becomes absolutely meaningless in her interpretation, there's nothing I can do about it.

Brecht didn't concern himself either whether they performed one of his plays in Greifswald or Plauen[151] correctly or incorrectly. He had a big machine working for him and could send out his assistants to check. But I don't have this kind of staff and, on my own, can't listen to every single person who sings my work or to everything that's recorded. I completely refuse to do that. Most of the time I find the recordings of my work dreadful and want nothing to do with them. But, I'm no Don Quixote and can't reform the record industry according to my own taste however much I would like to.

I did ban two records, however, because they were done so badly. Well, I went there (I had to rehearse once with these people) and said to them:

Dear friends, I wrote '*andante con moto* ($\quarternote$ = 112)' but you are playing it as if it were a tragic largo and by doing this, you are destroying the music. Why are you doing that? What else do I have to write over my notes to instruct you how to play the correct tempo? When you see a text that represents grief, you start grieving. But haven't you learnt that grief can also be sung cheerfully, which intensifies its effect much more than in your boring way?

Dear Doctor Bunge, I can't say more on this subject, I'll have to pin my hopes on the next twenty years. I can't supervise every performance of a symphony of mine, or my chamber music or one of my songs. Mostly they are played dreadfully, and I protest against it as much as I can without insulting those impossible singers, conductors and chamber musicians who are all doing their best (unfortunately, their best is not yet *the* best).

Which of the singers who sing your songs do you prefer?

I don't want to mention any names – except Ernst Busch's who really is a genius. Busch sings the songs to 'Storm' set to texts by Mayakovsky with incomparable brilliance in both East and West and I take my hat off to him. But apart from his, I don't want to mention any other names, and I don't want to drop any hints either.

My only concern is to fight stupidity in music. As you know, I'm working on an essay 'On Stupidity in Music' – I've published three chapters already. Believe me, that is the most important thing to me.

Six years ago, when I was in Paris at a concert of workers' choirs, I met an old friend of mine from England[152] who had also worked for many years in the workers' movement. After I had listened to the traditional, unintelligent singing of those polished, cultivated French working class singers, I said to him: 'My dear friend, I have, as you know, fought against stupidity in music since my youth, but today I can say that I have been defeated'. That doesn't mean that I won't continue fighting stupidity in music, even though up until now I've been defeated. I've really been fighting against it since my earliest youth. Well, you just have to persevere. It's not just about me. You mustn't get tired of fighting against the stupidities and by that I mean all bad musical traditions.

Believe me, no famous singer sings Schubert, or Schumann, or Brahms, or Hugo Wolf correctly. I can play you records by the most famous singers that demonstrate how badly they interpret the music; the barbarity in their musical interpretation is astonishing. Of course I won't make any difference. I'm no longer interested in whether or not I change anything, but I am really surprised how even the classics are misunderstood.

Even the best interpreters can turn Schumann into sentimental schmaltz and Schubert, the most original, nervous composer, into the creator of some kind of popular light music – it really is astonishing.

It is the same with symphonic music. A famous conductor[153] leading a course in conducting at the International Music Seminar in Weimar asked what he should teach the young people. I said to him, 'Why don't you show them how the first two bars of Beethoven's *Eroica* Symphony should be played?' That is [Eisler imitates:] 'Schrumm! Schrumm!' followed by the 'tum-ti tum-ta'. You see? This is how it begins and how it ends. The barbarity in music has been inherited by us from the petit bourgeoisie. We have to get rid of it.

Strangely enough, many of our cultural officials show such a respect for this barbarity, especially the stubborn ones, that it's often difficult for me to fight against it.

How far does the taste of the general public determine stupidity in music, by which I mean the stupid interpretation of music?

The general public isn't stupid, the specialists are. My favourite saying is: 'every human being is musical', that is musically talented. But when the music teacher is let loose on teaching a boy, that boy will lose his innate musicality within four years – which means (as every biologist can confirm) that the human being is born musical and it's only because of the way he's taught that he'll become non-musical. That's a very important discovery!

You mean if we had more of these better interpreters, the taste of the audience could be significantly changed in a relatively short time?

That would be a little too utopian, but I would say if we could educate the music teachers who teach music to the children from the age of four to six in the Kindergarten, then we would probably be able to get a new listening audience – by educating the children! With socialism in the GDR, it is mainly all about education.

It's of absolutely no interest how a man in black tie and tails conducts Beethoven's *Ninth Symphony*, but it is important how six-year-old children are educated musically in Thale, Thuringia,

Mecklenburg, in the little villages or on the collective farms. Which pieces are played (or not) at a symphony concert is important, but for me it's more important to educate music teachers so that they can teach children properly, teach their ears, their understanding of music. Our task is not only to teach or lecture but to educate teachers (those were my exact words when I came back from exile to the GDR in 1948), but unfortunately, we're not yet ready to do this even though it should be our most important duty.

Our government agrees with this, but there are huge difficulties. How can we suddenly send 20,000 teachers who have an understanding of music into the schools? These are the challenges, the growing pains, of the GDR.

But let us not be under any illusions. It's not about refining the taste of the concert audience (though it is about this too) but about fundamental musical education – and that starts at the age of six in the Kindergarten.

Could you please explain that? How would you go about that practically?

Educate the children's ears, teach them to have good taste, make them musical. They're already musical, of course; human beings are born with musicality but unfortunately music lessons cause them to surrender it. Music lessons have to be conducted in a way that ensures that a child's musicality won't be destroyed but rather

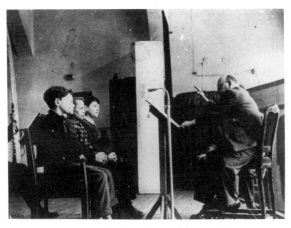

Rehearsing the Boy Trebles for Galileo *in the 1950s.*

developed. This can be done simply enough and there are a lot of practical examples of how it's done.

Similarly, Brecht might demand, for example, that children should learn to read and write; I would expect Brecht's audience to have at least read, heard about or seen a few plays by classic playwrights so that they understand how Brecht is different. What is the difference between Wallenstein and Galileo? Wallenstein in Schiller's portrayal is a very indecisive character, a kind of Austrian Hamlet (actually a Weimarian Hamlet). What is Galileo? Galileo is indecisive. Hamlet is indecisive. And Wallenstein's indecision is tremendous.

You are the literary scholar. If you wanted to carry out true literary research, you would have to undertake comparative studies so that the young generation could really understand something about literature (unless you wanted to rely on spontaneous talents alone) and that's the same for my field. It would be highly interesting but unfortunately nobody is doing it.

I've read a few things in our Republic about Brecht and I've also read about Schiller and Shakespeare, of course, but I'm yet to find one study that explores the connection between these three great masters. Take, for example, the problem of indecisiveness in a literary character. There are some great examples in literature where a person is depicted as indecisive yet his character continues to develop – but where is the literary research about that? Nowhere!

Now, dear Doctor Bunge, although you have a huge breadth of expertise in your field of literary research, you expect our primary school music teachers (teachers who are supposed to teach folk songs in some God-forsaken place, like in Klein-Winzig an der Unstrut[154]), you expect them to turn little children into musical experts on the spot. We don't want this and anyway it's beside the point. What we do want, and this is the difficult part, is that they are enriched by music, but unfortunately, teaching music is not as easy as teaching literature. And here I have to pause. Do we want our dear comrades from the Unstrut to get excited when a man, a conductor, conducts a symphony by Beethoven? Certainly, we want that as well. But what is the true mission of music? To what extent can music purify corrupted feelings or enrich and enhance a human being's life?

These are matters that haven't even been touched on yet. So, since you are proposing such things to me, I propose to you that in the literary field you demonstrate, for example, the development (or the indecisiveness) of a character, in a brilliant dissertation or a little book. Lots of people would learn a lot from it – audiences, writers, theatre directors. We now have this brilliant school, the Brecht-School (we all saw the production of *Frau Flinz*[155]), and somehow they were able to portray what I've just been talking about. I have to say it was magnificent.

Is it more difficult with music without words?

It certainly is more difficult. Music without words is not a natural phenomenon but a historical one because pure concert music, if we discount church sonatas and some court music, has existed only since the middle of the eighteenth century. You can't date it to one particular year but it has actually existed since 1750. We're talking about music that was composed by people for people who had a certain interest, and who took a certain pleasure, in so-called 'concert music' – 'pure music' is a totally absurd expression. Concert music, which initially was a copy of certain styles of church music, existed first at the courts and was only secularized in the eighteenth century.

By concert music we always mean bourgeois music and it begins when music becomes secularized, when it makes itself independent of the church. You can't pin a date on it. An extraordinary new phenomenon emerges: the autonomous human being who is able to express himself through music, something totally modern then and still extraordinary today. This is roughly where it all starts. Because concert music established itself under the circumstances I describe, it's not easy simply to integrate it into our early form of socialism. It's with great pleasure that I hear, for example, that in the GDR, Beethoven-only concerts are sold out. But with equal displeasure I hear that opera houses playing only Wagner are also sold out. We have accomplished at least one thing: a great many workers are running along to these events, especially to Beethoven concerts.

It's asking too much of me to explain this quickly. 'Pure listening' to abstract music (an idiotic expression that only means music without words) was a totally new experience in the eighteenth century and we haven't found a way of defining it yet. What we have is what we can see and hear. We've adopted a great inheritance, which is very challenging in terms of how contemporary music interprets it.

I'm just writing a symphony for the Gewandhaus Orchestra in Leipzig.[156] Believe me, I'm doing penance for all my sins because (a) who am I writing it for and (b) who is going to listen to it? Well, I'm writing it for the Gewandhaus Orchestra (they are marvellous musicians) and the people of the GDR are going to listen to it – but they know little about the classical music tradition. So I have to offer something new and bypass classical music. I often sit at my desk during the morning, racking my brains for ways to solve this problem and to find something practical and useful, but still new, to say without either boring myself or compromising the standards of my musical judgement. I find all this extremely complicated.

My best advice to you, dear comrade Bunge, is not to bring politics into everything. Let's exclude certain aesthetic areas from simple-minded politicization. There are traditions that still linger on today, for example the conductor in white tie and tails with his eighty musicians, also in white tie and tails – we don't have to subject that to political scrutiny.

On this subject, some of my friends have a silly way of politicizing popular light music, arguing about whether it's more, or less, American. I think that's idiotic. Over-politicizing in the arts leads to aesthetic barbarism. (That might be a new catchphrase – if it is a new one, then it's a good one.)

By 'politicizing' do you mean...

...a certain hollow aesthetic, a politicization of aesthetics that gets us nowhere. For example, our young people like to dance to boogie-woogie. Politically, we're against it, but aesthetically, the young people prevail because they like to dance to it. To argue about it is beneath us. Because we are communists and socialists, we already occupy the moral high ground, so we really don't have to scrutinize politically every piece of rubbish and measure it against our ideology. That's plain daft.

Opponents of boogie-woogie-dancing argue that other things will slip in alongside boogie-woogie and take possession of the young people.[157]

That's quite right. It's also very serious – and since my friends are not malicious, they'd like to allow young people the freedom to dance to whatever they want. However, they have a sinister feeling that with boogie-woogie (these days it's called something else)

Americanism will be smuggled in, which is absolutely correct. But American influence has to be fought politically, and not aesthetically.

Let's educate our young people politically so that they can (a) dance to boogie-woogie and (b) resist the political influence of America in the GDR. I've already said that in two party meetings and I openly admit I didn't have much success with this proposal. While the young people were delighted that I was for boogie-woogie, my friends in the presidium were against me for saying that it should be allowed.

But that's the problem: you can't politicize every aesthetic phenomenon. It's one thing if you examine things from a Marxist perspective; but a feeble aesthetic viewpoint just leads us into difficult situations (like where we are today, were yesterday and will be tomorrow) and will involve us in disputes for which we have no time, no energy, and no people. To give you an absurd example: I was asked to condemn boogie-woogie to 500 apprentices in a large factory and to recommend, instead, the English waltz.

Ridiculous!

Certain kinds of mass hysteria, such as those generated by American jazz or stirred up by some American religious sect, should simply be forbidden. I'm all for police intervention in such case. If hysteria escalates to the point where chairs are smashed up and the girls collecting the used tickets on the public transport have cigarettes stubbed out on their palms – and all because of the influence of boogie-woogie – then of course I'm against it and in favour of a police ban. I'd turn myself into a hard-nosed sergeant-major. But as long as that doesn't happen and we manage to control it, I'm all for boogie-woogie and for handling it with a degree of elegance so that we don't seem to be unworldly. A Leninist is not unworldly after all. If we turned the entire world's stupidity into a political question, we wouldn't be able to see the wood for the trees.

So, you don't think that boogie-woogie-dancing will inevitably lead to mass hysteria?

It could happen but it doesn't. We can only battle against boogie-woogie through the political education of our youth, real political education of true young socialists, and not with empty phrases. In my youth, in 1919, I jumped around in this way as you probably did too, dear Doctor Bunge. Dancing isn't the problem. But when people behave like crooks towards us and become politically malicious under the influence of the West, then the boogie-woogie can have a catastrophic effect.

Let's emphasis politics and not aesthetics. We have good young people and we mustn't base our approach on aesthetics just because the American entertainment industry, with its huge worldwide influence, has succeeded in turning entire nations into musical illiterates and continues to do so.

I read with great pleasure that the day before yesterday the pop singer Eddie Fisher sang some songs at a Kremlin reception during the film festival before the Minister of Culture, comrade Ekaterina Furtseva, and was a huge success. The Russians have so much more common sense than we do. We can't very well brush aside the appeal of American popular music with pointless political arguments such as, for example, 'It's not German' – which I did hear proposed. (The English waltz isn't German, nor is the waltz itself; it's Austrian.)

So, let's not politicize aesthetic matters but first ask ourselves what we can do? How can we use things to our own advantage? And let's not be too quick off the mark nor, above all, be over-confident in these questions. It's only too easy … it's the weakness of great Marxists in the realm of aesthetics often to make bad decisions.

Perhaps our problems are particularly evident because of those bad decisions. I remember such absurdities. At one time everyone in the GDR who wore jeans was ostracized.

When I was in America, jeans cost 98 cents. They were working clothes – workers wore them. But in the GDR they stand for a kind of Americanization. Of course these teething problems exist in our country, but we get over them. Today everyone can wear jeans. Nice! Why not make stupid decisions – aren't they inevitable? It's very difficult for our country: nothing is easy for us.

It's difficult when jeans, say, become some sort of symbol.

And they did.

Yes, when they first became fashionable. Now, fortunately, there are so many people wearing them that they're not seen as symbolic any more, even if they're worn in that spirit. But maybe we have to differentiate between clothing that is functional and the amusements (including the doubtful ones) that we spoke about earlier.

It's regrettable that on the subject of popular light music as well as of fashion, we're in an inferior position to America, the most successful industrialized country after the Soviet Union. America is at this moment in crisis with the percentage of its gross production below that of the Soviet Union. We simply can't deny that any mass production, not only of textiles, but also of products of the entertainment industry such as film, television, radio, fashion and jazz in all its forms puts us at a disadvantage. While we're still using manual means of production, the guys in America are already producing on an industrial scale. A big seller like a pair of jeans is mass produced. It isn't produced by one craftsman or by a single small business anymore.

We'll remain at a disadvantage only for as long as we fail to raise our productive output and become competitive. We can't do this at the moment because the first essential is to resolve this contradiction between a highly organized capitalist society and a less highly organized socialist society. You can abolish class distinction and certain distinctions between consumption and production. You can fight against them – within socialism as well as within capitalism. You can chew on one and the same problem, in two different social systems.

For example, England is at present in a dreadful economic crisis. On 25th July, the prime minister will announce an austerity programme. This means the gentlemen in England – what am I saying: 'gentlemen'? – the people in England will have to tighten their belts. Why? Because they're told they're not competitive. Now, I know England very well. Imagine if I were to go into a working class pub and say to them: 'Listen, in six weeks you'll have to pay ten per cent more tax and food will be more expensive as well. And do you know why? Because you're not competitive!' They would look at me like a wounded beast.

What does it mean: the worker isn't competitive? It's the English monopolists' industrial mass production that isn't competitive but the workers are held responsible for that – can you believe it! Suddenly, on 25th July, an austerity programme will be imposed on the English people, people who behaved magnificently during the Second World War, people who were the last, even after us, to end rationing. Suddenly, they're going to have something similar forced on them again (I'm not talking about rationing now), stuffed down their throats because they're not competitive.

Only a Marxist (and only a naïve one, a Leninist) will be able to comprehend the misery of a government saying to a worker: 'Dear friend, you're not competitive; that's why we're cutting your rations'. Workers, who probably want nothing more than a bit of margarine, a couple of mutton chops for their dinner and a pint or two down the pub. This is the sort of marvellous incongruity that only our friend Brecht the genius can describe accurately.

Something else that we can read about these days is the Pope's encyclical 'Mater et Magistra', the third encyclical letter about social problems. The first was 'Novarum Rerum', the second (forty years later) 'Tresi Dei', and the third one is today's. Whatever is it that the Pope wants to say to us we have to take very seriously – I warn here against ultra-left foolishness, because the Pope presides over one of the most sophisticated organizations! I wish to God we were at the point, as for example it is the case in South America or in West Germany, where we had an organization to which not only the smallest village community belonged but which also had a church, a cultural centre and a congregation. I wish to God we were that advanced, but we're not, and we must therefore take the Pope's encyclicals seriously.

The Pope acknowledges that, come what may, he supports the private ownership of the means of production and, naturally, we're tremendously interested in that because, as Marxists, we're totally against it. And then he comes out with all those tired old phrases that have been repeated endlessly since 1820, all those stupid, worn-out ideas and platitudes, like 'the gap between great luxury and the lives of poor people is unbearable' and 'workers must also have the right of veto in the factories' and so on.

Well, first and foremost, you can argue that the Pope doesn't understand anything about the matter. If he's in favour of the private ownership of the means of production, he hasn't understood that the private ownership of the means of production is *precisely* the cause of the social phenomenon of the concentration of wealth in fewer and fewer hands, in other words monopolistic capitalism. He probably hasn't read Marx. (Or maybe he has?) This is what creates the difference between rich and poor. But the Pope simply refuses to acknowledge it – incredible. You know I was a social democrat in my youth before the Great War. I'm embarrassed if today, in 1961!, comrade Noellen from the Social Democratic Party states that he's completely at one with the Pope's point of view, that the SPD is coming closer to the Pope's position.

What should we do? We should study the encyclical 'Mater et Magistra' very carefully because we can't mess about with religion. We have to differentiate between the so-called 'belief' of the common people (I say 'common' – that's so snobbish), the human being who believes in the ethical traditions of Christianity, and the church and its political role. You know that Marx, Engels, and Lenin too, warned against a political battle with the church. It has to die of natural causes. But when the church begins to assert itself and fights against us, we have to dispute things with them.

The encyclical 'Mater et Magistra' would be well worth a principled person sweating over – in fact, I've been trying to write about it for the past two days because I'm extremely interested in it. I want to demonstrate the contradiction between the Pope's humanistic position (one has to concede him that because he actually is against the difference between extreme luxury and poverty) on the one hand and, on the other the fact that he thinks he can resolve the difference while preserving the private ownership of the means of production. That's a classic case for us old Marxists. Between ourselves, we would call that a 'childish' position. Because Catholicism is so influential in, for example, West Germany, South America, Italy, Austria and other countries, it has to be discussed very seriously – we can't take it lightly.

You surely don't mean that the Pope is completely out of touch?

The Pope knows very well what's going on, believe me. I know a few Catholics – I went to a Jesuit college and know my Monsignor Scheiner, a Jesuit Father who was once a College Principal – and they're very educated people. Therefore, I have to say that I'm both surprised and disappointed that the Pope went down Shit Street to glorify the private ownership of the means of production. That, of course, is a huge mistake; the man's very old and the Cardinals are obviously worse than useless.

If I were Pope, I would have avoided this topic and would speak only about the difference between rich and poor (at some point mentioning Christian mercy). The first encyclical, 'Novarum Rerum' (in about 1890), was much better. In wandering into the field of economics, the present Pope (he's such a weak man) has unmasked himself and made a big mistake. Had I been a Cardinal (I would have made quite a good one), I would have advised him against saying those stupid things in public – his advisers are to blame. They handed it to us Marxists on a plate. On the one hand, the old man is lamenting the injustice of the world while on the other he no longer understands what's the cause of this injustice.

Let us not be under any illusions. Since the Pope is 'infallible', there won't be any argument. There aren't any arguments among Catholics, and then they reproach *us* for operating a cult of personality. For God's sake! (I say 'for God's sake', and immediately it becomes a sinister turn of phrase.)

What do you think about the complications that arose during the Church Congress?[158] *Did you follow them?*

They're not important. The Church Congress is of no significance but types like Bishop Dibelius, for example, are thoroughly unsavoury. Dibelius is a crook. I have an extreme antipathy to priests, mainly because I went to a Jesuit College where you had to kiss the priest's hand (You even had to kiss their hands! This is where, at the age of ten, my aversion started). Yes, Dibelius is a crook. We used to hear exactly the same speeches from him when he was in Potsdam with Hindenburg and Hitler. And as for his anti-Semitism …

The Church Congress certainly plays an enormous role in our country. Our churches are full. Whoever wants to dodge socialism prays to God – I don't know what you can do about that. It would have been crazy to allow the Church Congress to take place here; it would have been simply inviting in the counter-revolution: 'Please, come in. Agitate against us'. It couldn't be allowed. Let's not underestimate the influence of the church in the GDR – it's enormous.

That's why I was surprised when you said: 'the Church Congress is of no significance'.

Theoretically it's of no significance. But when Dibelius competes in the St Mary's Church with the State Opera House, 5000 people queue up to listen to this bastard. What's going on? How can every dimwit Catholic, who goes to school in Treviso or Bologna for five years (usually a farmer's son with no money who can't do anything other than become a priest), who hardly knows any Latin (just some sort of pidgin Latin), who doesn't know any real church leaders (as I do as an old communist who's had more than enough experience of them) and who, in a nutshell, is a completely uneducated idiot who doesn't know his way in bourgeois society, suddenly become a priest and preach to us the wisdom of the world? These people have no idea; they don't even know their own theology. The Evangelical clergy are the same. I would be delighted to engage Mr Dibelius, or a Catholic priest, in a debate about religion. The high clergy, like Cardinal Döpfner for example, are likely to be educated people, but I'm well educated too. I could easily cope with them. I'd like nothing more than a debate with these priests.

The common priest is the weakest, most low-minded, most uneducated and most stupid good for nothing who hasn't learnt anything and who's just a burden on us. It's perfectly all right for him to say to us, 'You're low-minded materialists', but when we say to him, 'You're a shit', he's insulted. It's unbelievable that every scoundrel, who went to a seminary for five years, all of the sudden thinks he can play the master in our country, while people who proved themselves in the working class movement for forty years and who understand a lot more about philosophy and theology are branded as 'atheists' and the like. I can tell you that *we* are the oppressed in the GDR – not the church. If I were to display my atheism, I would immediately be told by one of the comrades: 'Listen, dear friend, we can't afford to get on the wrong side of the church at the moment'. Yes, we are the oppressed.

I vividly remember that when *The Mother* was produced for the first time in Leipzig after the war, in 1952,[159] the Party wanted the scene in which the Bible is torn apart to be deleted. We complied and cut the scene in order not to upset the church. That's how bad it was. We must praise our Party for its tactful, big-hearted position, its generosity towards those dimwits who think that, just because they've taken holy orders, they can preach the same old worn-out messages in church, those shitty priests who create problems for us every single day. What a huge step backwards!

Here's another example. After the publication of the Pope's encyclical 'Mater et Magistra', social democratic MP Noellen made a statement, that he – in the name of his party! – agreed with the Pope. This is what things have come to with the working class movement. If the world perishes, then it's the SPD's fault, I'm certain of that. But I think we can prevent it.

I would like to get back to Brecht again, if you don't mind. Was Brecht mathematically talented?

Dear friend, there's no reason to talk about that.

But we've already touched on this topic once before.

About how Brecht didn't understand Pythagoras' theorem? What's the point of me standing at the foot of my friend Brecht's grave pointing out like a scornful fool (since every schoolboy knows Pythagoras' theorem) those subjects that he hadn't fully studied? He used to talk about how he 'out-calculated' his stories, his tales – that was the expression he used and it made sense. But he had no understanding of pure mathematics – why should he? What else do you ask of Brecht? That he dances? Plays the violin? Knows mathematics? With all due respect to the genius of Brecht, I think that's asking too much.

I'm not asking about whether he was able to do these things. I only wanted to hear your opinion about certain of Brecht's ideas. What did he mean, for example, when he speaks of 'out-calculating'?

What Brecht meant by 'out-calculating' was, first of all, to strip a thing down to its bones. It would have gladdened every mathematician's heart to hear about his relentless logic and rigorous demand for simplicity. It was marvellous. But mathematics was a different matter.

Remember that Einstein (as you know, I knew Einstein) was a poor mathematician; every physicist can confirm that. In my youth, in 1925, I met a certain man called Romm with my professor Hans Ludwig Hamburger, at that time professor of mathematics in Cologne (you'll find his theorem in the maths books). Hamburger was a great mathematician and a student of Einstein's and he told me that when Einstein, who was teaching at that time at Berlin's Humboldt-University, wrote a formula on the blackboard, this Romm (a pretty down-and-out bohemian type who usually hung out in the Romanisches Café) would put up his hand and say: 'Professor, that's wrong!' and would prove it there and then. Einstein could easily make mistakes within a formula. This was told to me, because I'm in no position to judge, by admiring mathematicians who sat at his feet and regarded him as one of mankind's most astonishing geniuses. But this Mr Romm, who unfortunately became morally depraved and has been forgotten, was a true mathematician.

It would be downright childish to call Brecht a mathematician. But higher mathematics is a completely different field and Brecht was interested in a kind of advanced abstract reasoning for which he had an inherent aptitude. But someone who has never done any maths can't suddenly become a mathematician at the age of forty – Brecht really hardly understood Pythagoras' theorem.[160] Even so, I'd give fifty mathematicians or more for a tenth of Brecht, for his stories, for his way of thinking. However, there's no point in wanting to pin him down as a mathematician.

I don't think anyone does that. But if he himself used expressions like 'out-calculating'...

The mathematical process of 'out-calculating' is no more than the application of logic. He should have called it 'logistics' (Brecht might have used the wrong vocabulary inadvertently) but what he meant was that the moral of his stories must be unassailable. Logistics here means the same as it does in the military. Like me, you've been in the military and know what logistics is – something, that needs to be calculated, the movement of an army corps. This corresponds with mathematical ideas in that there's only one way to do certain things: if one thing works, then something else won't. In this respect Brecht was a great logician. In fact, he was relentless even towards himself. But in terms of school mathematics, even Einstein wouldn't pass muster. Any third-rate professor from a small provincial university would beat us hands down.

And how did Brecht apply it in Life of Galileo?

It wasn't only mathematics – it was politics too! Don't forget that. The first version was called 'Die Schlauheit des Überlebens' [The Cleverness of Survival], a great title. Those people who worked as physicists during the fascist period, physicists like Meitner and Hahn who discovered nuclear fission, behaved exactly as the character in the first version of *Galileo*, which Brecht sent to me in America. I understood the play to mean this: 'Keep your head down when the going gets tough'. Well, Hahn did more than that. He passed his knowledge on to the outside world.

You should understand that Hahn (he's still alive, he's eighty) really did act precisely like that. He could have handed over his findings to the fascist government but he didn't. He gave them to Mrs Meitner, a Jew who worked in Copenhagen with Niels Bohr. She understood the message and gave it to Bohr. Bohr flew to New York and joined up with anti-fascist (mostly Jewish) émigré physicists. And they informed Roosevelt that the Germans could, if Hahn...But Hahn didn't reveal his findings to the fascists and remained silent until the end. That is true nobility. He was a different kind of Galileo. At first, Roosevelt said that he wasn't interested but then received a letter from Einstein: 'Listen, Nuclear fission...when the Germans can do it, the whole world will be in danger. I suggest that you begin work on it immediately'. You know what that meant? It meant thousands of millions, billions of dollars; it meant establishing a huge industry, which they did – on the strength of Einstein's letter. What clinched the argument for Roosevelt was that a Hungarian émigré or maybe it was Fermi, an Italian émigré who'd successfully split the atom in a practical experiment, had told him: 'A man who had invented the steamboat went to Napoleon I and said: "If you use my steamboat, you can conquer England" but Napoleon threw him out'. Roosevelt was terribly impressed by this story – and by Einstein's letter.

So we had this man Hahn in Germany who could have told Hitler about his discovery. The procedure of nuclear fission was very complicated and the German physicists, by which I mean the fascist physicists, were working on a false theory: they used heavy water instead of plutonium. This could be said to correspond with Galileo's first phase although you can't compare the development of physics (physics as practised to the doom of mankind) with Galileo. You must guard against such comparisons! Brecht wrote a historical play to show how difficult it is to enforce the truth. How long can you fight before being crushed? How long does it take to see things through to the end, still passing on the truth and acknowledging yourself to be a weak man? Suppose you are a physicist with the last thirty years in fascist Germany at the back of your mind and you watch *Galileo* – you wouldn't compare yourself to it. It would be like comparing a murderer with Macbeth. In fact, you might as well compare anything with anything. Physics is simply the hook, the backdrop against which we see a human being fighting cruel authority, then becoming changed and distorted. He sells himself out, regretting it and finally exposing the sell-out. You shouldn't take *Galileo* literally.

Thank God our audiences are not educated in such a way that makes them feel queasy about this. I don't mean to complain about them – quite the opposite. They see something very heroic, in fact doubly heroic, namely, the new human being within the old society, and that, of course, is Brecht's magnificent achievement. What's important is not Galileo's attitude towards the Inquisition, nor that he finally gives in (with the result that he's put under house arrest, guarded by two clerics and his daughter, with one pupil visiting him) but that he always strove for the truth. What you have to understand is that Galileo's great tragedy is his hunger for the new, his craving for it, his imperative need to study – not the social circumstances.

There are scenes in which physical experiments are performed. Did Brecht seek advice and information?

Yes, from Bohr's pupil.

And later in America from Reichenbach?

Hermann Reichenbach,[161] yes, the old professor. That was for the second version. For the first version, when he lived in Denmark, Brecht consulted Bohr's pupils at the Institute in Copenhagen.

Physics doesn't change. What does change is Galileo's attitude.

The second version really is marvellous. The first version is mischievous. It encourages Galileo's sell-out. The second version doesn't – it condemns it. If I were to say 'I live in the GDR, I'm cleverer than our government but, secretly, I'm withholding my discoveries', that would be a dirty and indecent attitude, wouldn't it? Brecht exposed that attitude. He didn't want to describe some kind of bighead who thinks he knows more, in his own narrow field, than the working class – a Smart Alec, like a Chinese sage who finds a way to wriggle through the powers' net. Wouldn't the West have liked that! Brecht took that away from him (I think he did this brilliantly) and the problem is rectified in the second version.

There were changes to only a few passages, though.

Recognizable, for example, in the final monologue.

And this makes the matter complicated. There's so much left in from the first version that in the second version you often only see the sly Galileo who wants to survive.

Let's be honest, that's a respectable attitude too (as an old communist I'm allowed to say it) – wanting to survive at any price while keeping faith with the noble sentiment 'I have the monopoly on the truth and therefore I have to pass the truth on', like in a relay race. For an old communist like me, the image of the bearer of the great truth is, of course, enormously attractive. But, at the same time, it's also demoralizing – do you know what I mean? If we'd all behaved like that, there wouldn't be a working class movement at all, only sly, crafty people with a monopoly on the truth, wanting to survive. For Brecht (at that time I was with Brecht a lot, we were in Finland then)…to depict this immoral behaviour demonstrates his greatness. Brecht was Schiller's best pupil. For him theatre was a true moral institution. Although he wasn't a philistine in aesthetic matters, for Brecht aesthetics had reached the point where it ceases to exist and morality begins. That Brecht added this morality into the second version, when the first one was far more attractive…For example in West Germany, the message of the second version would simply have been the most acceptable for many people. But it is one of Brecht's greatest achievements that he undermined that and added, as you say in English: 'Welcome, brother rat, to the gutter!' (This is what Galileo says to his pupil when the pupil praises him.) Just 'wanting to survive' would be a brilliant, attractive stand point, attractive for every Smart Alec, but not truly revolutionary. The fact that Galileo is criticized for this attitude once more sticks in the throat. That's why in West Germany they find Brecht so hard to swallow.

I have to say this undermining is an astonishing achievement by Brecht, I remember discussing it with him. I have to confess that in the beginning, I didn't like the second version. To me, the first version was marvellous. When Brecht showed me the second version in Hollywood I was a bit sceptical. In fact I found a strange heroic glorification, an over-glorification, taking place. The first version already contains a heroic glorification: to keep silent under force, but to carry on a monopoly of the truth. In the second version, there is a double heroic glorification: Galileo (a) carries the truth on, but then says (b) 'I'm a pig, I'm a wretch, and I should never have hidden it'. Highly interesting! Today it's like talking about it after a hard battle. When the great battles over art are finished, you, dear Bunge, and I, the old Eisler, can get together and discuss them. Then, I insisted on only one thing that I think Brecht also

accepted: 'Let's have him devoured at the end'. Because he holds
on to the truth, illegally and blindly – he says he's blind – Galileo
is supposedly heroic. He hides the truth in the globe and when his
pupil appears, Galileo gives him the globe. The pupil praises him
and Galileo replies: 'You're praising me wrongly, I should have
resisted', and so he is cast as a hero. Well, that was too much for
me, which is why I said he should be devoured at the end. It should
be made quite clear what Galileo was up to.

What I hold against Brecht, I hold it against him but with
utmost admiration for this great master, is that he over-glorifies
Galileo. Because he lets Galileo acquire two attitudes. I would
have been happy with just one. The first is a very difficult one,
to keep a monopoly on the truth under oppression, to continue
working blindly and to pass it on to the pupil. That alone would
have been a huge achievement. But Galileo does something else:
he admits his own depravity. And at that point we find echoes of
the Renaissance in the conditions of the years 1939/1940. Those
are tricks that of course only a genius like Brecht could have
pulled off.

Were you to ask me today which version I like more, I'd have
to think long and hard about it. I've said, for me Galileo was too
heroic. The generally held view is that Galileo's heroism starts
when he scolds the pupil, which he doesn't do in the first version.
Instead the pupil finds it extraordinary that a man, a blind, sick, old
man who's under the greatest pressure, writes down the truth and
passes it on. People say the curtain should fall at this point. But it
doesn't, because Brecht carries on: Galileo acknowledges his own
moral depravity... You have to admit this is an enormously heroic
attitude.

So you can see that Galileo, not without reason, is one of the
great heroes of the working class movement. He was always one
of its greatest role models as he was for me when I was a small
boy. Social democratic youth organizations taught you that. At the
end, Galileo says, '*Eppure si muove* – And yet it moves!', which
Brecht simply left out. Brecht's relentless political position becomes
aesthetically attractive and this aesthetic attractiveness turns into
politics. That's the reason why he is performed all over the world.
If he had included the sentence 'And yet it moves!' he would have
represented one side of Galileo only. And to think that I would
have been happy with the first version and was against the second

version. Thank God Brecht was wise enough, as always, not to listen to the voice of his friend Hanns Eisler.

'As always' is overstating it.

My dear friend, I don't want to start a hero cult here. As you know, Brecht's death hit me very hard. It's really not just sentimentality when I say that we miss the man terribly now. But let me put it like this: Brecht was a great man who wasn't swayed by me. That's a fact. Don't think I was some kind of *eminence gris* because I wasn't at all. I don't want it to appear that I had a secret influence on him. That would be silly and I would certainly object.

It was about collaboration.

That's right – it was real collaboration, especially in 1929. This was the time of the great success with *The Threepenny Opera* and *Mahagonny*,[162] right up to *The Measures Taken*, when I actually functioned more as a messenger of the working class movement than a significant figure. I used to tell Brecht some of the practical details about the working class movement, which, because he was very sensitive, made an impression on him. When I say 'sensitive', I mean sensitive to people's attitudes.

In the final scene of both the first and second versions of Galileo, *you see Andrea going over the border. This scene was printed but never performed.*

I know, never. For myself, I would have liked to see it performed – it's a marvellous scene. Brecht himself took it out for the first performance in Hollywood. I have to say that the works of the great masters – be it Shakespeare, Johann Sebastian Bach or Bertolt Brecht – will be performed in a particular way at a particular time. Don't forget that Shakespeare was completely distorted for 150 years.

Thank God Brecht can't be similarly distorted because we have the Berliner Ensemble. So what if some scenes are taken out? In twenty years they'll be put back in again. I wouldn't worry too much about that. In September, Harry Buckwitz will direct *Galileo* in Frankfurt am Main and I'll suggest to him that he includes this scene because it's so interesting. It would have to be elegant in form (Brecht is very much for elegance) – it's true that it's a bit 'top-heavy', as they say in English (there are certain laws of the theatre). But to include it would be pleasant and amusing. What makes Brecht's enemies so tired and angry is that, as well as his magnificent language and the mastery of the theatre, Brecht wants to be elegant and funny as well. Maybe I can convince Buckwitz to include the scene in Frankfurt. He probably will because as the play is performed a lot, he'll want to present something new.

I think the scene suits the first version better than the second.

Yes... if Brecht were sitting opposite me now I would have a good discussion with him about that. He always listened and you could convince Brecht of things... He'd probably say: 'You know what? I'll give it a try'. Brecht's greatest strength was that he tried things out (I can't stand artists who don't try things out and neither could Brecht). Without trying out there would be no art. It's different for different art forms. With music, the only thing we can try out is the impression it makes on the listener. We can't try out to see if the clarity of thought is correct. What Brecht meant by 'trying out' was that the thought comes over correctly and is understandable. Then the right thing is being understood correctly. This is 'trying out' in a higher sense. It's not about what's technically correct, or difficult or easy to understand.

With music 'trying out' is quite complicated. I often have to 'try out' whether my audience can still keep up with my work. I have to confess that I frequently (and impertinently) simply disregard them and tell myself that in twenty years' time they'll probably understand my music. This is a crude, vulgar attitude, but I have no other choice, particularly with works that were written during the exile. What can I do? Now, in 1961, I can't very well 'try out' all the pieces I wrote in 1935. My audience just has to get used to the different types of my music. Whether they're right or I'm right remains to be seen, I say.

Where Brecht is concerned, we can conduct our discussion at a higher level because in literature and in poetry (Brecht is above all a poet, even in his plays) it is much easier to express the truth through concrete means. However, when the truth is presented in an over-complicated way, the means of presentation is often incompatible with the simplicity of the truth. But here we're entering the field of pure aesthetics and this is when I have to call upon my beloved master Hegel. If you seriously want to talk about art, these are the real problems.

But who wants to talk about art seriously in these times, apart, of course, from you, dear comrade Bunge, and me, especially when we talk about Brecht? An opportunity such as this to talk seriously about art would be a talent of Brecht's, and when you talk about Brecht there's nowhere to hide – neither politically nor aesthetically. Politics and aesthetics, contradictory as they are, blend together and you have to confess to colour – and the colour is red!

Earlier you said that Galileo *is a historical play. One could think you meant it's a play about the historical figure Galileo.*

That's wrong, and if I did say that, I must have expressed myself inaccurately. Imagine a play about Professor Hahn who, as you know, wasn't a physicist, but a chemist, and was the first to discover, observe, together with his assistant Meitner, the possibility of nuclear fission. Hahn shared this discovery with Meitner, a Jew, who had, in the meantime, emigrated to Copenhagen, but he concealed it from the authorities. Is this Galileo? Absolutely not. Hahn was left unharmed until the English arrested him. They picked him up somewhere in 1944. After six or eight weeks' imprisonment in England for appearance's sake, he was released back to Germany because of an indiscretion…Well, Hahn didn't want to inform Hitler about the possibilities of plutonium fission with the mass number of 233. I'm sorry if I got that wrong. So he wrote to Copenhagen and Bohr flew… but I've already talked about this. So, this is not Galileo – Galileo is a much more complicated type living in a more difficult time. Galileo had to assert himself against the church whereas Hahn had only to keep silent and drop a note to Copenhagen. Galileo's achievement was to separate the idea of religion from the Bible, although given the circumstances of his time, this ought to have been impossible for him. For Galileo it was one of the most difficult situations in which a human being could find himself and without ever wanting to! He didn't want to get rid of the Bible or religion. This is actually the tragedy of the specialist.

Are you now talking about the historical Galileo?

Yes, I am, but I'm also talking about Brecht's. Galileo is the *Spez* [Specialist] as the communists say. It's a somewhat contemptuous term for someone who's an expert in a particular field, someone you need, someone you have to call upon but who causes trouble. Remember the scene where he asks, 'Where is God?' and then answers, 'I'm a mathematician'. That's Galileo, the specialist – this is the tragedy of the specialist – one can only understand him in this light. To describe Galileo's character correctly, you would have to call the play 'Life of Galileo or The Tragedy of the Specialist'. That would be its correct subtitle.

So that means from the historical Galileo there are ...

... some vestiges in the play, yes. But it doesn't matter what these are. What did Shakespeare include of the real Henry IV or Henry V or Julius Caesar? The real historical figures are not important. This is the tragedy of the *Spez*. I'm using the abbreviation on purpose because that's how we communists say it; we use those abbreviations. You know how relentless we are. And furthermore, we don't have morals. We exploit every specialist. Given that a dog trainer who's good at training dogs will immediately be employed as a dog trainer, imagine what we'd do with a physicist! Now there's an interesting idea. The tragedy of the specialist who causes problems for everyone by persisting in returning to his specialism. In this respect, Galileo has a great deal in common with the physicists of today, and that's what makes the play exceptional.

Similar to our physicists in the GDR today.

Yes, I'm afraid our physicists are against us. Some of them have even run away to the West because they felt that their children weren't free to take Christian confirmation. We allow the children of doctors, or minor officials, physicists or engineers to take confirmation if they so wish, but if one unfortunate little functionary mentions that they should have the socialist ceremony, the *Jugendweihe*[163] as well, they think they're restricted in their rights and desert the country. These people aren't Galileos. If these people are stupid enough to think that a badly educated little cleric who hasn't learned any Latin to speak of, who can hardly interpret the Bible, who doesn't know his church fathers any better than I do, is a suitable comforter of their children's souls, and if they run away because they can't manage without him, well ... then we have the tragedy of a different kind of specialist. Galileo was better in that respect. He stayed.

When you say: 'Brecht was a great tryer-out' and 'let's try out and see if the last scene works', do you really mean that you can only decide whether or not a scene can be played at all when it's on the stage? Surely, first and foremost, it must be an investigation of the text that determines whether or not it's 'right'.

That comes first. But this last scene in *Galileo* is relatively simple. It won't take much time to try it out on stage, in the run-through.

Does that mean that it's solely about theatrical effect?

No. It's about whether or not it comes across in the run-through. When Galileo has that huge monologue at the end, you can't have another scene such as the crossing of the border following it because it obviously is the end. This scene was added to the first version and it's very attractive. But after this huge monologue (which, I must remind you, is an important poetic work) you can't, I think, add another scene. I can't explain why, you'll just have to accept it. But maybe Buckwitz in Frankfurt could be persuaded otherwise. I think I could manage it.

That would be a completely different end of the play.

Actually, it wouldn't be.

But if the main weight is not on Galileo's self-condemnation anymore but on the work being taken across the border to...?

Galileo wants the work taken over the border. He wants the work taken to safety, which is why he gives it to the pupil (and note that he wrote it as a blind man because he doesn't want honouring as the clever man). The pupil, still in shock that Galileo has entrusted him with it, praises him for writing it under the most difficult circumstances. But Galileo refuses to be praised.

Conversation 7
22 August 1961

'Hotel Room 1942' – Hölderlin

What have you chosen to sing or play?

Your advice was very good. I will try to play a song called 'Hotel Room 1942', although it will be inadequate and feeble and, as I said once before, it'll sound like a sick dachshund. The poem, by Brecht, is written in very simple language with great craftsmanship – it's high art really. Using the same simple style, I tried to transpose the poem into the language of music, in the same way you preserve a fly in a piece of amber. I'll try to sing it and if it doesn't work, I'll try again. As you know, the text is:

Against the whitewashed wall
Stands the black suitcase with the manuscripts.
Over there stands the smoker's kit with the copper
    Ashtray,
The Chinese canvas, showing the sceptic,
Hangs above it. Also the masks are there, and beside
    The bedstead
Stands the small illuminated loudspeaker.
At dawn
I turn the switch and hear
Reports of the triumphs of my enemies.[164]

This poem was written in the days when all the radio stations in the world bombarded us with news of the incredible victories of the fascists. I hope I can sing it in that cheerful spirit with which I set it to music then – and, by the way, also in a hotel room. [After listening to the playback:]

It doesn't sound very optimistic. Let's do it again and describe what's happened.

We've moved the microphone a bit further back now.

That should improve the range of the sound. But it's quite possible that the real problem, musically speaking of course, is not the distance of the microphone but the range of the performer's voice. Let's try it once more. [After the second playback:] I have now published Volume V of my *Songs and Cantatas*. I always try to begin each volume with a special motto. For example, in Volume VI, which is already at the printer, I composed a motto to Brecht's poem 'On a Chinese Tea Root Lion'.[165] [Eisler's poodle barks.] I'll stop this recording now. Puschko, get out! Now my snarling dog has been thrown out, I can continue.

When I was in Leipzig, I bought another edition of Hölderlin poems and from this I composed a motto for Volume V. I put it immediately before the poem 'Red Wedding',[166] probably one of my favourite workers' songs, which I composed in 1928 and which are known for a certain coarseness and roughness. Hölderlin's poem, it's really only a fragment, goes as follows (I quote only a few lines):

Indifferent to my wisdom
The waters hurry by, but even so
I like to hear them, and they often move me
And make my heart strong – the mighty waters;
And, while not along my channels but their own,
They find their true course down to the sea.

Musically it sounds like this … I can hardly sing it and I can hardly play it, but I'll try. [Eisler sings the song.] Unfortunately, in my performance of this song, and I hope I can improve it sometime, we once again hear the sound of the sick dachshund. I'm afraid that this 'sick dachshund' sound represents the petit bourgeois in ourselves, which we have to fight every day: there is a certain complacency in the way we accept that not everything works in the way we'd like it to – an apologetic rationale of the petit bourgeoisie, which one has to overcome in oneself. I'll try to sing this song again and hope I can avoid the whining sound this time, although the 'beauty' of my voice at this time of day has greatly diminished – if indeed it ever existed in the first place.

[A phone call interrupts the recording. It was decided to continue with the interview two days later.]

Conversation 8
24 August 1961[167]

On Stupidity in Music I – Hölderlin

Why don't you ask me why I look so pale and whether I'm sick or if something is troubling me?

Eisler, you look pale. What's wrong? Are you sick or is something the matter?

I've had a lot of trouble. In Zurich I met a man who had read my essay 'On Stupidity in Music'[168] and thought I was an opponent of modern music. I simply replied that I'm against modernity if it produces only stupidity, or that's what I wanted to express in my writings. Needless to say that sounds not only bad but incomprehensible. So let me repeat: I'm not against modern methods in music. I've used them myself ever since I was a young man. What I am against is the misuse of modern methods in music if they produce stupid results. This man's observation made a big impression on me. I think my enemies are right (and I'm happy to learn from my enemies). I should organize my thoughts much more carefully. I should express myself better so that I am understood by the people I want to understand me, by which I mean either my enemies or those audiences who don't rate me very highly. Let me try and compare today's situation with the historical one. We've learnt from Hegel to observe things historically and I want to apply this approach to music.

Since my youth, I have been reproached for being a rough, plump man, whose working class songs are so powerful and loud that bankers' daughters and spoiled audiences at musical events find them impossibly difficult, aesthetically speaking. And this admonition is correct: I was rough, inelegant and loud. So if someone like this man, or even a few of my working class listeners, says something against my music, then I am reminded of the old times. I was, as you know, unfortunate enough to receive a good education from the Jesuits.

And it leads me to ask myself how was it possible for new art forms to forge ahead 1500 years ago when things were every bit as complicated and as interesting as they are today. A musical expert could have been able to hear in my first compositions a new function, a new style, a new method as well. I'm going to compare that now but it won't be very good because I'm finding it very difficult to concentrate on speaking tonight.[169]

Let me give you an example. In 475 AD there lived a poet called Sidonius Apollinaris[170] at the court of the Franks and Visigoths that is to say at the court of Bordeaux. He was a poet of the classical Latin school who wrote poetry and epics. He said: 'It's impossible for me to write poems when I see all these new people who smear butter into their hair'. And indeed there were these people, among them the Teutons, who rubbed butter on themselves (they must have stunk to high heaven). 'I can't write an ode to the goddess Venus if these Germanic barbarians come here and I see with horror that my children are already starting to learn the German language!' He particularly disliked the blue-eyed Saxons who reeked of rancid butter and couldn't speak Latin and whose only specialism was killing. And this man wrote a very beautiful poem about all this, which nobody knows about. I'll try to read it in Latin – not that anyone today will understand it, but maybe our pupils in twenty years' time will understand Latin better than I do. I wrote this poem down when I was in hospital in Vienna after my heart attack.[171]

What Apollinaris wanted to say was this: 'It's atrocious that these stinking barbarians are coming here because I can no longer talk about art at all. All I want to do is write magnificent epic tales about the past – but now along come these new people!' Now this strikes a chord in me. It reminds me of my youth and it reminds me of today because, and it's extremely important to understand this, a new culture, a new function of culture, often seems so barbaric that the old guard, who want to write about the goddess Venus, grow pale and become distressed. Let's not forget that the poet Sidonius Apollinaris, 475 AD, also met the future Shakespeares, Schillers, Goethes and Brechts – but he didn't recognize them. They stank too much of rancid butter.

Today it's much simpler. We know that Brecht is one of the great masters, and not only of this century. However, it isn't useful to reflect on art in this way; we have to free ourselves from stupidities and look forward, not back – not the easiest thing to do, but very important.

Unfortunately, I didn't understand this example. Apollinaris was silent because the new people disturbed him?

Yes, they stank too much for him. The new stinks of the new and Apollinaris had an old nose.

So, the Teutons with the buttery hair could only kill.

Yes – but, dear Doctor Bunge, haven't we been through some experiences in the past twenty years which, as a German, you can't refuse to acknowledge?

You said Apollinaris was silent because he didn't understand the new, and you're suggesting that we don't look back but forward. You see the new as a revolutionary element, but in the example of the Teutons you don't define it as revolutionary but as something strange that came into the country.

You're right, Doctor Bunge, I expressed myself poorly. I only meant that the poet Sidonius Apollinaris, 475 AD, couldn't comprehend the new. The new came into his room stinking and he despised it. He didn't understand that the children of the children of these stinking Teuton barbarians would one day become the Shakespeares, the Goethes and the Brechts of this world. I only want to warn our enemies, and we have plenty of those, not to underestimate our new beginnings even if they seem barbaric at times. I made up the example.

Unfortunately I can't read these marvellous verses because the light is no good. As you know I'm over-meticulous with hexameters. But what I'm trying to say is that inherent in us Marxists is a marvellous skill to recognize progress in whatever way progress comes along. Brecht has a fitting sentence about this in *The Measures Taken* – I won't quote it, it's a terrible sentence and Brecht and I cut it out.[172]

Maybe we can quote another one: 'Everything new is better than everything old'.[173]

Certainly, although 'everything new is more painful than the old' would be better because, believe me, to make something new in politics is as difficult as in art or in our private lives. Let's not delude ourselves! It's an enormously complicated political process of which we're both part. As an old man of sixty-three, who's done penance for a few things and seen a few things, I'm telling it as it is. It's very complicated – but that's what I like. I always say: we've overcome the old difficulties and now we're looking forward to the new ones.

And what does that have to do with what we originally wanted to talk about: stupidity in music?

Music is an 'archaic' thing (Carl Jung's word, not mine). The development of the ear lags behind the other senses. The eye and the intelligence have progressed, at least in the socialist countries, but in the capitalist countries the ear lags behind. It's archaic, numb. It's lethargic and lazy, it hasn't kept up. It's somehow a backward look at the old collectives of hundreds of years ago. To listen with the ear actually means being backward in development. The eye is much more agile, so is the gesture of the hand. But precisely because the ear is retarded, it's able to bring a certain humanity into our time.

I grow pale at the thought of such complex ideas. You told me at the beginning that I look pale. They're very difficult to put into words. So, the fact that the ear lags behind and can't take in new elements of social development as quickly as the eye provides an opportunity for us musicians. That's why I'm so strongly opposed to stupidity in music! Because the ear is something archaic, I fight against bad listening, bad interpreters and particularly bad composers who express stupidity, pomposity, rubbish and lies in music. I've been fighting against these things since 1918 – and now, in 1961, I admit defeat.

But even the losers don't give up the fight – as you, a Marxist, know, comrade Bunge. As long as I have the strength, I'll fight on.

When you speak about the backwardness of the ear and bad listening, do you mean that because the ear has a slower uptake than the eye, it takes longer for it to absorb modern impressions and it continues to yearn for traditional sense impressions for the longest time?

That's correct although it's somewhat daringly phrased. I believe that the ear couldn't keep up either with the eye or with human intelligence; awful for conductors and composers, I know, but it is the truth.

And awful for doctors too?

Doctors have ear specialists among them. Look, Doctor Bunge, let's be serious here. Music for me is a very serious matter. In the last fifty years we have never investigated music's potential influence on medicine. It's only in the last two or three years that research has started into what music really is. My God, when I think of the history of music and what we once had and how much have we lost... Don't look at me with such tragic eyes!

But it sounds so tragic.

Think of Orpheus, the great mythological figure of Greek art. He made stones dance (as well as being torn apart by some women). Just imagine that I, as a musician, could rebuild the Stalin-Allee. Or think of the walls of Jericho: some musicians came along, played a little piece, unfortunately not one of mine, and the walls of Jericho collapsed. Now, that's what I call a function of music! It's very good, you have to admit.

It's brilliant fiction.

It's not fiction – it's the archetype. Music used to play an enormous role. The Orpheus saga isn't a fairy tale; it's a real experience in human history. Brecht wanted to write a ballet with me (a topic not worth mentioning any more) on Orpheus and Eurydice. I'll tell you my unauthorized version of the story. Now I'm too old to set it to music, so nothing will come of it, but I did write it down. The great singer Orpheus lost his wife Eurydice, his finest audience, and when she died, the whole of nature fell silent. The gods became angry and said that without music the world wouldn't function: cows couldn't give milk, shepherds couldn't graze their sheep and men couldn't live. Now Orpheus can't go to the underworld just like that to get Eurydice back. But because music is dead, and with it the whole of mankind, for Orpheus, an exception has to be made, just like one of those special permits you can get these days. Jupiter speaks, Orpheus receives a special permit to go into the underworld and visit Eurydice and bring her back, on condition that he only looks forward, and doesn't look back. Looking back is also a bad thing in politics – you have to look forward.

Now you're smiling, dear Doctor Bunge, but this is the Orpheus saga exactly as I told it. When Orpheus entered the underworld, horrible ghosts approach him such as the Ghost of Stupidity who said: 'I'm deaf'. Then there was Cerberus who didn't want to let Orpheus through to Eurydice. (Do you know Gluck's magnificent *Eurydice*? [Eisler hums a few bars.] Just brilliant.) But Jupiter had decreed that Orpheus should be allowed to lead Eurydice back, and so they climbed up the stairs into the light. But when Eurydice says: 'For God's sake, look back!' He looks back – and Eurydice is lost again. You see, if it's art worth talking about, it means it is great art. These are the great parables from the cradle of mankind, when mankind was naïve. Thank God we're not that naïve today. And now, if you could say something intelligent to me, I would be most grateful.

You put the words into my mouth. The condition was: don't look back. But you've been looking back yourself all evening. You talked about the effect of music in earlier times. The fact that music played such a vital role in the past might have been because it was one of the few art forms that could be performed by everyone. Were you not to look back now, for once, but forward ...

I have to interrupt you, because looking back also means looking forward. In order to look forward, I have to look back. For example, I'm often busy abroad and most of the time, because I can't fly, I take the sleeper train. I always travel with Hegel's *Encyclopaedia of the Philosophical Sciences* and *Lectures on the History of Philosophy* and that's when I look back. And from looking back, I learn how to look forward – who wouldn't do that automatically? There's no question that in order to understand 1980, I have to read Marx and what he wrote in 1860. Now, I have to acknowledge these are cheap points, dear Doctor Bunge and I don't want to play the clever man here. But life today is complicated and we have to prepare for this. It places a lot of responsibility on intellectuals. I'd be extremely interested in your reply.

Unfortunately, I haven't yet found a plausible definition of stupidity in music either in our conversations or in your publications. It's probably very difficult to determine precisely what stupidity in music is.

You're absolutely right! You've got me there, Bunge – as always. I freely admit that it is very difficult to define what stupidity in music is, or to write against it, because such stupidity is so immense. Little things are easier to express but when stupidity is enormous, what can you do?

Can I suggest that the two of us go to a performance of the *Ninth Symphony*, under any conductor, the greatest or the most insignificant, and listen to the stupidity in the performance, the pomposity, the fraud, the rubbish. Or we could go to a violin concerto or a vocal recital. Then you'd see how backward music is. You wouldn't believe the rubbish you'd hear – you'd never accept it in your private life. But because music is music, you go along with it. And then there are the composers (and I don't mean ours in the GDR) who despite their frequent use of modern methods are backward in a way that I find really surprising.

So, when is music stupid? If it's not at the same level as our understanding of present times. If I compose a *Miserere mihi* – which, after all, I'm perfectly free to do here in the GDR – then somehow I'm mentally deficient. Who is supposed to take pity on me? What is supposed to happen? Now, a lot of people, my dear friend, compose such things, maybe well, or maybe badly, but unfortunately the form takes over the content. The whole thing is somehow useless when an individual simply begs for mercy.

Neither my friend Brecht nor your friend Eisler has ever begged for mercy. My music has a completely different tone. Take for example Brecht's poem 'In Praise of Dialectics', which I set in a happy, cheerful way – I tell you, dear Doctor Bunge, only a communist could have set it in that way. Any other composer would consider it criminal to treat it in a humorous way. I also set Brecht's verses 'because the defeated of today will be the victors of tomorrow!' humorously, and although it's not what is expected of a great composer (though history will be the judge of that). At least I behaved like a Marxist. Revolutionizing the world is a hugely complicated matter.

I think putting stupidity and finesse side by side is particularly difficult. I probably haven't explained myself clearly enough and you're right to criticize me. One has to work with contemporary methods, with the latest sophistications of modern music – but one must work with intelligence.

And not just be simply formalistic...

Absolutely right.

... to, if I may express myself rather succinctly, secure advancement or continuous striding forward?

Allow me to object to 'striding forward' and 'advancement' – that strikes me as too idealistic.

I have to acknowledge your objection because I'm just as vague as you are.

I'd put myself on the lowest rung of the ladder in the fight against stupidity. Let me put it this way: in order to cut out stupidity it has to be abolished and you're absolutely right, it's all about progress. As an old Marxist, I'm all for progress.

Would you agree if I said stupidity equals anachronism?

You're right, but unfortunately I'm such a trained Marxist that I can't accept the idea that anachronisms can be equated with stupidity because stupidity is a particular vice. Anachronism and stupidity are both special types of depravity; they can complement each other. We can't simply call an individual stupid if we think he's anachronistic. It's a lamentable situation. It's such a struggle for a Marxist to have to deal with such complicated circumstances. But we can't relax in the face of our enemies. We have to fight with a variety of methods.

But we're only interested in stupidity in its social context.

Yes, that's what I meant.

But then it's ambiguous if you say stupidity is a vice like ...

... like smoking opium.

Or like any other enjoyable bad habit.

I possess lots of bad habits myself, but that's not the point. Nor is it the point to single out an individual composer and declare him to be stupid. That would not only be rude, but politically completely wrong. I see stupidity in this case only as a social phenomenon.

I seem to recall a lecture Marx once gave about the veil that's drawn over the production of goods, which results in people not being able to recognize the means by which the goods are produced. This same veil is hanging over music and despite all our failings and virtues, we have to push through it because if we don't we'll be trapped forever in stupidity. The lamentable fact is that this is a general vice or, to put it entirely politically, it is the late phase of monopoly capitalism.

When Marx says the veil of goods production has to be pushed through, he explains in detail what he means by goods production and where and how it's obscured. But in our debate about stupidity in music, we haven't, in my estimation, come far. It's not much good if you say that it's difficult to explain and that we have to fight against stupidity because it's stupid and so forth. I would like to hear a concrete example. To be fair, you have given examples of where texts have been set to music and where the composer has, let's say 'misunderstood' the texts and even I can see what's stupid about that. But if you want to take a lay-person like me to some concert conducted by any conductor to listen to the Ninth Symphony, *then I really don't know how I could recognize, in concrete terms, stupidity in such a work.*

It requires education, training, experience and intelligence. Because the opposite of stupidity is intelligence, isn't it? It's rather difficult in the field of music, but I'm afraid that you've really ambushed me. I'll have to think about it immediately and try to come up with something sensible.

Stupidity in music is about the replication, in musical term, of the stupidity in every-day human life. If I were to sing you a really wonderful song by Schumann [Eisler sings: 'You are like a flower, so fair and beautiful and pure...'], you will admit that my singing is idiotic – but this is exactly as you hear these songs performed. So, what's wrong with this? First of all, this poem, written by Heine, is second rate. Heine is a genius and I admire him greatly, but this poem is...well...mediocre. Then, my singing of it is like a sick dachshund before he goes to the vet.

In music we have to prove that the behaviour of a person is wrong. A musician is not someone who stands outside human society. I can't very well sing [Eisler imitates an opera singer] 'Come, my dear Doctor Bunge...' What I have just sung is Richard Wagner's *Lohengrin*, second act, the Bride's room. But it's not at all the way to talk to each other, in fact, it's impossible; the gestures are wrong and that sort of behaviour is wrong. Music must behave much more cleverly. It doesn't only have to be responsive to our time in an agit-prop way, as our enemies think. Music has to do it *intelligently*. I can't lie to you by singing [Eisler imitates again]: 'Today is Monday morning'. This sentence, which I've just made up, would be sung by an opera singer without any scruple and he'd earn about 5000 Marks a month for that. It's not on.

We have to cleanse our feelings. Music is all about feelings, and unfortunately they become polluted through music. I've been fighting for this for forty years and it's a hopeless undertaking! What I'm talking about is the solemn presentation of human stupidity in music. Marx talks about 'the shallow and the solemn misery', and this is what I mean by 'stupidity in music'.

I can see by the doubt in your eyes, dear Doctor Bunge, that I have again been defeated (actually, I've been constantly defeated). But it's all highly interesting.

There are such operas and songs ...

Not just operas and songs – it's everything, everywhere where music is made.

Perhaps it depends mainly on the listener. Does he have a critical attitude to what he hears? Does he think a song is beautiful just because the text is by Heine and the melody by Schubert?

Unfortunately you're right, that's the reason he thinks it's beautiful. Now you can see the prejudices and traditions I have to fight against. Gustav Mahler said: 'tradition is slovenliness'. My works are performed dreadfully something I spoke about in our last meeting, and I won't get the chance of finding out whether they'll ever be performed better. Stupidity reigns supreme in music. Just look at the way a conductor conducts!

You have to admit, my dear friend, that I'm quite a good musician and the rehearsals are every bit as important as the performance in the evening. I know conductors who never rehearse but who display themselves in their tails purely for the benefit of the audience. Music begins with rehearsals, with seriousness, diligence and stamina and what you do in the evening in your tails is of absolutely no interest. If I could ban conductors (this is an ultra-leftist point of view, which I think my party, the SED, would castigate me for), I would outlaw them immediately through a kind of musical state security service.

In all honesty I don't really hold with these ultra-left ultra-views, but they deserve to be heard at least once.

Do you think audience expectations are taken into account here? Everywhere I hear people complaining that the conductor's name is featured above everything else on record covers.

You're absolutely right. Robert Schumann (from Saxony, like me, but from Zwickau not from Leipzig – I say that with indignation) has already protested about that. The musical personality cult was vigorously resisted during those great days when we were creating a new German music... until about 1948. After that our resistance grew weaker. Nowadays you can't just have in small print: 'Conductor X performs Beethoven's *Ninth Symphony*'. Personally I couldn't care less whether my name is mentioned or not, I'd be happy enough to have one of my pieces played at all. It's very seldom that any of these conductors performs anything of mine – and do you know why? Because it's too difficult. He would have to study it, think about it. He'd have to have five rehearsals instead of two. That's the reason why I'm not performed in the GDR, this good, dear country where I feel completely at home.

But this doesn't matter. I'm not fighting against the stupidity that lies behind all this because my music isn't performed, but, and here I speak as a Marxist, because of the social situation. My own situation supports the theory: if my music isn't performed, then the music business is stupid – an impertinent thing to say, but correct I think.

My political friends would reject this as a deviant, ultra-leftist point of view. Why shouldn't Rachmaninov (who, by the way, has always been an enemy of the Soviet Union) be performed? But Eisler, the old communist – why not perform Eisler? God! It doesn't really bother me much. A performance of my music is really hard work. I have to go to three rehearsals to do battle with the conductor (which is always so annoying); so I really don't care. But don't run away with the idea that I want to be performed more often. My doctor has strictly prohibited me from attending rehearsals, for heaven's sake. So, it's on doctor's orders that I'm not performed.

As an example of stupidity in music you recently mentioned the setting of Goethe's text, 'To wander on through wood and field' by a contemporary, living composer. You were very sharp in your conclusion. But you yourself have set texts by Goethe, Hölderlin and others to music. Therefore, my question seems justified: where does the difference lie?

That's a serious question. If we're speaking about socialist realism, that comes from within you. What I select, what I read and what I choose to work on is under my own control – it's controlled by my temperament, my talent, my political experience and my intelligence. The way I read Hölderlin, of course, is different from the way a petit bourgeois would read him. I also read Beethoven in a different way – and Bach. I could play you Bach's B minor Mass in such a way that you would be surprised at what a wonderful example it is of the great humanist age, even measured by our values.

When I set a poem, for example, first of all I have to choose it and then I shorten it – I only use fragments. Brecht said to me in Hollywood (you'll find this remark in his Journal): 'It's really astonishing the way you knock the plaster off Hölderlin! You choose some lines, set them and afterwards it somehow works'.[174] He was partly horrified because he thought it an act of vandalism and partly pleased because some of Hölderlin's poems are four pages long. My friend Arnold Zweig felt the same. So I chose eight lines from the poem, and it worked. Well, it would have been impossible if some writer or a great poet like Brecht or Arnold Zweig had said to me: 'Eisler you're criticising Hölderlin!' I couldn't possibly have accepted it, because I wasn't criticizing Hölderlin, simply quoting him. That's a big difference. To return to stupidity in music – a stupid composer wouldn't dare to do what I did. Another composer might have more musicality and talent than me, but he can't outdo me in the way that I select and set poems [...].

Intelligence is not only about the selection of texts but also what you do with them. Were I to identify myself completely with the text, empathize with it, cling on to it, that would be absolutely terrible; a composer has to challenge a text first of all. I like to look on the bright side of the tragic and I remember how enthusiastic my friend Brecht was after I set 'In Praise of Dialectics' to 'happy' music.[175] I resist the obvious content of a poem and interpret it in my own way, thus demonstrating intelligence in music. Anyone who doesn't do likewise is a fool. If I'm praised one day, then it will be for having resisted the text.

That means, therefore, that a certain work of art is not fixed in
time, but that it changes. When it is reconsidered at a later date, it is
given a specific meaning that is relevant to the context of that time.

What a brilliant remark, Doctor Bunge. Yes, artistic conventions
do also change. When I came back from the Great War in 1919 I
could never have set a poem like 'An eine Stadt' [To a City][176] for
example, because I was sick and tired of patriotism. It was only
the brutality of emigration that led to nostalgia and the art of
remembering.

You know, it's a great art – remembering. You won't be able
to empathize with this because you're much younger than me.
If you'd emigrated for fourteen years and had remembered this
damned Germany, then you'd have a different view of things. One
remembers...free from sentimentality. Brecht had some wonderful
things to say about this. In the hands of a stupid composer,
remembering becomes sentimental rubbish but the way I remember
is, and this is a contradiction in itself, dispassionate, gracious and
tender. But the fact that you remember is part of intelligence in
music.

Is sentimentality in each case and every form to be condemned?

Sentimentality, yes, but not sentiment. The Germans are, as you
know, an unfortunate people. We have only these two horrible
qualities: the sentimental and the brutal. We either exterminate
people – gas Jews and send our young men out against Russian
tanks – or we're sentimental and sing: 'Ich weiss nicht, was soll es
bedeuten' [I don't know what it could mean],[177] although I would
change it to: 'I *do* know what it could mean'.

This is our 'national weakness' although it isn't national and
can be explained by Germany's production methods. Germany
was industrialized very early. Its industrial revolution started in
the first third of the nineteenth century, and this resulted in certain
weaknesses for Germany, namely that a central government never
really came to power as it did in France under Henry IV or in
England under Elizabeth I. Germany wasn't able to unite on a
national level and national unification, a miserable unification, only
happened after the war of 1871 when it was imposed from above by
Prussia. Marx made his expectation clear in his writings about the
war against Napoleon III. Through unification he hoped for a larger

roof over German workers' heads, not a workers' movement on a
local level but on a national level. It makes me happy to think of
Marx saying this.[178] I think it's brilliant. Serious mistakes, however,
which had nothing to do with nationalism, race or anything like
that, were made during this unification process and its weaknesses
persist to this day.

How long did the unification of Germany last? From 1871
until 1945. That's all we had, nothing more. For a nation, if we're
going to use such a grand term, it's not very much, is it? But this
isn't a national question; it's a question of economy. Today we're
separated all over again and, quite honestly, we deserve it in spite
of the fact that the Germans have among them people like Karl
Marx, Friedrich Engels, Karl Liebknecht and Rosa Luxemburg, not
to mention culture's finest flowers, the poets and artists.

During the difficult emigration period I wrote a song,
'Erinnerung' [Memory],[179] which drained blood from Brecht's face.
My poem is a fragment (I used only eight lines[180]) of Hölderlin's
poem 'Lied des Deutschen' [Song of a German]. 'Good grief, how
can you compose something like that?', he asked me, beside himself
with anger. 'You're being nationalistic, ain't yer?' (I'm deliberately
using his slang). I *was* being nationalistic for the reason that, during
the emigration I did indeed sometimes think about Germany, not
in a sentimental way, but in the way that Hölderlin did. As you
know he was an early Jacobin. I wrote this song around the time of
Stalingrad and I'd like to sing it to you so that you can see how, at
the same time you were so nationalistic, dear Doctor Bunge, I was
nationalistic too, only in a different way. I wrote it in 1944[181] a time
where nobody would have given a penny for us Germans. I think
that, you, dear Doctor Bunge, were somewhere in a POW camp in
the Soviet Union, and I was in Hollywood. I was well off. It rankled
with me that these poor Germans were and are such bastards. They
were bastards. I'll read you the poem now:

Memory
O sacred heart of the peoples, O Fatherland!
Enduring all, like silent mother earth,
Unacknowledged still for what you are, while strangers
Plunder the treasures from your depths!
They harvest your ideas, the essence of your spirit,
They like to pluck the grape, but they deride

You, the vine, for your misshapenness, for
Twisting your crooked shadow on the ground.
But you do not keep your inner beauty from me.
I have often stood surveying your green pastures,
Your spacious garden, from the high, light air
Of your mountain tops and drunk you in.
And on the shores I saw your cities grow,
Those gracious places of quiet industry
And science, where your sun
Softly warms the artist's noble purpose.

When I played my song to Brecht, he was horrified by my
nationalism. You'll find a note about it in his Journal.[182] I admit
that it was completely tasteless to compose something like that
but, in the hour of the German people's deepest degradation – a
people of whom, unfortunately, I'm one, as are you, there's no
denying it – I was provoked into doing it. When the Russians
reached the river Oder,[183] and I wrote: 'They harvest your ideas,
the essence of your spirit,/They like to pluck the grape, but they
deride/You, the vine, for your misshapenness...' I knew it was in
bad taste to compose something like that but, nevertheless, I did
it. And do you know why? I said to myself, 'When I return, I want
to be able to say "You bastards! But at least I composed something
for you!"' It belongs to an artist's dialectic. What do you think? Is
this going too far?

No. There is a similar text by Brecht...[184]

Yes, he wrote it after I wrote mine. I don't mean to slander my
friend Brecht, but when he saw me setting Hölderlin to music
(this poem we've been talking about was only one of about
twenty Hölderlin poems that I set), he drooled with enthusiasm
and repeated: '... where your sun softly warms the artist's noble
purpose'. Brecht was absolutely spellbound. He had never read the
poem before and was completely carried away, even though he'd
accused me of being so nationalistic.

*You make huge demands on the audience with regard to their
understanding of dialectics.*

Yes, my demands on the artist's intelligence are enormous.
Imagine me, an old Communist, sitting in America during the

emigration watching the tank battles. I watch as you, dear Bunge, sacrifice yourself for a wrong cause. And I write a poem to the glorification of Germany. You have to admit, if dialectics exists, this is it. Wouldn't you agree?

Yes, I would. I can think of other examples as well. In the bitter times of the emigration, you wrote the German Symphony – *for how many chorus members?*

Four hundred people – a hopeless enterprise.

So that's a symphony that you could really only perform at the Deutsche Staatsoper of the GDR.

Yes, but Bertolt Brecht wrote *Chalk Circle*, which could also only be performed in a country where the proletariat has the power. In a nutshell, we wrote for the dictatorship of the proletariat as it manifested itself in what we now call the German Democratic Republic. But is that any reason to praise ourselves? No. I tell you, we had no other choice. We could have gone over either to the bourgeoisie or to the working class in which we were brought up. Remember the famous Brecht poem: '... I'd like to go to school again...'[185] We were the pupils of the working class and we had no other choice. There's no particular merit in that, no virtue, no courage, nothing. Pupils follow their master and that's that.

You just wanted to survive.

Not even that. I just wanted to pass something on.

Isn't that the same?

Yes, it is. Imagine that, in the event of my having a fatal accident, I'd wanted some of my music to outlast me, so that the German workers would be able to say: 'We know this lad. He delivered'. I wanted to be like the messenger who arrives gasping, breathless, having done his duty – that was what I had in mind. Fame was always of secondary importance. My position as an émigré made it impossible for me to become famous, and what was I supposed to do with fame anyway? But at least I could deliver something. The most important lesson I learnt from the working class movement (from the days of my youth actually) was the idea of delivery, of doing something useful, of being the messenger who has to deliver something that endures.

Can I sing that song for you now? My voice is already very hoarse but I'll try it. 'Memory', Hölderlin fragment, composed in 1944. [Eisler sings and afterwards listens to the recording.] That's so badly sung – it's more of a bawl, like a nationalist club, as in 'In Treue fest' [Steadfast and faithful for ever].[186]

I can't agree, I have to protest!

My dear Bunge, even at eleven o'clock at night I'm so keen to discuss things with you that I'm happy to deliver a hoarse, bawling performance in the hope that, one day, it will be understood.

I'd like to add some afterthoughts. It's well known that the early Christians were only able to meet illegally consequently many rumours about the true nature of Christianity arose. Even among zealous, religious people it gave rise to misunderstandings, of which – a graffito in the Palatine – is one example. The graffito shows Christ, with the head of a donkey, hanging on the cross, with the words 'Alexandros prays to his god' underneath. This Alexandros was, supposedly, a North African or Egyptian soldier who transposed Egyptian gods with animal heads into Christianity, which he didn't understand but felt attracted to. That's exactly how I saw miners from the Borinage area in Belgium demonstrate during a general strike. They carried a badly painted picture of Marx (probably done by a house painter) looking like a menacing miner with black skin. He didn't look much different from the people who were striking. Such comparisons are very useful in helping us to understand history, although it's not always so easy. No one owns a monopoly on the truth – one has to work hard to acquire it. Class struggle can appear, and does appear, in many different forms and our task is to be in the midst of these struggles, to recognize their different forms and join in.

When I talk about the Borinage, I'm reminded of early feudalism and the completely different demands it made on the people. Take a knight for example – and I'll quote this in English: 'A knight was supposed to enjoy music, poetry and dancing and to be adept in the "gay science"'. Raoul de Houdenc wrote that in 1230, and we communists have to take hold of this sentence, alienate it and rephrase it. The 'new man' of socialism should not only adopt the knight's 'pleasures' (it's only a basic list) but a lot more besides – the new can only come from the old, as Brecht already said in the 'Moldau Song'.

The stones of the Moldau are stirring and shifting.
In Prague lie three emperors turning to clay.
The great shall not stay great, the darkness is lifting.
The night has twelve hours, but at last comes the day.

The danger is that, because we want something completely new and are fighting for it, we forget the old, the knowledge of the things that are inherent in us. It might sound banal, but unfortunately it's true.

Conversation 9
25 August 1961

Hans Mayer's book on Brecht – Brecht and Georg Lukács

Can I begin by saying that last night my voice was already very hoarse and the way I sang the Hölderlin song weighs particularly heavily on my soul! I beg you to erase it once and for all and when I'm in better voice I'll try it again. Do you promise me this, Doctor Bunge?

Of course.

That's a deal, because it was just bawling and on top of that, we had been drinking champagne, which is very bad for the voice.

I'm not such a strict critic as you.

That's extremely nice of you but we really have to erase it. I don't want it kept because I can do it better, especially when I'm well-rested.

Today we want to talk about Hans Mayer's book *Bertolt Brecht und die Tradition*.[187] I read it last night, finished it this morning and find it tremendously stimulating. Mayer certainly depicts Brecht as a great personality and as a universal thinker, although he did leave out some elements relating to his working practices. (You can't include everything.) Although I can be called an expert on Brecht, there were many details I wasn't aware of. For that reason alone the book was great to read and very informative. Do you have any criticism?

It's a question that actually only you can answer. Mayer writes, 'meticulous preoccupation with Hegel, dealings with the economic

theorists of Luxemburgism, relinquishing of party commitments –
all of these must have brought even the Marxist politician Brecht
into opposition with Marxist orthodoxy'.[188] *He continues: 'Brecht's*
speech at the First International Congress of Writers for the
Defence of Culture in Paris in 1935 makes that especially clear'.[189]
Mayer then explains that the Congress was called to find common
ground between all exiled writers from different camps in the hope
of building an anti-fascist front. In contrast to that, Brecht, who
came to Paris from his Danish exile, proposed in his paper that the
ownership of property should be investigated as the root of all evil.

Yes, that's right, I mean, the fact is right but I think it's futile to
look for an opposition between Brecht and what my friend Mayer
calls Marxist orthodoxy. 'Being orthodox', if we understand the
word correctly, applied rather more to Brecht than anyone else.
I was there for the first preparatory conference of the *Front
Populaire Allemagne,*[190] which, by the way, Walter Ulbricht also
attended. I enjoyed the calm, reasonable, but strongly principled
tone that prevailed in the negotiations between the social democrats
and the independent émigrés in order to bring about such a *Front
Populaire.* Brecht spoke at a writers' congress and not at the
Congress of the Popular Front. We have to distinguish between
them. At a writers' congress anyone can stand up and express an
opinion, especially if he's not a member of any party. However, the
KPD's position in exile, especially after the Brussels conference and,
finally, in 1935, really was: 'Let's all stay true to our principles but
also investigate our politics. What do we have in common?' That
was a very simple formula, which later came into practice in Paris
in 1936 with the *Front Populaire Français.* Let me remind you of
the Daladier government: the enormous progress in Social Welfare
Legislation; the massive strike; Franco's escape abroad – at that
time there really was a revolutionary atmosphere in Paris. I even
came over from London. Brecht didn't experience that. He was in
Paris the previous year and he had an insurmountable dislike for
the Popular Front in Paris. We really got up each other's noses over
this in Denmark.

Because of the French Popular Front?

Yes, he thought it was *Rabitz*[191] as he called it. We seriously fell
out without doing each other any harm, because I thought, the only
possible step for one of Germany's neighbours was to bring the best

of people together in a united government. I wasn't for a moment under the illusion that this would be the way to introduce socialism. And on top of that, the end of the Popular Front government marked the beginning of the war against Germany. Daladier wasn't a socialist either and the communists were outlawed not only under German occupation but, even before that, under Renault's government and later, under the Vichy government.

Of course Brecht lacked practical political experience – and how could it have been otherwise. He came to Marxism via a different route from that of his friends of the same age. I came to Marxism actually through my involvement with the organization 'Socialist High School Pupils' in 1912/1913, where we read the easier texts by Marx and Engels, and then, finally, through the First World War. But it was different for Brecht. Mayer is correct in his analysis that for Brecht the war wasn't the first step towards his becoming a socialist. Brecht, as you know, made his final step into Marxism during the great depression of 1929 and collaborated with the party from then on.

I have to say the relationship between Brecht and the KPD was excellent and the rumours that Brecht was disliked or was seen as orthodox by our KPD friends are simply not true. The term 'orthodox' just seems out of place. We weren't at all like that at this time. A left-wing writer speaks at a writers' congress about the true roots of fascism, the social conditions, the ownership of property, and we neither rejected those ideas nor made them our top priority. And nobody would, could or even wanted to prescribe what Brecht could say. A party-affiliated writer like Johannes R. Becher for example, or my friend Bodo Uhse, yes, they spoke differently. They dealt more with the practical demands of the current situation, which was the question of how we could unite?

Well, history has shown us that all that survived from this writers' congress was Brecht's great speech and nothing else. Very little else survived as we look at the current situation in our divided Germany. But what remained, and it belongs to a different phase, is the magnificent GDR. With all its shortcomings, I think the GDR is magnificent. You couldn't predict the situation we're in today and we should re-read the other speeches given by our friends or our enemies during that congress. I'm sure they're quite trivial. Brecht left us a fairly classical document that we read with great pleasure even today. I'm sure tactically it was wrong, but I don't care in the least about that.

At first, there was no movement towards a Popular Front, neither among the writers nor among the émigrés. As far as I know, the Popular Front's slogan to unite all anti-fascists originates from the conference in Brussels in 1935...[192]

...of the party and later in the Comintern, in the famous speech by Dimitroff.

But if I'm correctly informed that was after the Writers' Congress in Paris.

I was there in Paris in 1935 on the first preparatory committee to form a Popular Front but this had nothing to do with the writers, only with the political exiles.

For that reason I'm confused about Mayer's portrayal. He was in Paris then, wasn't he?

He was very young at the time and we actually didn't know him then. It was a congress called by the party, attended by social democrats, independent people, artists, scholars and most of all politicians. It wasn't a party congress, but a preliminary meeting that explored the question: is the unification of all the anti-fascists possible? You can't equate this with the Popular Front. The term 'Popular Front' is actually only a derivation from the French *Front Populaire* and there was nothing similar in Germany.

This preliminary meeting was an experiment to see if unified actions in political exile are possible. Nothing much came of it. The incompatibility of the communists and the émigré social democrats, who never wanted to get into bed with the communists, was insurmountable. The people most likely to work with us were independent from any party, the so-called outlaws; those who would have liked to join a powerful political émigré organization, to operate within it better.

Two things about Mayer's report rankle with me. First, he makes out that Brecht wanted to educate the party about what was important. Was it in Brecht's nature to point the party in 'the right direction?'

No! Once, in Hollywood, I said to him: 'Listen, this is actually not what we [the party] would like to achieve', whereupon he said: 'Where I am, there is the left' (or the other way around) 'The left is where I am'. He never presumed to teach the party anything. As any reasonable man would, he offered mostly productive criticism by making practical suggestions. There was no need for him to hold forth about the ABC of Marxism among communists. But I repeat, it wasn't a communist conference. It wasn't even political – it was a conference for writers. Thomas Mann, who by the way, didn't attend as far as I remember, or Schwarzschild, who was there (in those days, he was a well-known journalist and during the exile he continued to publish a journal called *Das Tagebuch*, which he had begun in Berlin) or Josef Bernstein, also a well-known journalist and other such people... of course they talked about all sorts of things. They went on endlessly about culture and about freedom of speech. In contrast to that, Brecht just offered a sober statement: what are the fundamentals of fascism?

He was absolutely right in principle and I think you're confusing here, or rather Mayer is, simple facts. At a congress for writers many different people get to talk. Brecht certainly took up a Marxist position, but, by the way, not the orthodox Marxist position. The term orthodox in itself is already a criticism because it means 'excessive'. Brecht behaved entirely reasonably on that occasion, which in this situation was very valuable. I remember some physicists I knew in Paris – they were thrilled by the precision of Brecht's explanation. Unfortunately, nothing came of it.

My second objection is when Mayer writes: 'Although already gravely ill, Brecht, who is collating material for his fifteenth (and last) journal Versuche, *decides to include his 1935 Paris speech in this edition'. According to Mayer this was a deliberate tactic of Brecht's to demonstrate publicly, for the benefit of a critical future generation, the opposition (albeit an opposition established by Mayer himself) between Brecht's political views and 'Marxist orthodoxy'.*

No, because Brecht thought, as we all did, that it was a brilliant speech, worth keeping. The 1935 issues are no longer relevant – unless you see things the way our enemies do. They use the term 'state philosophy' and mean Marxism. Marxism is a science with its roots in economic fundamentals. I don't need to lecture you in social sciences because you already know as much as me. Well, I don't understand Mayer here. It seems to me a weak point in his book, but otherwise the book is brilliantly written. It gave me a lot of information and I read it with real enjoyment. Mistakes always happen – unless, of course, you never do anything. If you don't do anything, you won't make mistakes.

I agree, but it can't just be a 'mistake'. Mayer explores first how the speech was received at the time …

It was very well received. Everybody knew that Brecht wasn't a party member. The speech was the breakthrough of a famous writer into purely Marxist questions, which are: let's really investigate how matters have come to this, and not just carry on making speeches about it! Brecht insisted that his bourgeois fellow-writers should concern themselves more seriously with the phenomenon of fascism. And that was absolutely correct.

Mayer asks what further effect this speech had and let's not forget the fact that Mayer teaches in the GDR and is regarded as our most famous literary historian.

Undoubtedly he is – and not just in the GDR. I can't think of anyone in West Germany who comes anywhere near him.

I agree with you, but sadly he publishes his book only in West Germany.

He has the right to do so.

But then it won't be available here. It should at least have been published at the same time in both countries. Maybe there were reasons…

As you know, Mayer did have difficulties although they're long buried. We're glad to have such a first class man teaching in the GDR. These difficulties belong to the past and Mayer is not an elephant who never forgets, but a very intelligent and lively man. I think he has a need also to be recognized in the West. He's very well received there – famous even. His lectures are full to overflowing because he really animates these young people with his enormous knowledge and his brilliant presentation. Well, it had to be said once. I don't mind if he wants to publish in the West.

It's just – if the book is published exclusively in West Germany and the story of this speech is described in this way, which is not at all right…

... not exactly right. He should have sought better advice.

...and if he claims that Brecht would have acted against the party by reprinting the speech in 1956 ...

Which is absolutely wrong!

...then he feeds the Western perception that Brecht was in opposition to Marxism.

Not to Marxism!

I mean with 'orthodox Marxism' as Mayer phrased it.

I don't really know what 'orthodox' Marxism is. You embarrass me. I know what sectarian means – the politics of sectarianism. Brecht didn't oppose Marxism at all, quite the opposite. There is this particular thesis by men like Melchinger & Co arguing that a distinction has to be made between the poet Brecht and the Marxist Brecht and Mayer's brilliant analysis shows that this is completely wrong. Only his reciprocal, contradictory penetration of dialectical materialism plus his poetry adds up to the phenomenon that is Brecht. That is what Mayer worked out brilliantly, even though he might be wrong in this little detail. I think this minor matter sets you off on the wrong track and I don't agree with you, dear Doctor Bunge because I think the whole book will reinforce the impression that Brecht really was a Marxist and that Marxism and Brecht can't be separated. Mayer's book makes the way people from the West approach Brecht more untenable and even forbids them, as much as possible, from taking this approach – even with this little error.

Mayer lets this example run through the whole book. He refers to it in two or three passages. In the West, people don't question that Brecht was a Marxist but they do say that Brecht practised a special or personal Marxism. And my opinion is that Mayer's point of view supports this argument.

That would be wrong – quite the opposite is true. I can tell you from my own experience that, whenever the party wanted something from Brecht, whether during the Weimar Republic or in our Republic now, Brecht was the most helpful, enthusiastic collaborator. He was never in opposition to the party, not to the

KPD or the SED. He criticized a few things (and who wouldn't have!) but he criticized in a loyal way. Brecht always felt like a communist, like a Bolshevik without a party card, as they say in the Soviet Union. Brecht was the classic Bolshevik without a party card – as, by the way, was Mayakovsky, who wasn't a party member either, or Eisenstein. This has to be emphasized. It was enough for Brecht to get a call, often from an insignificant party functionary or from the government itself, asking for advice or help or for a statement on some issue and Brecht immediately dropped everything and got on with it. He was tremendously loyal.

Being loyal doesn't mean the blind loyalty of a believer to his church. It is a critical loyalty. Any different kind of loyalty would have been pointless. It's just... once the party makes a decision on something, the criticism has to stop, otherwise the party can't function at all – and Brecht understood that. That's the old practice of the revolutionary working class party: discuss for as long as you want and as heatedly as you want, but once we agree on a decision, then please follow it through! Brecht understood this principle as all comrades do and always have done. If we don't adhere to this, then we'd turn the whole thing into a very interesting debating society, which can also be useful and can even coexist. It's especially important to observe this way of decision-making when a party governs a state. You can't talk things over for ever.

Brecht often accused his young people of cynicism if they responded to an issue too cynically, too carelessly et cetera but he also had some great young people to whom cynicism didn't appeal at all. I know of one case when Brecht accused someone of cynicism – it wasn't Wekwerth or Palitzsch or Rülicke... no, it was me! Well, in my defence I told him, it wasn't cynicism, but there wouldn't be any other way of approaching this particular matter. It might have been a bit abstruse what I said there, I don't remember the details. Brecht withdrew his accusation when he realized that he had hurt my feelings and said: 'Now I understand you better since you explained it better'. This is how far Brecht went.

Is there an explanation for why Brecht never joined the party, neither the KPD nor the SED?

We never discussed that and I wouldn't have thought it a good idea anyway. Brecht wasn't the man for that kind of discipline. It's a serious step as it's not enough just to join. You also really have to conduct yourself in a certain way.

Do you think the Politburo or the Central Committee of the SED also preferred Brecht not to be a member of the party?

Look, the party never gives a thought to why a valuable man isn't a member. Joining is a completely voluntary decision, there is no pressure. When defectors from our republic claim they had to escape because someone tried to force them to join the party, that's just childish. Just between you and me: it's actually very difficult to join. You have to give the names of two guarantors, then you have to tell them your life history – in your own handwriting – and then you have to answer all sorts of questions. So it's not particularly easy to become a member of the SED.

I think defectors who tell the lie that someone tried to force them into the party are absolute gangsters. I know how difficult it is to be accepted. There are also many people who aren't accepted because the party doubts their usefulness or objects to them for other reasons. The party never asks: 'Are you a card carrier?' The party asks: 'What are you doing practically?' And with such a great poet as Brecht – well that's for Brecht to decide.

From my own experience I can confirm what you said.

Correct. As you know the party has a lot of members, I don't know how many members there are now – a million or seven hundred thousand or so? Well, we don't exactly need to tout for customers, quite the opposite. What the party needs are genuine, serious members it can rely on and since the party itself is indistinguishable from these people, it needs people who are able to rely on themselves. There is no distinction between party and party members. When things are unstable, in particularly complicated situations, you need reliable people.

It often happens that non card-carriers are the most reliable and people with the party card are not. It takes all sorts to make a world. However, that was never a question with regard to Brecht. When Walter Ulbricht delivered the funeral oration at the 'Schiffbauerdamm theatre',[193] he spoke only of 'comrade Brecht' and the word 'comrade' was used time and time again and deliberately emphasized: 'Our comrade Brecht'. Brecht was treated like a Bolshevik without a party card.

Can we get back to Hans Mayer, please? Maybe you can comment on the following statement Mayer makes: 'For the Marxist and émigré Brecht there was only the whole truth or no truth at all. Concealing factual knowledge for tactical reasons, as the organizers of the congress (he means the writers' congress in Paris) obviously tried to do, was unbearable for Brecht'.[194]

That's another mistake. A man who says there is only the whole truth or no truth at all must be someone without the slightest idea about how to live a practical life. What does it mean? It's a purely idealistic phrase, it has nothing whatsoever to do with Marxism any more.

At the same time Brecht wrote and published Five Difficulties While Writing the Truth. *You can't deny that this is a tactical instruction...*

It is the absolutely perfect ABC of how ingenious you have to be to smuggle in the truth through hard times. I think Mayer is mistaken here, but that doesn't mean that this book doesn't have real value.

I'm not denying that and that's the reason why I have selected certain passages from the book.

On those two points unfortunately I have to agree with you. When next I see my friend Mayer I will suggest to him that he might make a correction or two in the next edition – not to toe the party line but for the sake of the truth, because those statements are wrong. I don't intend Mayer to make corrections simply because a friend puts pressure on him – there's no sense in that. What I'm going to say is: 'Listen, you've made a mistake'. It's obviously wrong too to attribute the poem 'Das Stundenlied' [The Hour's Song] to Brecht. It's from 'Des Knaben Wunderhorn' [The Boy's Magic Horn] (unfortunately I haven't been able to find it yet, but I'm sure of it) and Brecht just added a few verses to the poem for a composition by Gottfried von Einem.[195]

It's a small mistake by Hans Mayer – and who is supposed to keep all of that in his head if it's not his main subject? Mayer ought to revise those two passages, they're wrong. Brecht wasn't an obstinate dogmatist but Mayer tries to turn him into one. Brecht was quite the opposite and I have never ever met a more astute man than Bertolt Brecht in my entire life.

Mayer writes: 'between 1929 and 1935, the Marxist Brecht, by comparison, frequently took the standpoint of an ultra-left, abstract and dogmatic communism'.[196]

Yes, strangely there is a grain of truth in that. When people take on a new point of view, they often want to lecture about what they have just learned. It's characteristic of what the Americans call a 'greenhorn'. I know a few old greenhorns who would like constantly to lecture the whole world. It's so very decent of them but unfortunately this is not the way to do politics.

Let's go to the border with the Western sector and write on a blackboard in big letters the famous statements of the heirs of Karl Marx and hope by doing so to set right the whole of world history. Of course that wouldn't achieve anything. Brecht never believed in such foolishness. In his younger days, about 1929/1930, he had a certain, well, let's say, obstinacy but this evaporated soon after. Just read the play, *The Mother*. I don't see any point in asking about his private life. What matters with Brecht are his works. Nobody can claim this is a doctrinaire play! The mother's behaviour in particular, is that of a shrewd old woman. Let me remind you of the magnificent dialogue when the mother visits her son in prison, pretending to feel motherly love, which indeed she does, in order to discuss politics with him.[197] This is an action that cannot be interpreted simply. This man Brecht can't be called doctrinaire, impossible! The play was written in 1929.[198] Brecht might have had certain inclinations, as we all have. I was also doctrinaire sometimes. But people develop. You don't always stay the same. It is unnecessary even to bring it up.

Earlier you mentioned Mayer's phrase 'slave language'.[199]

That is a very well known classic phrase. When Lenin came back to the Soviet Union in 1917 he said: 'Finally I can stop writing in this damn slave language!' It's a classic expression originating in the working class movement.

I wasn't attacking the slogan, but you yourself said that somebody objected to this phrase 'slave language' being used by Brecht.

Someone criticized it, yes.[200]

Mayer talks in more detail about the contrast between Brecht and Lukács.

It was a huge contrast. Since Lukács is under scrutiny at the moment, I don't think it's necessary for me to add fuel to the flames. Whole books have been published against him and I don't want to be part of all that. For one thing because he's a very old man and, for another, because I'm not interested. In the past I had an extremely bad tempered public correspondence with Lukács. I had written a really strong open letter to him. You can find it in the 1936 back issues of *Die Weltbühne*. In it I accused Lukács of nearly every charge that could be levelled against him: that he's a hopeless idealist (for Lukács even the concrete becomes metaphysical – I mean, he's a hopeless meta-physicist and even the most concrete things vanish into thin air)…that he can't speak German and that he can't think, politically, that is. You can read it all in there. I don't feel like repeating it today.

The attacks on Lukács are not that severe at the moment.

Brecht didn't know what to make of Lukács.[201] More to the point though, Lukács didn't know what to make of Brecht.[202] In all of Lukács' big books, Brecht is mentioned in perhaps one line. Lukács was preoccupied with all sorts of other things. One of his favourite writers was Wilhelm Raabe, a writer whom I can barely read. Lukács thought he was the great revolutionary, pre-revolutionary or bourgeois (call it what you like) writer. I can't stomach that stuff! Fontane is a different matter, he's a great bourgeois writer. And Mörike…Lukács called him a little squirt. How can you call a magnificent poet like Mörike a little squirt!

Lukács is doctrinaire and so what doesn't conform to his doctrine is written off immediately. I remember his downright childishly naïve polemic against the scene at the agricultural world exhibition in *Madame Bovary*, which is a montage. While you hear the cries of: 'Pig – pink – 200 Francs bonus' (or whatever it says), Madame Bovary has her first romantic conversation with this young traveller. Lukács argued that this scene was put together in far too contrived a way and he compared it, foolishly I think, with the scene at the races in *Anna Karenina* – the scene where Anna Karenina faints when she hears that her lover has fallen off his horse and might even be killed…while competing during the race.

These were the passages that Lukács compared. He said that in *Anna Karenina* the scene is organic – Lukács' so-called organic – while in Flaubert the scene is contrived. I think *Madame Bovary* is a brilliant achievement which I would put, without hesitation, alongside *Anna Karenina*. *Anna Karenina* is weakened by the double narrative which makes the book difficult to read. The progressive landowner Levin, who just pops up every now and then, is an extremely boring character but apart from that, *Anna Karenina* is enchanting. The dual story does make the reading very difficult and takes away some of the book's beauty, whereas *Madame Bovary* is of course tightly constructed right down to the smallest detail.

To make such a comparison in the first place simply reveals that in this mighty brain of Lukács there lurks a dreadful schoolmaster. He very much reminds me of my German teacher. On the other hand, I have to add immediately that some of the things he accomplished were significant but there are always these fundamental mistakes. He also polemicized unbelievably against me. He tore me to pieces, and then I gave him as good as I got. After that we were best friends again. That's how it is in the working class movement: you beat one another up and if you meet again a year later, everything is perfectly all right. We had our good reasons to lay into each other but time was the referee. The next occasion I saw Lukács was at the peace conference in Wroclaw in 1948. He came over to me, embraced me and in his speech immediately spoke of his friend Hanns Eisler who was sitting there in the auditorium – all was forgiven.[203]

You said Lukács is a schoolmaster. Maybe you could then say that within Mayer the Academic and the Feuilletonist *are at war with each other.*

Dear friend, you're right. We should restore the term *honourable feuilleton*.[204] What Mayer is writing, in the most refined way, is succinctly informative, extremely stylish, and very clear and well-constructed – everything in its place and in harmony. Why shouldn't a very well written *feuilleton* have its place? I'd prefer it to some unreadable heavyweight tome.

Hans Mayer teaches students in his capacity as a literary historian.

Yes, and obviously brilliantly. Käthe Rülicke is a student of his and she is a good student.

I agree with you. Brecht wrote an essay in 1938 called 'Popularity and Variety of Realistic Writing' In the introduction, Brecht takes a position 'against the tendency of formalistically setting limits to realistic writing'. He reflects on an essay by Lukács, which was published in Das Wort.

Yes, in two editions of *Die Weltbühne* Ernst Bloch and I published a discussion about expressionism and other topics. It was heavily attacked by Lukács. He attacked me in particular. Bloch's name wasn't even mentioned. He gave me a real going over because for him German literature means Thomas Mann – this line of late bourgeois literature. He looked with suspicion at everything else: the rebellious, the not-so-easy to handle, the fragmentary and the wild; everything that developed in German literature in the years after the Great War.

It occurred to him for example and he really must have been having a funny turn at the time, to compare, of all things, expressionism with the USPD. According to Lukács, expressionism would be a similar movement to the USPD (which, as you know, was founded during the war). Well, what expressionism has to do with the USPD I will never be able to fathom. That's an argument he pulled out of thin air. Here, in a contrived way, Lukács takes us from the wild bourgeois opposition, the petit bourgeois radical opposition that was expressionism, to the strange post-war construction that was the USPD when many of them (if my memory hasn't failed me, I think it was 1920 during the party congress in Halle) joined the KPD. So, from the Spartacists to the USPD to the new KPD. Lukács had these weird fads. I was there myself. There were fiercely contested discussions between Brecht and Lukács during the Weimar Republic. Sometimes I was embarrassed by Brecht because he was so rude. He hated this little, intelligent, nervous yet very significant man, Lukács, from the bottom of his heart.

Mayer, who reflects on Brecht's answer to Lukács, obviously suspects that Brecht wrote that essay for publication in Versuche *in 1954, while in fact the essay was written in 1938. That is an irritating mistake.*[205]

Correct. I would suggest that you write a little letter to my friend Hans Mayer and make him aware of these things. It would help him to correct these little mistakes, which can so easily occur. The man is working very hard, has a lot on his plate, and travels often.

You have to consider that as well. He's extremely versatile. By the way, he also plays the piano very well and is very musical. He told me once that he even wanted to become a musician. He has a deep understanding of music. One has to help him to clear up things in the next edition of his book. If I'm right about the poem, that the 'Hour's Song' is indeed from 'The Boy's Magic Horn' (I still haven't found it yet), I'll write to him as well.

There are a few little things I have to point out anyway to him, for example, Brecht's play is not called The Horatians and the Curatians, *but* Curiatians.

Those are lapses of memory, he probably confused it. He puts the losers first and the winners second.

No, it's about the missing letter 'i' in Curiatians.

He knows Latin extremely well, maybe there is a different grammatical form for that? He must have had a reason.

I'm afraid it's an analogous construction to Horatians. *Mayer probably overlooked it or he read it too quickly.*

Yes, that's probably what happened. Although I can tell you his knowledge of Latin and Greek absolutely exceeds the average educated European. But, I would point that out to him as well.[206]

And then he should on all accounts try and publish the book in the GDR.

Very good suggestion! That's a really good practical suggestion.

You wanted to say something about 'Das Sichellied' [The Sickle Song].

'The Sickle Song' originates in Julius Bittner's opera *The Mountain Lake*. When I was a student I had to read the proofs in order to scrape a living and I liked it so much, the poem, not the music, that later, in Denmark I suggested it to Brecht as 'The Sickle Song', which he immediately took on board. That's that. These four or eight lines are by Julius Bittner and we used them. With that, the brave Julius Bittner managed, at last, to grab a bit of immortality.

Conversation 10
4 September 1961

The Music to *Schweyk in the Second World War* – On Stupidity in Music II

The meeting on 4 September 1961 wasn't intended to be one of the 'conversations'. Edouard Pfrimmer, a French friend of Eisler's, came to visit to get some details for a programme article for a French production of Schweyk. *Eisler dictates a brief version of his curriculum vita to him and while Pfrimmer writes up his notes Eisler elaborates on his collaboration with Brecht on the play* Scheyk *and later suggests talking on the subject of stupidity in music again.*

[…] Yes. About the music to *Schweyk*…Is this actually necessary? If you talk about the collaboration with such a towering master as Brecht you always feel like an idiot – and you actually are an idiot. Nevertheless, I can tell you the following: I began the work on *Schweyk* in Berlin. A year before his death, Brecht asked me: 'Can't you do the music for *Schweyk*?' I said: 'But you told me yesterday that I have to do the music for *Simone Machard*'. 'Forget that' he said, '*Schweyk* is the priority now'. So I wrote the music. Three of the pieces were songs I had already composed in 1942 in Hollywood and which were only later included in *Schweyk*. Among the songs are: 'Ballad of the Soldier's wife', 'German Miserere' and 'March of the Sheep'.

Not the 'Moldau Song'?

No, that poem was written while the battle for Stalingrad was still going on. It's a sign of Brecht's greatness that he wrote poems like that in such dark times. I had the opportunity eight weeks before his death to play all the music to him. He said: 'It's very interesting that you can be so amusing'. That was one of our last talks about music. But he listened to it once more and I can still see him smiling at my weaknesses and his strengths.

Actually I had finished the music for *Schweyk* in time for the first performance in Warsaw. Since then, every time someone performs it, I try to improve it. Planchon's production gives me a brilliant opportunity to perfect the score. I believe that the first performance in Paris of *Schweyk in the Second World War* will be Brecht's true legacy in the French language.

On the subject of stupidity in music: unfortunately, these days, people often accuse me of having something against certain styles of music, but that's absolutely wrong. I support every style as long as music is able to express reason instead of stupidity. Right from my early youth I've been tormented by music that stands on the side-lines and doesn't reflect our actual social conditions. In his own way, Arnold Schoenberg also commented on this. He said somewhere: 'The presence of an audience seems essential because an empty hall doesn't sound good'. (I can tolerate audiences as space fillers, but I could do perfectly well without them.) My friends will probably be terribly upset about this and will accuse me of bourgeois decadence. But when you look closely at an audience for an evening chamber concert or for a symphony concert at the state opera, then Schoenberg, in his very accommodating way, is simultaneously both right and wrong. It is ridiculous of my friends to make fun of electronic music or simply to call it decadent, because, if the bourgeoisie decays, its great geniuses and great talents will also decay. We shouldn't fail to remember, after all, that there were great talents within bourgeois decadence.

When the working class rises to power, geniuses such as Brecht and Gorki will rise with it. But every human being can't be instantly awarded a certificate for being a genius because he belongs to a certain class. Unfortunately, nature didn't make it that easy for us. One has to think historically. Maybe we won't live better lives, but we'll be able to see more clearly.

If we think about it, all this revolting music coming out of the radios, televisions, gramophones, insulting our ears daily, hourly, morning, noon and night...then I have, at the very least, to congratulate every serialist composer for his abstract protest against this slimy filth. Just imagine my situation, Doctor Bunge, how hard it is! First, this filth, which torments us daily and which manipulates us into abstract and decadent behaviour (by the way you can find a little note about applied music in Brecht's Journals)...well then, how it manipulates us into totally affected and abstract behaviour – 'foolish behaviour' my friend Willie Bredel calls it. How hard it is to avoid this ghastly bland trash, this mindless drivel. You can therefore only fight against the modern styles, the refined electronic, abstract, serialist music, if you fight against the general trash at the same time. You can't ban the garbage on the other side unless you confront the garbage on your own side as well. I'm repeating myself. Doing battle with the abstract stupidity of our young people can be successful only if, at the same time, one also takes up arms against the disgusting rubbish that pours out of all the Western and Eastern media. Otherwise we will turn ourselves into bourgeois music masters and then it will be all up between the young people and ourselves.

Conversation 11
6 November 1961

Hölderlin Poems – On Stupidity in Music III

[...] Tonight we have a dull November evening and therefore I read in a Hölderlin volume of the *Kleine Stuttgarter Edition*, an edition by Friedrich Beißner, which you, by the way, don't like at all.

Actually I like it very much![207]

I have compiled a few verses to set to music. As you know it's been one of my hobbies for twenty or thirty years to arrange verses from the great poets for my own use. For what I can make use of today, I look in Hölderlin in particular, because he writes with an over-abundance – that was Schiller's reproof by the way: Hölderlin's over-abundance. I read Hölderlin with the eyes of 1961. I will recite you a montage of a few lines from a Hölderlin poem that I've put together. The original poem is called 'Der Gang aufs Land' [The Walk into the Countryside] and can be found in the second volume of the *Kleine Stuttgarter Edition*. I suggest you read the original poem later, which I won't read now so that we don't waste time. My montage goes like this:

Come! Into the open, friend! Although the day sheds little light
And here below the sky oppresses us.
Neither are the mountains risen nor the
Laughter of the forests' peaks, no singing in the empty air.
It is dull today; the paths and streets are sleeping
And it almost seems to me a leaden time.
Yet still desire prevails, the knowing

Have no doubts. Although our songs are frail,
They belong to the life we want.
The blessing-bearing swallows will come,
Always some, before the start of summer, into our land.

I have taken these few lines from a much longer poem and I
anticipate with pleasure the brouhaha it will cause among literary
scholars, but as I said earlier, Brecht for example, found the de-
plastering of Hölderlin and his re-interpretation from a contemporary
perspective very useful. I see you want to say something, which we'll
come to in a minute; it was just an intermezzo 'during the perusal of
Hölderlin on a dull November day'.

*I would actually like to ask you something about that. Do you
have any guiding principles when you're doing such a selection and
compilation?*

The strange thing is there are no principles because it's not a
scientific process but an artistic one. I read the poem and try, without
butchering it, to summarize what seems important today. It became
clear that the poem expresses a great uncertainty – that's what the
poem is about. 'The one in the know' (or as Hölderlin has it, the
orthodox) doesn't have *a moment's* doubt – there is a great idea
behind it, namely that a communist is going through a bad patch
but doesn't generalize the problem. He simply calls it a bad patch.[208]
This seemed to me a real poetic concept that ought to be preserved
in the music and I will set it to music, otherwise something like that
will get lost. I've said it a few times already: the mission of music
is to preserve such poetic concepts and images like a fly in amber,
otherwise they'll be lost. Who is going to read in the second volume
'The Walk into the Countryside. To Landauer' by Hölderlin – if not
comrade Eisler when he's got some time on his hands?
    Another concept is the 'Come! into the open, friend!' This is a
very beautiful phrase rich with meaning. Translated into prose it
would be, 'Let's speak about the matter at hand!' – namely there
is 'no singing in the empty air' and that was also precisely the
condition the composer was in when he wasn't composing anything
at that particular moment and 'it is dull today' as well.
    Time too seems 'to me a leaden time' – that is one of Hölderlin's
most brilliant images, very unique to Hölderlin. It reminds one of
Ovid, of the *Metamorphoses*: the iron time, the golden time and

Hölderlin speaks of the leaden time. Lead means here dullness, repression and insipidness – all the things that speak to one in a dull hour. The poem continues 'yet still desire prevails, the knowing (I call them that, Hölderlin says orthodox) have no doubts'. I have already explained that.

I do think it's remarkable that we, who not only believe in but also practise the social function of art, now also celebrate the antagonism.[209] 'Although our songs are frail, they belong to the life we want'. This is a magnificent sentiment – it contains both the positive and the negative. Of course, every artist and every musician believes that what he does is relevant to the whole of society, but Hölderlin says: 'Although our songs are frail, they belong to the life we want' – which is far more concrete, wittier and better than a somewhat dull naivety, which thinks it can rescue the world through a song. Having said that songs like 'The Marseillaise' and 'The Internationale' did make an enormous contribution to world history – it has therefore to be demonstrated from two points of view and I show the singing's other side.

Finally, there is also a coquettish attitude in it which is particularly amusing. 'The blessing-bearing swallows will come, always some, before the start of summer, into our land'. That is the coquettishness of the artist who says he is way out ahead and he brings the summer, the summer that hasn't been recognized yet, like swallows that arrive too early. That swallows that come back too early are in danger of freezing to death is another matter altogether, but this coquettishness of Hölderlin and the beauty of this coquettishness – let's not call it coquettishness but a certain kind of wistful nostalgia: this coming too early, this must also be preserved like a fly in amber.

You see, this is a little insight into my method of working when I compose songs. You've dragged the explanation out of me by asking, as I didn't have these thoughts when I was reading the poem. I chose the verses simply for their poetic beauty and poetic beauty for me is only what's useful, something that's intellectually useful. So it's just an instinctive action that I tried to explain to you because you asked.[210]

Your explanation belongs to our old theme 'On stupidity in music' ...

Correct.

... by giving a positive example of how an old and almost antique text can be made useful today.[211]

But you have to read critically and that is very difficult. It requires thorough training and, I have to say, a certain maturity. It needs, and this is very banal, a certain life experience and by that I don't mean the petit bourgeois life experience, in the petit bourgeois sense, but the life experience of an old communist. He needs to know exactly what is it that matters, what he can say and what is useful in what he has said. In this case it's for the benefit of the socialist listener.

Many clues in the poem point to what is generally called the 'theme tune', which is autumn. I politicize autumn; in a way I socialize autumn. For bourgeois people that will sound like terrible vandalism, but strangely enough the socialization of the autumn... It's a horrible phrase, but let's stick to it: I can't get rid of my political views even if autumn is coming, they still apply even then, it's like a reflex.

If you're used to thinking and feeling politically, then consequently your emotional life can be enriched, it can be purified, and with that you can advance to understanding. Once they listen to my autumn song, people won't be taken for a ride by autumn anymore. I'm probably exaggerating, because many people will still get depressed by autumn. But not me! And as far as it is within my powers, I'll try to prevent people becoming gloomy about autumn, you know, all this – yellow leaves are falling, the mist in the early hours...[212] – and instead come to regard autumn with relish because it is a very beautiful season and people can gain by looking at it.

You're absolutely right, in normal music that is if we speak of poetry and you look, for example, at the composer's great poetry, you'll not find such moments. You will of course find other tremendously important moments. I remember a song by Brahms, 'Auf einem Friedhof' [At a Cemetery], I think the words are by Storm,[213] where the poet goes to a cemetery. Brahms' setting is exceptionally beautiful. It was a rainy day, he has been to the cemetery, looked at a few graves and the final thought of the poem is then 'all the tombstones bore the word "Saved"'. That is a protestant, excessively pious position which, ever since I was young, has made me want to throw up, because I don't believe that death is the salvation but simply the end. When I went on holiday in Thuringia, I went to a little village cemetery, at the entrance it said: 'We are but guests on this earth'. That's a famous quotation from The Bible. I stood there in the rain, I remember it was a dull, rainy day, and got very angry, because I asked myself: 'So where is the host?' and: do we have to endure the whole shebang to have been nothing more than a guest? Such a low-down outlook on life can only originate in religion and this particular sentence really upset me.

Let's summarize: we have Brahms' song 'At a Cemetery'; my memory of those little graves in this village cemetery in Thuringia where I read: 'We are but guests on this earth'; and my objection to it and this contemplation of autumn, because Hölderlin's poem is about an autumn day. You mustn't believe that those are now artistic principles. Behind it all is nothing more than a man (and there are hundreds of millions of men, or at least there should be) who has dialectical materialism running through his veins. The man looks at a flower, admires it and then something else comes into his mind – really, those are not intellectually contrived positions, no, what I'm doing there is a completely normal process, in the same way that you would drink coffee or go for a walk.

But I still think it is a question of one's standpoint, and therefore more to do with principle than this method of…

I have trouble with the word 'principle'. 'A question of one's standpoint' – I can't very well see the world in any other way than the way I see it.

I don't insist on the word 'principle'. I refer only to the practical standpoint that emerges from the philosophy of dialectical materialism.

That's right and then autumn becomes twice as beautiful, the leaves are a nicer shade of yellow than for the metaphysicist and sadness becomes more moving than for the stupid ass who's into religion. Further, the decline and even the decay of the autumn is more impressive and more stimulating than for the poetic blockhead. So, for the dialectical materialist the beauty of nature becomes more radiant and its specifics (spring, autumn, summer and winter) become more significant. Indeed, the beauty of nature is able to raise you to a general position, to a general feeling. Feeling is therefore not abandoned and replaced by something that windbags call 'practical thinking' – as if that would ever be possible – it's not reduced to practical thinking, quite the opposite. Autumn flourishes more brilliantly to me than to the metaphysicists and in this way acquires its individual meaning. If you ask me a personal question whether it puts me in a better mood, I say no, because a better mood is not a matter of art but one of personal well-being.

Is this process really as naive as it seems now? Is the montage only a product of coincidence? Did it really only come about because you took a volume of Hölderlin from the shelf? Would you have been able to come up with the lines yourself in the same way as you have put them together now?

Listen, I'm not a poet ...

My question is devious. Hölderlin reflects reality in a poetic image and the accompanying explanations of your montage were also poetic. What is the essence of poetic explanation?

I was already infected by Hölderlin. You can only describe poetry poetically. What I want to say is this: as important as the term 'naïve' is in art – not only for Schiller (in 'On Naïve and Sentimental Poetry') but also for Brecht – nevertheless, whether or not something is 'naïve' is a question that I actually don't find relevant any more. The superior level of consciousness that we Marxists possess makes the term 'naïve' redundant in the following way. Naïve is actually only the incorruptible eye that takes in stimuli, feelings and situations as they first appear. For Marxists today naivety would be the initial step in the thinking process. Before reflection can begin, the subject has to be looked at. In that sense, 'naïve' is appropriate. First, I have to look at a tree before I can describe it. The process of looking at something is naïve. In the same way that curiosity is the source of philosophy, if you think of Greek philosophy.

I think you have to be very careful with expressions like 'naïve' and 'intellectual' – they are opposites really. It would be better if you'd use naïve – un-naïve, i.e. if I look at a tree in an 'un-naïve' way then I look at it in order to discover something and that would not be naïve, it would in fact be non-artistic and non-scientific. The most naïve physicist ever is Einstein. Naivety exists in his case because he looked at things as if nobody had ever looked at them before; he looked at physical processes in a naïve way. But we have to cleanse the term naivety in order to work with it. I suggest you repeat the word 'naïve', as it is now understood.

You interpreted Hölderlin's verse 'Come! Into the open, friend!' as 'Let's not beat about the bush'. Is there a practical explanation for why you assembled the poem in this way at this particular point in time?

No.

Which are the references to our present time?

Well, they're very simple and, if you so wish, once more naïve. Namely, it was a somewhat dull afternoon and I read Hölderlin. There is nothing more to it. I didn't plan to read Hölderlin when I got up in the morning and I worked on something else before lunch. However, in the afternoon, at four o'clock, when I had nothing else to do, I picked up a volume of Hölderlin to pass the time and as I leafed through it I found this poem. That isn't a naïve process, but a process of coincidence, which has a certain place in art – with small works, large works need planning.

Poetry in particular often has some spontaneous and accidental quality. I would even say, and the literary historians will cross themselves, a partisan quality. In the literary woods I find a poem, almost always by accident, it's as if you would stumble across something. Even when I set a poem by Brecht, I have found it somewhere at a certain time and in a certain mood. As far as small projects are concerned that don't require great planning, the composer's partisan attitude is very important for the creative process.

Such a simplified explanation will hardly do. Someone who gets to know your 6th November 1961 montage of a poem will think about the context and perhaps fall victim to speculations because he thinks there must be, with particular references to today, concrete reasons for your interest in Hölderlin's poem. Are my assumptions overstepping the mark if I presume the same?

No, you're not going too far there at all. May I say, we're both in the same boat. It's typically German that with a certain pedantry (and for us Germans it is very honourable that we are so thorough), we're always trying to systematize something that doesn't exist. I only need to look out of my window to see that it's autumn, or walk up and down in my garden, which I avoid doing because I get bored after a short time, the falling leaves bore me too.

By the way, in one of my volumes you'll find the *Buckow Elegies*. Once, when I visited Brecht out there in Buckow, I wrote a text and set it to music. On this occasion I wrote a poem, which I seldom do and shall continue seldom to do because I'm not a poet, in which I described the falling leaves. I called it 'L'Automne Prussien' with lines like 'The trees, always robbed of...' I can't remember how it goes anymore; you'll have to look it up.[214] I chose a French title for this poem – it's the classical method of *Verfremdung*, that an observer looks at autumn in Brecht's garden and describes it then as *L'Automne Prussien*. Brecht found that incredibly odd and was amused by it.

These are just simple reactions to everyday events that happen to one. In the case of Hölderlin's poem, the matter was much more accidental. Had I grabbed a different book, Mörike for example, I probably wouldn't have found anything. I enjoy reading poetry; it's part of my profession. So, now and then, when I have time on my hands I grab a volume of poetry. I have to describe this on such a simple level, Doctor Bunge, otherwise you, with your formidable talent, will come up with a powerful literary theory for the composer, a composition of words, which unfortunately won't be true. There exists, and we can find it in politics too, something which I call the 'partisan quality'. Let's embrace spontaneity, the partisan quality, and we know it can even go as far as anarchy although this spontaneity does have to stay within limits.

Perhaps I'm able to demonstrate the absurdity of a certain theory with my questions.

That would be good.

Among Brecht's Buckow Elegies *there is a poem about the crows that are sitting in the trees in his garden. These crows annoy Brecht and then the poem ends with 'because the surroundings are otherwise bird-less, I'm quite happy about them'. So in the end he accepts them...*[215]

Oh, this is of course absolutely wonderful. 'Better than nothing' is what Brecht meant.

But in Buckow there are thousands of other birds and it is impossible for Brecht not to have noticed them. What I would like to emphasize is that Brecht poeticized here something that ...

There is something very strange and ambiguous about Brecht's observations of nature. If he leaves out the songbirds in his garden and mentions only the crows, well of course that seems very strange. I haven't thought about it and I'm a bit surprised because I can't recall these verses, but I do find it very interesting.

What comes to mind (you are the one who's familiar with aesthetics, not me, I'm only the object of aesthetics) is that our works might be received too mechanically. For example, the creative process sometimes relies on just a mood and Brecht had those moments too – as in the poem about the crow, for instance. I can say that I had the opportunity to observe Brecht for a long time and he sometimes wrote things down spontaneously, but that doesn't mean that what is created on the spur of the moment and partisan-like is not substantial. Major works, however, can't rely on mood; they have to be planned.

But it's possible that the source of a great work originates from a mood. I remember clearly how, on a tour in America, I got tired of telling the Americans each and every evening about Germany's cultural barbarism. It was monotonous (I nearly always gave the same talk with very little variation) and so I decided, in order to have something to work on, and it was a similar dull autumn evening in a hotel in Chicago, to compose the *German Symphony*. The spark was a mood, a mood that then lasted five years. And again it was a mood when Brecht sat down for a year and wrote *St Joan of the Stockyards*, wanting to repair the damage done by *Happy End* – that cheapjack comedy that Brecht and Hauptmann threw together. The mood behind it was that he didn't want to sell the good ideas from *Happy End* so cheaply. So, in this small way, planning is identical with mood.

I don't want to give up so easily.

That's good, maybe something will come out in the end.

Let's be precise then. Although the verses are by Hölderlin, in the end you chose and put them together so that a poem by Hölderlin and Eisler was created. Were you interested in the montage because the poem is a poetic description of the current political situation? Or is that going too far?

It is going too far as the concrete political situation has nothing to do with the poem. When you remember the phrase 'the knowing have no doubts' you already got your answer. This poem, and the composition, doesn't reflect the current political situation, but it is, nevertheless, an important idea that the strong people should reveal their weak moments. However strong one is and whatever one's convictions, one should also display weakness, which comes naturally – in the same way as sleep or, for whatever reason, a bad mood. That is also part of the creative process.

If we artists want to be creative we can't hide the weak moments either. I'm not sure I would call the song 'The Weak Moment'. It could be called 'The Autumn or the Weak Moment' and with that I have provided you with sufficient assurance that the poem is in no way an interpretation of the current political situation. A situation that will not of course, as with all great endeavours, exclude a certain bitterness because you can't undertake such enormous projects without it costing lots of sweat and bitterness. There'll be a lot of trouble.

The verse that you quoted just now is the one that impressed me most when you read the poem, but I interpreted it differently from you.

How did you interpret it?

Very optimistically. I thought it to be a response to the 22nd party congress of the CPSU. The bitterness about the revelations of the past was repudiated by the provision of a new perspective 'the knowing have no doubts'.

That's very good.

I probably read too much into it.

No, dear Doctor Bunge! It makes me very happy to hear you say that. I didn't think of it in such detail. I already told you that the montage of verses is an artistic-musical process for me and the poetic stimulus of these verses is for me...Would you please quote it again?

'The knowing have no doubts'.

That could be from Lenin. That's why I liked it so much. Well, there you have it all: the bad mood; the current situation; the 22nd party congress; and the general standpoint of an honest communist. That is why this phrase is so great.

That is exactly how I understood the poem and so I wanted to find out whether this is what it really meant.

Unfortunately, in this respect I have to be a little more modest. I didn't think of the 22nd party congress but of autumn. But they're the same. If, for example, the Stalin-cult dies, then it is autumn for Stalin. He falls like the leaves. You know I only get it now after you've told me this. Now, I can't really pretend to be an especially spontaneous person here: it didn't cross my mind.

But you see how well I selected: you made an association and in my selection I have, by artistic means, purified your feelings and influenced your mind. Therefore, the choice was superb because if a man like you makes such associations then I'm very thrilled to have reached into this particular drawer one afternoon to pass an hour's time.

The phrase 'the knowing have no doubts' is one that you and other communists had to say to yourselves for years to keep your spirits up. This position has proved to be right and therefore stood the test of time.

Correct! I'm delighted with the choice of these lines from Hölderlin because they touch the central nerve of our current situation, a situation that is wonderful because we're energetically sorting out our dark past. But, dear comrade Bunge, I didn't think of that when I set it. It would take me much more time to come to terms with the past. I wouldn't be able to express that in this short Hölderlin quotation.[216]

There is this other song of mine, which was composed way before the 22nd party congress, even before the 20th: 'Chanson

Allemande'. I'll read it to you so you can see how I expressed it then. In 1953 I set the following poem:

> Whoever wants to be sad, will maybe read me
> And he will think between the lines.
> Yes, this person has also been sad,
> But can his sadness heal mine!
> You should ask yourself about the reasons
> Of sadness, you human being of better times.
> Mine will be told by History to you,
> The milestones of my sadnesses.

There you have it much more clearly. I'll even try and sing it to you if you want. [Eisler sings the song.]

I'm still with Hölderlin. It's a pity that you didn't use these two lines from his poem: 'May the carpenters speak from the high point of the roof, we gave our best as well as we could'.

Well, dear Bunge, I'll put that in as well. It fits after the swallow too because the swallow nests in the ridge. That's a really good suggestion. I'm very grateful to you, an excellent idea.[217]

Eisler proof reading in the 1950s.

I'd like to come back to the song you sang. I found a great resemblance to a song you composed for the play The Playboy of the Western World.

I have no recollection of that. I think it's a coincidence. I myself don't see any similarity but there might be one. Such similarities are totally unimportant because in music the context is what produces the actual original.

In the three essays 'On Stupidity in Music' that you have published so far, it puzzled me to find that you speak about stupidity in music as something absolute and definitive without defining it. I asked about it once before: obviously there must be difficulties in providing an exact definition?

I don't think so. The term 'stupidity in music' derives from the general stupidity in society. What we find with stupidity in music is not a particular musical characteristic but the stupidity generally inherent in human beings. What I mean by that is the failure to keep abreast of actual circumstances. Let me repeat it once more: what is stupid is when human thinking fails to keep up with its time, with its social development. That is what I would call stupid.

For example, and this is quite astonishing, music preserves stupidities, which each of the different classes in human society has long abolished – but these stupidities continue to exist and are practised in music. And this is why music is the most distant from the world of practical things and what that means is that music is underdeveloped. I have articulated this idea several times already but I'll repeat it: because of music's distance from the practical world, where all arts – literature, painting, sculpture, architecture (Hegel by the way doesn't think of this as art)... well, because of music's failure to keep abreast of practical things, it has that dull, archaic quality. Music is, if you so wish, the breeding ground of stupidity.

That is what many scholars have recognized already in their own way, especially religious scholars. The scholars of the early church such as Thomas Aquinas and Saint Augustine have had very significant things to say about stupidity in music. They tried to fight against it by using music for their own purposes, but with the secularization of music, namely its becoming bourgeois, the doors were thrown wide open for stupidity to make its entrance.

If we are driven to describe the musical history of the bourgeois class, which can't be pinned down to specific dates, as some of my precious but dear and naïve colleagues are trying to do, we have to set the point at which music became bourgeois, when it sought its independence from the church. This is not a clear-cut process and there are overlaps like musical forms that came into existence within the bosom of mother church that are bourgeois in character, but they are purely hedonistic, while the actual purpose of church music has already been forsaken.

You probably know that Saint Augustine, for example, said that the sole purpose of music is to compel the listener into a state of penitent remorse. That's not a stupid thing to say. In his time, when there was still a naïve and primitive society, music had a real function, music was restrained and harnessed like a horse, it served a purpose. And Augustine further warns the composer not to get over-preoccupied with great beauty, because such great beauty only distracts from the actual purpose of music, which, once again, is penitent remorse. With the same portentousness, the use of musical instruments in church music was forbidden because it would bring too much luxury, potentially seductive to the listener.

In its own way the early embattled church tried to eliminate stupidity but in the process it suppressed something else – folk music. There were, of course, ordinary people who sang and made music. But the church forbids this and because of that a schism developed between popular music and church music. Church music in its classical posture employed most of all Gregorian chant. The common people's infiltration into the church occurred through Luther's hymns. Luther, with his gentle hands, 'corrected' popular music to make it 'Christian' (his words) by transforming into pious hymns popular songs that were often obscene. The Protestants would be very surprised to discover what the great-grandfather of a hymn such as 'Now Comes the Gentiles' Saviour' was once like a popular song.

For as long as music existed in the church it wasn't stupid, it was only dull. It was more an exercise than an art. Looking at it from a composer's point of view it also seemed to be something you could manage by applying a few formulae. Imagination had no part in it. Stupidity in music replaces the dullness of early Feudalism, where intelligence and stupidity don't yet play a part – that begins from that point on when the free citizen asserts himself.

But our conversations about stupidity in music are not about looking at things from a historical standpoint, but from a current, contemporary standpoint. When we speak about particular social circumstances, then we see that even great musical masters are not abreast of their times with regard to their social points of view. I know it sounds strange, but I have to say that even mankind's greatest musician, Mozart, still included in his compositions the clinking of the aristocrats' dinnertime crockery, and not to mention Haydn. These are not stupidities yet, these were merely naïve responses to the circumstances in those days. But today composers, conductors and musicians take on these attitudes of earlier times without analysis, and by doing so produce a strange kind of idiocy and stupidity in music.

Is that why you are so aggressive towards composers and conductors and take the listeners' side, because the composers and conductors are not doing enough to introduce other themes, other material and other music to their listeners? Aren't the composers in a dilemma, either to satisfy the audiences' existing needs or, when playing modern music, be met with incomprehension and disapproval, because education and experience are missing?

Yes, it's clear: the listening is lagging behind, and music, concert music of the newer kind, encounters great difficulties. The music of the romantic and classical period and also a certain conformist music of the twentieth century is a music that demonstrates an old attitude. Now, you have to admit that I'm not someone who is against an attitude or expression like 'through night into light'; really, I'm not. I think it has its place. Beethoven demonstrated that most magnificently in the *Fifth Symphony*, in the last movement, but when thousands of composers now, without any real reason, compose 'through night into light' – *per aspera ad astra* or whatever it is called – then that slowly but surely becomes routine and we can no longer believe in the colossal triumph of the final movement. Instead we become sceptical or bored.

The wear and tear of certain musical effects is a question that hasn't yet been investigated and it should be approached very critically. I remind you of a very fine statement in Hegel's *Aesthetics*, which hasn't unfortunately as yet been correctly interpreted. He said: if grief for a loss is expressed in music, then the listener should immediately ask why this grief came about and what for?

It is the damn Protean-character of music that invites this idiocy. You only need to turn on the radio at any time of the day and you'll hear an abundance of stupidity, which you will immediately recognize as stupidity even though you are not a musical expert. You have this certain pathetic zest for life, which is mostly expressed in waltz form or there is the kind of pseudo-militaristic behaviour that expresses itself in marching rhythms. There is this kind of sentimental affectation of the so-called important symphonic works – Brecht always said it's like a man who can't digest dumplings or like stomach pains. All of that has lost its real function – but how to change it? First and foremost, you have to change the audience.

But who or what is at fault if the listener can't keep up?

The general social circumstances of course, it's not only the composer's fault. He has been subjected to the same influences as the listener. What we need is an excellent music education – stupidity can only be driven out with education. If, for example, we give our six- or four-year-old children the right musical education, then one hopes in ten years' time, a stupid composer will be laughed at. He will only need to use four trombones and keep on quoting 'through night into light' and the true listeners, listeners who have truly come through night to light, will roar with laughter because that won't be the way for them to come through night into light – they'll know of better ways.

And what's also missing is cheerfulness in music – especially in Germany! – a certain elegance, a certain lightness. We carry the evil burden of *esprit allemande* round with us. In symphonies you have for example this kind of pompous 'world view' – I say 'world view' in inverted commas because that is what is really meant by 'through night into light'. It no longer has any meaning whatsoever for us. It meant something to Beethoven, but using it today is as common as muck.

But with all that I still haven't been able to explain the real stupidities, nor can I really. The real stupidities have to be described in a very particular and painstakingly detailed way. I can't do that at the moment.

Conversation 12
5 July 1962

Eisler on Classical Literature, on the Function of Art, on Cybernetics and on Napoleon

I've just been re-reading Goethe's conversations with Eckermann and I've come across something that's depressed me because it reminds me of the difficulties the Germans have in claiming their own classical inheritance. The facts are well known. As they themselves have admitted, the authors of the classical period wrote for the educated classes, although their education was rather idiosyncratic. It will be difficult for the working class to catch up to their level. It will need time and it won't always correspond with our immediate concerns.

I understand that there are difficulties in reading Goethe's play *Tasso*. Someone said to Goethe, and I quote: 'Nevertheless in Germany they consider *Tasso* to be difficult, so they were surprised when I said I was reading it'. Goethe retorted:

> The main idea in *Tasso* is that one is no longer a child and that one won't achieve anything without a good education. A young man from a good family with sufficient strength of mind and spirit and an adequate academic education, which comes from associating with the finest people of the upper and higher classes, will not find *Tasso* difficult'.

You have to admit, dear Doctor Bunge, that this is a bleak prospect for us. Of course we'll catch up eventually, but to catch up today, *hic et nunc*, there are bound to be difficulties, especially when we think of our Bitterfeld Conference, where we came up with the slogan: 'Let's conquer the summits of culture!'[218] What do you think, Doctor Bunge?

When he spoke of 'the upper and higher classes' Goethe had a specific section of society in mind. Which would be the corresponding social strata in our country – and what function do they have?

I can only say that in my youth those upper strata were educated in a sort of democracy – in the sense of the monarchy of late capitalism. That means every petit bourgeois son or aristocratic son, but rarely a working class son, was able to receive an education at the monarchy's State Grammar School. The working class was excluded. In my year, for example, out of forty-five pupils in the k.u.k. State Grammar School Number Two there was, I think, just one working class boy…on a scholarship and even he pulled out after a few years because he couldn't keep up. It has to be said though that in 1912 the education available to the aristocracy and high society was also available to the petit bourgeoisie – so, we can be optimistic. We can say that when our education system develops further we will also reach this 'class aim'[219] and I mean this in its double sense.

That shouldn't prevent us from acknowledging both the brilliance and misery of the German classics. Just think, for example, of the great literature of nineteenth-century England. Everyone was able to understand it, either if they could read or if they knew how to interpret what was read to them. This literature even influenced the law, through the novels of Charles Dickens and Thackeray, for example,[220] and before that, in the eighteenth century, great novels were part of the fabric of society.[221]

I also refer to French literature of the eighteenth and nineteenth centuries and of the broad strata of people who were literate and understood it[222] and last but not the least, there's Russian literature during the time of the Tsars, which was also a popular literature.[223]

Our German classics leave a terrible aftertaste of exclusivity. I have to say, of all the cultured countries, Germany is the only one in which the classics were not only great but also a curse – they were totally exclusive. We have to keep this in mind when we educate our young people. I was told that very intelligent young students in the GDR don't find anything that they can relate to in Goethe's *Wilhelm Meister*, for example. This work of Goethe's assumes such high standards of education, such understanding and knowledge of mythology and of particular social conditions that no longer exist. I don't know how this part of our inheritance can one day become the property of the people. For it to become their property it has to become 'popular', by which I mean on an abstract level where the best works of the classic period in music, art and literature become accessible to everyone. I don't know how to achieve this.

Is it even necessary? I don't know if it is necessary that two of Goethe's wonderful works, *Tasso* and *Iphigenia*, will actually one day achieve the popularity they deserve. (My friend Brecht would say no!) I can't pass judgement on that. It depends on our schools and teachers – a slogan springs to mind here once more: educate the teacher! That's the be-all and end-all.

We could also ask whether Homer, who was popular among the educated circles in eighteenth- and nineteenth-century Germany, might become 'accessible' again. Those are things that worry a culturally interested man like me, but it's a productive worry. One has to think about what is the outcome – and for whom?

To be absolutely clear about this: you think it's essential that as part of general education our working class should be familiar with works like Wilhelm Meister *or Tasso or Homer's* Odyssey?

Absolutely essential! It may sound somewhat academic, but that is what's needed. Take for example Odysseus' journeys – one of the most amazing works of art in the history of literature. By the way, Karl Marx says that too in his third foreword to *Political Economy*.[224] To try to make the *Odyssey* popular today reveals only the difficulties we face when we really break with educational privilege and attempt to bring the pinnacles of world culture into the so-called national ownership – like a VEB [People's enterprises].

Maybe the 'Bitterfeld Way' can be seen as some kind of preliminary stage to this. When the worker's respect for literature is no longer just reverence for something exclusive, and when he gets to know great literature, which was practically impossible in the past, then he might even attempt it himself, and it's possible that he may discover an interest in ways of expression that he thought up until now were exclusive to other classes and social strata. Maybe that is the way to gain access to literature? If so, then certain conditions of a class-ridden society would be corrected by the 'Bitterfeld Way'.

That is absolutely right. I'm not agreeing with everything, but the 'Bitterfeld Way' has, with all it wanted to give expression to at least achieved one thing – it has put culture in its appropriate social position among our young republic. That means that the working class has been newly appointed both as a receiver and a producer of art. I have doubts about the latter, but the whole concept is absolutely right. One can't live in socialism and babble about socialism in culture without applying it practically. With all its imperfections, the 'Bitterfeld Way' is a way or a beginning, which at least points us in the right direction.

Bearing this in mind let me develop my thoughts and perform an enormous leap. Please don't be too surprised about what I'm going to say. When I look at Goethe's pure class standpoint, his actually writing literature and creating art for the most highly educated circles, then I have to think of something, which I would now call a 'retraction'.

I've read in a book about the cave paintings of prehistoric times that these paintings of bison, for example, were done in the darkest corners of the cave. They weren't done for the viewer because, in a way, the function of these cave paintings was to overcome the animals by drawing them, to bewitch the animals before meeting them in reality. The animals were conjured up first before they were actually killed.[225]

This is highly interesting because the original primitive function of art, as in this practical example, reminds me strangely enough of the function of art that is embraced by the revolutionary working class, and I include our friend Bertolt Brecht here. And here I see a tremendous retraction. If art history can be explained at all, then it is through the division of labour that individual art disciplines come into existence. Art's secularization, its emancipation from religion, from rituals, from myths occurs in its becoming bourgeois, or modernized! That means, at this moment, when art is separated from its practical use, and ritual is a form of practical use, then it becomes what we, from our progressive point of view, call art.

Now, one part of late bourgeois art (late feudal art as well, and especially the art of the revolutionary working class) apparently went back to the original primitive functions of art. The secularization of art was just 'culinary'. Art became an object of consumption. It changed from the myths of simple societies into an individual work. Art became fun instead of a compulsory communal task. That is why we have to concede that in these times (and also the resolutions of the Bitterfeld Conference) that actually – and it sounds awful – we are back at the stage of cave paintings.

We need potatoes – let's produce a potato-cantata! We need to increase certain areas of production, therefore, you composers and poets, write songs and cantatas to increase production! A completely honourable task that I would support and you know how long I've been involved in the working class movement and how much I've tried to achieve in this field. In philosophical terms, however, isn't this a remarkable retraction of secularization? Hasn't art already been liberated from its most primitive needs to serve society rather than to entertain society? Now, I have to admit, and you too, that there isn't really any opposition between entertaining and serving. The older Brecht has shown that in his *Organum* [226]: to entertain the serving and the entertained can serve. Nevertheless, in the turbulent years of the Weimar Republic we saw art going back to its original functions, where art, in a primitive way, only served social needs.

Here, and I'm jumping again, I'm reminded of one of Hegel's marvellous observations. He said that in a finally liberated society, it's highly likely that art will die and into its place will step philosophy.[227] Well, is this the great philosopher's insolence against us artists or is it a shrewd assumption? What Hegel means is simply that when the being is complete, specifically the communist being, we won't need the currently fashionable, entertaining and pretty facade of art any more. Alternatively, I would say that the function of art must be redefined so that it can become what art really is about and which exists today only in its most trivial forms: fun, diversion and entertainment.

I admit that by saying this I'm contradicting nearly everything Brecht and I once believed, but I'm not going to take back what I said just now. What I said should never be an excuse for all the talents to avoid the current tasks facing art and declare themselves content with the way things are in a time when, for example, the all-important issue is peace.

Look at this marvellous journey: from Goethe's remarks about class back to the cave paintings, to Brecht's productions and his friends in the Weimar Republic (slightly improved by Brecht in the *Organum*) and to Hegel. With our insight into the dialectics of history, if we don't want to find ourselves falling behind theoretically, I think we need to have the courage to question all our previous beliefs and be prepared to liquidate ourselves into a newer future – a painful but useful process.

How am I supposed to understand this? How do you want to liquidate yourself?

I'm not talking about liquidating *myself*, I mean our ideas. Young people have to be careful not to become sectarian by criticizing both our ideas and their own. That might not have any practical consequences at the moment, but, as an old man, I have to be prepared to question my position and to forecast the next 100 years, because this is also what our politicians do. As comrade Khrushchev said, we're planning communism up to the year 1980. I'm planning new theories of art, which may not be feasible today, but I predict them with joy.

I can say that the current theories underpinning the role of art in our dear republic are sectarian, that's to say to the left of Brecht. They do hold good for a certain period but they will have to be changed. And they will have to change not because of theoretical arguments but because of the general development of social conditions.

Our thinking needs to include the new sciences – automation, cybernetics. They will have an ever-increasing role to play! I'm not confusing science with art. I can't tolerate that banal opposition any more, but I do believe that a society that can organize even the process of thinking by means of machines will be less able to know what to do with the poet's or composer's naïve spontaneity.

Of course art will still be of use to society. It can be predicted that the brain's social powers, and also those of its intellectual production, will become more ingenious. Consequently, then the demanding Adagio movement for warming the emotions will play an ever-decreasing role. Is that to mean that our art should be automated? I say yes and no. Art will certainly be influenced by this tremendous development, I do hope so! It will then emerge that this loyal, spontaneous composer's view will become ridiculous!

Young people in the Soviet Union are already thinking along these lines. They're totally sectarian by saying what good is art to us these days? Science is supreme! Good ... I admit that as an artist myself I have to say: 'What a good idea'. It won't turn out that way and their saying such things is more precocious wisdom or pre-precocious wisdom than real wisdom but I enjoy it when the artist's sweet gaze is brought back to serious matters. Things can't continue as they are, especially not in music. The whore music, who has sold herself to everything good and bad in society, will one day also be called to account for her behaviour because of the general development of society.

You're seeing at the moment a great contradiction between art and philosophy?

Yes, I still believe there is an enormous contradiction. In philosophy everything has to be defined down to the smallest detail and cybernetics, for example, is having a tremendous influence on human thinking, on philosophy, even on psychology, not to mention physiology. Well, the cyberneticists are busy studying Pavlov and are trying to apply his 'conditioned reflexes' to machines – one has to study brain functions in great detail in order to apply them to machines.

I don't know if you're interested in this, but I've been thinking about it now for a few weeks and I'm a complete lay person, but I have read up on a few things.[228] There are two schools in the Soviet Union that say that people will be able to build machines which are more intelligent than people. It sounds perplexing but it's possible. There are already machines that are stronger than people; a lever crane is stronger than a man. Why shouldn't it be possible to construct a better brain than a man's? That's the idea of one of the schools.

Well, do you believe that those inventions will leave art untouched? One day we'll have machines that can compose symphonies, or make more accurate medical diagnoses than a doctor on the basis of symptoms. The symptoms will be fed into a machine and it will diagnose the illness much more efficiently than the physician. So you see those are things that can't bypass art.

The artist's sweet gaze will be abolished! Not as a result of my sectarian standpoint but through actual circumstances and we can, of course, also observe here another tremendous development. Our unalterable, class-conditioned positions of the last forty, fifty years – and, if you like, those of socialist realism as well – will be amended. Not through theoretical discussions but through factual reality. I really can't imagine that further developments in cybernetics, for example, can leave this lyrical composer unchanged.

Despite all those stupid experiments with electronic music in the West, I think they are useful. I accept that mechanical reproduction will carry on and also that the scientific, electronic methods in music will play an enormous role, that the sweating trombonist Müller, and the conductor in particular, will be replaced by machines. I think this is enormous progress. You know about my old battles, especially with conductors and I don't have anything against sweating musicians, I simply feel for the man, even if he blows badly.

I see incredible possibilities here, they're already there and you can read about them. Why should art stand still? Art will have to follow suit. Hegel has given us an important starting point, although as usual in a very strange, abstract and off-the-cuff remark. My descriptions from the cave paintings to Hegel to cybernetics could give you a foretaste of how tough it will get for you with us artists, dear Doctor Bunge, when we artists get involved with the flow of the times and start thinking ahead. I'm not interested in producing an art where you have to leave your brain behind in the cloakroom.

I think this progress is necessary and important and I can't tell you exactly how it will happen, but I know tremendous changes will take place and since I am, as you know, always in favour of change I look forward to them with great pleasure, even if they call into question my previous opinions.

That would be a starting point for us to have the conversation I asked you about once before: about the influence of cybernetics on art.

I'm not educated enough about it, I can't really say anything about it. I have only had a glimpse, a sniff at cybernetics, so to speak. It seems to me a significant development. With cybernetics begins not only what they call the third industrial revolution but something more. It will begin a new chapter in the history of mankind, which we can't predict. What we have now are just presentiments, the morning before. We artists have sensitive antennae and if the new smells so bizarre and looks so strange, that makes me, as a composer, very excited.

As theorists we should take that to heart especially because I think that our literary and musical aesthetics are nothing but metaphysics. Not once has anyone, not even a scientist, really investigated the effect of a piece of music on people. Not even the most primitive trials have been undertaken: whether the blood pressure rises or falls if one hears music of a certain style; whether Brecht's blood pressure falls or rises; what physical and psychological changes occur in a person.

You see, all that hasn't been done yet. We talk about aesthetics in the same way that country bumpkins discuss a tractor that they haven't yet seen. Those explorations have to happen. There are some trials being undertaken in Czechoslovakia, in the Soviet Union, also in Sweden where, at last, they will really study the effect of art on human beings. Then I can do aesthetics, otherwise, it's just ridiculous. I reject an aesthetics that doesn't take the new methods on board.

You're the only artist here whom I have heard talking about such things.

Yes, because my colleagues are obviously not thinking enough about it. Or maybe they're thinking too much, or they're not reading enough. Well, it's not a question of who says something first but that it's said at all. In any case, aesthetics, including Marxist aesthetics, is dethroned by me as metaphysics. I demand precise experiments before we talk about art.

We have all the potential to do it. We can establish a little department at Humboldt-University, for example, or the Charité-Hospital where we can conduct trials in the effect of music on people. Until that happens, I reject any other explanation about music as completely tedious and obsolete. It's the same for drama et cetera, effects have to be confirmed psychologically and physiologically.

And suppose we discover that certain music is harmful. What do we do then? Certain music raises the blood pressure. When you reach fifty you shouldn't listen to this music anymore because arteriosclerosis will have set in and certain pieces should no longer be played because they lower the blood pressure in people who already have low blood pressure. That sounds barbaric but I think it's only reasonable.

I say that all jokingly now and it won't really happen like that but it might as well. I have to insist on such experimental trials in music, otherwise we get completely muddled up with the old hermeneutics and the old metaphysics, of which I have had quite enough.

With drama it's a bit more complicated, because it's less about blood pressure than knowledge. Although I also think that Brecht's idea of fun and pleasure will become the main function in eighty or a hundred years' time or maybe in fifty or, optimistically, even in only thirty years' time. A society that educates itself needs to be taught by the stage only as long as education is fun – where education isn't fun any longer it's already obsolete. Certain schematics and sectarians, who include some of my friends of the Brecht-school, will most certainly be totally liquidated by history and therefore, as Brecht's friend and because I also belong to that school, I eagerly anticipate my liquidation.

It won't be fundamentally different from how it has always been. Each epoch scrutinizes which of the old certitudes can survive and which cannot.

We're doing it right now.

What is still valid will still be performed.

Absolutely correct and that's what I predict will happen. Until we come up with something better we should stop here. Let's listen to what we've said. [After listening to the recording] Afterthoughts: I've said that all very spontaneously, although you know how much I disapprove of primitive spontaneity. What's happened here perhaps is that I have tried to articulate for the first time some ideas that I have had for years. What I've said has to be more accurately expressed because it's not right. It is too distorted but I think I have touched on some important topics.

More details need to be provided about secularization and about the emancipation of art as the real indicator of progress in a class society. Historically, the bourgeoisie has, of course, achieved the greatest emancipation. As it is with the economy, so it is with art. I just want to remind you of the *Communist Manifesto*: of the bizarre achievements of the bourgeoisie with all their crimes in colonial countries; and the development of an economy (do you remember these phrases?). We also need to remember the progressiveness of the bourgeoisie, in fact how they industrialized primitive societies through incredible crimes.[229]

In this respect, I feel on familiar ground with my dear friends Marx and Engels. As with the economy, the emancipation of art in bourgeois society also has its drawbacks: its decadence and its one-sidedness. So what I've said is compatible with the *Communist Manifesto* when it argues the transformation of feudal economy into free enterprise.

Processes that took place in the past can't be retracted and I'd like to add a political example here. The freedom achieved by the Jacobins was, of course, pure bourgeois freedom. Originally intended for the whole nation, it was reduced very quickly to the freedom of young entrepreneurs, the up-and-coming bourgeoisie (and here Napoleon comes into the equation) eventually ruling the whole of Europe! Nevertheless! In the same way as it is certain that the freedom of art is not retractable from its primitive social function, albeit circumstances made us [Communists] retract it. We had to retract the term bourgeois freedom and replace it with the dictatorship of the proletariat. However, I believe that in a perfect society, a free society, a communist society, the idea of bourgeois freedom, reframed as a socialist concept, will resurface. In a class-ridden society, we weren't able to achieve the so-called freedom dreamed of by the Jacobins because when we eventually came to power we had to bring the class enemies under control. We had to restrain the bourgeoisie, its henchmen and its associated classes. That's why the pure idea of bourgeois freedom didn't get its chance in our society, just as it didn't for the Jacobins.

But you can't take away a society's dreams. It has already been calculated, predicted and approved that the free individual will, on a higher level, make himself whole once again through communism. So, the restricted class dreams of freedom will become true freedom, but they will be the grandchildren of freedom, the same as in art. Art, freed from primitive social function will then become art that is truly free.

Although the term 'pure arts' (*poésie, musique, ballet* – even *l'art pour l'art,*) sounds derisory under capitalism – and is a criminal phrase in our strict society today – we will preserve even this term by giving it a new function. This means that what existed once in society is going to be redefined in a new classless society. These are straightforward predictions that will indisputably be fulfilled. We'll have unlimited freedom within a free society where the Jacobins will seem like mere beginners. We will have an art that is finally liberated from the everyday necessities of society. It's totally uncomplicated. Society only needs to free itself from the everyday necessities and art will achieve a completely different function. I won't have to concern myself with increasing production by means of rousing songs or that all people are brothers. (I've said that very clumsily.) Then we won't need the *Ninth Symphony* any more either, although every now and then it will still be performed in large museums to the delight of a new society, but there will be no further need for this kind of new work because reality will be more powerful than the attractive surface.

We're not going to publish this but even so I'd like to warn against dividing history artificially into periods. I think that we in socialism are not doing this correctly and it sounds like a dry, academic thought, but it implies a radical change. If you were to ask me seriously, and I hope that you do ask me seriously Doctor Bunge, I would say that in the GDR we have established the primary basic fundamentals of socialism, that is as much as we can say about socialism in the GDR: the socialization of the means of production, the collectivization of the land with a deficit-economy and the distribution of power is socialist. And the working class, supported by its allies, is in power.

Unfortunately I have to say that the Soviet Union is also still only at the basic fundamental stage although on a far more advanced level than the GDR. For forty-two years now they have made advances in socialism with tremendous heroism and energy. But we can call it socialism only if there is no longer a deficit-economy. So, the unavoidable price increases of, say, meat and butter in the Soviet Union, which I of course understand, are a sign that we don't yet have fully matured socialism there, but simply a country that now has the potential to build socialism.

The view that by 1980 we'll have fully developed communism there is, I think, an inappropriate periodization. I don't know what things will be like in 1980. We'll have a higher form of socialism then than we have now in 1962, but, as with each phase, we also have to divide the societal form of socialism into phases as Marxists have always done. We talk about an early bourgeois phase, early feudalism in middle development and late feudalism. In propaganda terms with regard to our allies – the workers of the West – we will make a huge mistake if we periodize wrongly and call things by the wrong names.

If we say that in the Soviet Union we're building on the securely grounded fundamentals of socialism and that we'll have socialism only when there is no longer a deficit-economy, then we'll probably create more effective propaganda than if we tell the American worker, who already enjoys a high standard of living, that what we have now is socialism. I'm not saying this to engage in a theoretical argument but from a purely practical point of view. Let's acknowledge our situation and stop boasting so much! Then we'll feel better historically as well. I do want to listen to that now. [After listening to the recording:]

Today bourgeois capitalists work against socialism by using the word 'freedom'. My observation, therefore, that freedom is determined historically within the circumstances of social class is a very politically important remark. The bourgeoisie today has such a precise class position that we can't defeat it with theories alone. You also need the 'soup and dumplings reasons', as Heine once said in a poem about rats[230] but here, my theories become superficial. Many points are unclear and I probably ought to correct myself.

The simple thought that there can't be any going back, no retraction – neither in industry nor in general social conditions nor in fields such as freedom and art – is...

It's a completely heretical thought but even the term *l'art pour l'art* can't be retracted although art for art's sake will, of course, be the natural function in a truly completely free society. The class struggle character of art will dry up if there are no social class distinctions and art will become a general social matter. Once we're there, many things will change. In any case, and this is also important in current discussions, we can examine these terms only from a historical-critical point of view. Today *l'art pour l'art* would be nonsense, but I'm not going to let the bourgeoisie appropriate the term for themselves, nor the terms 'bourgeois freedom' or 'the inviolability of the person, housing and private property'. I'm not going to surrender those terms to them. *L'art pour l'art* is not at all useful to us at the moment, but we will use it ruthlessly against the class opponents of the proletariat. I'm not surrendering it – I'll need it one day. I'll also save *poésie pure, musique pure* and *ballet pure* as well as *théâtre pour le théâtre*. I'll save them all for better times. None of them is useful to us at the moment, but I'm not gifting it to them just like that – especially not to those gangsters of the capitalist world.

Now! What I'm going to tell you next is for a bit of fun. I found, by chance, in an antiquarian bookshop the memoirs of the k.u.k.

General Commander, Freiherr Auffenberg-Komaróv. Normally I wouldn't have been interested in it, but this guy commanded the 15th Infantry Group Division in which I had to serve as a soldier in the 48th Regiment, second Battalion. So I was very intrigued to read how such a member of the top brass speaks about my poor – please note, 'my' poor – division just because it's interesting.

These memoirs were written in 1919 and contain one delicious sentence. He writes: 'In the end I was well able to distinguish between our own and the enemy's shellfire'. I have to say that is an astonishing statement from a General, an army commander. I could distinguish between them on the spot while he only came to this amazing conclusion after a few weeks or after a few observations.

This Auffenberg-Komaróv was arrested as General Commander in 1916/1917, I think, because he'd done some shady business on the stock exchange in 1912 when he was Minister for War. Even though he denied it, there was some murky correspondence in existence, et cetera. I wouldn't usually be interested in that and I'm accustomed to the fact that war stories are inextricably linked to shady stock exchange deals. Eighty-six generals were called back to Vienna during the war in order to sit in judgement on this man. He was acquitted, by the way. These connections were self-evident to me. I would have been surprised if he hadn't done any stock exchange deals.

This General had a problem-child in his army, the 15th Infantry Group Division. What he says about us is just awful. On one occasion he says: 'Horrible losses in the 15th Division. A scandal! The officers are obviously not much good'. Then he says: 'Astonishing that this decimated, starving unit is still holding on'. And a third observation is: 'This 15th Division is unbearable – they always run away'. A fourth is: 'The colossal attack of the 15th Division surprises me'.

Looking like a fly at a monstrous bear, that's how I see this man discussing a unit in which I had to serve. I find that extremely funny and the way in which this general writes about battles – I quoted him earlier – is incredible. You couldn't even dream it up. What's more I never even saw the soles of this General's shoes because the Divisional Commander, General von Krauß, was already elevated to invisibility. That's all actually; it's just a little memory from my military life. I had the greatest pleasure reading about this division's terrible adventures, escapes and attacks. It won't mean anything special to you, old soldier, but it was a great pleasure for me to read that, after a few months, the man learned to distinguish between the enemy's and his own shellfire when I could do it after two minutes.

You also read Napoleon's memoirs some time ago.[231]

Oh yes, they're magnificent! He's a great man, albeit a terrible great man. There are a few gems...You have to dig deep into the ten volumes of this stuff to find the gems. Like a great chess player one of Napoleon's unique qualities was to develop things in an unbelievably roundabout way and, after the battle, no matter whether he won or lost it, to make an analysis. Now I thoroughly despise the appalling butchery that lies beneath the names of those famous battles. The slaughter of nations is abominable and you don't always understand why it's happening, but at least I read some really interesting things as well.

A gem: when Napoleon returned from the burning Moscow to France in a sleigh with Count Caulaincourt, he said he really should have had most of his generals shot for corruption. He didn't do it because he needed them, especially the Prince Murat, who behaved like a real snob. He could live only in castles and was unable to manage without his court chef. When the Russians caught his chef, dressed in a fantasy uniform with an epée, they thought they had captured a general – instead it was only Murat's chef [...].

Another gem from Napoleon: it was in the period before the battle of Leipzig when things weren't going well for him. Austria was still uncommitted. Napoleon was related to the royal family and tried every method to secure Austria's neutrality. If he couldn't have her as an ally against the great Russia–Prussia coalition with some other German states, he wanted her neutral. Saxony was an exception and, because that's where we're both from, we'll talk about that later. And so he was talking to Prince Metternich, who was an old fox. He had been commissioned to drag out the negotiations so that Austria could have time to conscript some more troops in Bohemia in order to join the coalition and break the celebrated peace contract. Although Napoleon knew about this through his spies, he thought that it might be possible to make a deal so that the Austrians wouldn't support the Prussian coalition. Well, he made a big mistake. He was already quite nervous and excited because he knew it wouldn't end well. The next time Metternich was at the main headquarters, Napoleon paced up and down the room and Metternich, playing cat and mouse, prevaricated: ' ... yes..., no..., but we have no plans Your Majesty ...' Napoleon grew furious and said: 'Metternich, tell me, how many millions did you get from England? I've already given you twenty million francs. Do you want a further two hundred and twenty million?' In his rage he threw his hat on the ground and Metternich went pale as this was a deadly insult to him. Of course he had received money from both Napoleon and from England, but that Napoleon should offer him even more money and in such a crude, explicit way, he found – tactless. That an aristocrat like him should receive such an offer from an upstart like Napoleon? Tactless! Then Napoleon writes: 'Now I saw my mistake. A week ago, if I'd dropped my hat Metternich would have immediately picked it up, but we walked straight past my hat and I knew that my cause with Austria was lost. He no longer picked up my hat.' This is a great story. It could have come from Brecht, by the way [...].

These books reek of blood. If you think about all those who were slaughtered and all for nothing! Unbelievable. Eventually, it's disgusting. The books are written in the style of Julius Caesar's *De Bello Gallico*: first he talks about himself as Napoleon then in the third person, as Emperor. It's brilliantly written, tremendously pedantic and incredibly boring in parts. You have to leaf through it for a long time until you find the gems, but there are quite a few [...].

Oh, yes, here's another very nice story. Napoleon was politically very skilful in Egypt, especially with the Moslems. He had the Religious Council, the Divan, called together in Cairo. Needless to say he had studied the Koran very well beforehand. As is well known he had a brilliant memory and knew the Koran inside out. The Council was beside itself at how this French guy, this stranger, had mastered the Koran. He told them: 'You know, I think the Koran is quite outstanding. Perhaps Islam is the best of all religions. I'm considering whether my troops...' He said that in order to win time and avoid those terrible partisan battles against his army. 'It is very likely' he said, 'that I and all of my troops will convert to Islam'. That was a hugely wicked thing to say. And the Divan was completely taken in by it. 'Just imagine' said the clerics, 'that the whole French army led by the famous General Napoleon suddenly become Moslems'. Napoleon says: 'Of course you have to tell me the conditions under which that can happen'. The Divan withdrew into private enclave. After two days they come back with two conditions. 'First, the whole army has to be circumcised and second, nobody is allowed to drink alcohol.' Napoleon replied: 'Well, let's leave circumcision on one side. But Frenchmen need wine. I can't do it. Go and think again if there's a way round it.' There are two more meetings of the clergy. When they come back to Napoleon they said: 'Well, we have considered the following: we could do away with the circumcision since it is a benefit of Islam and not compulsory. It's a gift. We will allow wine to be consumed if the soldiers surrender their everlasting souls.' Napoleon said: 'Listen, I can't tell my men to become Moslems if all they are left with is nothing.' These meetings really took place.

And what was the result?

Nothing. But he kept them busy for a few weeks. In the meantime there were great rumours going round in Cairo that all the French were to become Moslems. That was enough. He needed two weeks. But you have to admit it is a devious offer. And the clerics were clever too. One thing is a benefit and the other can be permitted at the expense of the everlasting soul, of course. That was a good idea.

Napoleon had taken French scholars with him. Egyptology in its early form already existed. They were called donkeys because they were always so laden with manuscripts and all sorts of devices used by the army. The scholars were appreciated later but at first they were shunned as mules. The conditions in Egypt at that time were awful. The achievements of the French army were legendary. Just consider the distances they covered when they marched. Absolutely magnificent! The Napoleonic army marched up to seventy kilometres in twenty-four hours. That is unimaginable today. That's according to Napoleon. Maybe he's overdoing it.

When I was a soldier I participated in marches of up to forty kilometres. And that finished us off. At thirty-five kilometres we were completely wrecked. How you can march seventy kilometres in that climate seems to me impossible. Well, you didn't have to march in the Second World War as much as I had to. It was absolutely horrific. When you march with 200 bullets, five hand grenades, a steel helmet, rifle, iron rations, baggage, clothing et cetera, it is unbearable. Just ten kilometres. But forty kilometres finished you off. And they marched seventy kilometres and didn't have any less baggage than us.

Probably more. You wouldn't have had that many motor vehicles.

In 1914 we had no motor vehicles. All the troops, including us, had to go on foot. The baggage and the artillery were driven as well as the wounded. But healthy soldiers had to march even during the First World War. Well, we had to in the Austrian army and I think it was the same in the German army.

At the moment I'm reading a magnificent book, *Education before Verdun* by Arnold Zweig. I recommend you to read it again. There are unbelievable hardships described. And the characters were only bargees. The physical work of a bargee was downright shocking.

Napoleon is a great man yet he's not interesting, which is a common thing. There is no doubt about his historical significance and he is absolutely uninteresting today. I read it as a hobby. I didn't get much out of it. My knowledge was not enhanced. I read other stupid things as well. I read crime novels for example. Well, these things about Napoleon are repulsive, utterly repulsive. Once after he went and visited a field hospital for the wounded, Napoleon felt sick because it stank so much. Or when he surveyed the battlefield of Borodino, he had a bad turn. There had never been slaughter like it. He experienced something that Hitler also experienced – the Russians wouldn't withdraw. They just dug in until the last man. Napoleon experienced that once in Borodino and that was a horrible massacre.

Because other troops either surrendered or withdrew, he bust the whole Austrian army after Ulm, the famous encirclement of Ulm under General Mack. The whole battle lasted only fourteen days, although he marched from the coast to Bavaria and that's a long march. He bust the whole Austrian army in fourteen days. He was often lucky because the other side lacked manpower. Very good; those were brilliant achievements. But in future we don't want this kind of personality cult ever again.

What are our chances?

Enormous! First of all it's not a question of being a personal genius, which Napoleon absolutely was, but a question of how to take stock of the historical situation. Undoubtedly, Napoleon created a completely new legal system. Even our Berlin Magistracy only came into existence after Napoleon conquered Berlin. In the

Rhineland, the entire legal system hung on to the Code Napoléon although I don't know for how long. The Byzantines called it the 'Code Napoléon'. Of course he didn't invent the code all by himself. But he was the president of the meetings and made sure his voice was heard. I recommend you read the Code Napoléon – the Code Civil. I've read it. It's amazing: the law of shares; inheritance law which is tremendously complicated; orders of procedure. Those were all very new. Mothers with children born out of wedlock were, in practice, made equal. The juror courts. Jacobinism has made itself manifest here in monumental concrete form. Napoleon was the Jacobins' greatest enemy. They were his arch enemies. [...]

One should, by way of contrast with Napoleon's memoirs, read Stendhal's unfinished writings about Napoleon. I don't know whether you know them. They knock Napoleon's memoirs into a cocked hat. As a soldier, a young lieutenant Stendhal went over the St. Bernhard with the French troops to Milan. He didn't take part in any of the battles. Then he left the army. But he talks in his writings about how Napoleon met up with him. He knew everything in detail. He was war commissar under Napoleon. He was in Russia, in Moscow; and during the most disastrous retreat Stendhal was impeccably washed and shaved. Napoleon said to him: 'You're a brave man'. Because it was astonishing that Stendhal was the only shaven officer or war commissar. He met Napoleon three times in all. Stendhal calls it 'The astonishing decadence of the great army'. First you are promoted for competence in battle and after that it was a question of who you knew. The army was completely decadent, even in 1804–1806. That is when its downfall started. It wasn't about competence any longer but about your connections. Stendhal was very clever to observe that.

One should read much more about the phenomenon that was Napoleon. But there is little interest. It's always amusing to see how in particular the great Germans like Hegel and Goethe admired Napoleon tremendously. Hegel called him 'world history on a horse'. And Goethe was simply enthralled by him. Goethe's son, the little August, was also a tremendous follower of Napoleon. Breathtaking!

Then Napoleon accomplished the liberation of the Jews, which had already been decided upon during the great Congress of Vienna but he put it into practice in Germany. Ludwig Börne, for example, could become lieutenant of police in Frankfurt when the French ruled. After the victory over Napoleon he had to quit his job because he was a Jew. The Jews were liberated under Napoleon. That is why in Jewish families and in French families there is traditionally a great affection for Napoleon. Napoleon was a great man for my Jewish father. That was somehow passed down through the generations. I think that is all we need say about Napoleon.

Conversation 13
14 August 1962

Serious Songs – Eisler's Plans for a Symphony

On this day, Eisler and his wife were in a particular good mood. They celebrated two events with a bottle of champagne: the first flight into space by two Soviet astronauts and the completion of Eisler's (what they were then still called) Seven Serious Songs. *Bunge was allowed to have a look at the freshly printed manuscript.*

[...] I'm happy that I was able to read the texts of your Seven Serious Songs. *I'm glad that you wrote them and that you want to publish them.*

Yes, I'm glad too. It cost me a year of my life to write these songs alongside a lot of other work. To be precise it begins with a short introduction followed by seven songs. I often asked myself why I did it. Something inspired me to speak about the past and about old age. I'm sixty-four years old, and age is an important concern of mine and it somehow seems to have something in common with autumn. There are Hölderlin's superb verses, which inspired me to write about or, rather, sing about equivalent subjects: namely the recollection of old times and looking into the future. Those verses have a corresponding weight for me. Autumn is also the autumn of human life and it's the autumn of politics, too, if you like: looking back and looking forward.

When I think about those two incredible astronauts flying around in space, today my work seems trivial to me.

I think both can happily co-exist. These songs must also be published and performed.

They will be performed in March in Dresden.[232] I'll send them to my publisher the day after tomorrow to include them in Volume VIII of my *Songs and Cantatas*.[233] That's all very well. But far more to the point is, I can't explain why I actually wrote those damned songs, because I just followed my instincts. There is this one poem, for example, 'The 20th Party Congress'. I didn't write this poem, nor is it entirely by Helmut Richter, because I took some lines of his and called the new version 'The 20th Party Congress'. I think it's an artist's responsibility to describe everything we've gone through as it really was. This isn't always a straightforward process. I'd much prefer to have written a good march, although as you know I've often done that as well. This time, however, I don't want to write good marches, but serious songs instead.

Among the poems is Hölderlin's 'Come! Into the Open, Friend!'[234] about which we talked about nine months ago. Were you already thinking about the Serious Songs *then?*

Yes. My adaptation of Hölderlin's poem was in fact a preliminary work to *Seven Serious Songs* and about eighteen months ago I wrote a piece, which is now called 'Epilogue', with a text by Stephan Hermlin, where the song of autumn, as it's called, is expressed. God knows why I wrote that! It's some comfort to me now to have done it, rather than have nothing at all.

I'm able to identify the authors of four of the poems: Berthold Viertel, Helmut Richter, Stephan Hermlin and Friedrich Hölderlin.

There's another one by the great Italian poet Leopardi, called 'The Despair'. The poem must have been written in about 1880 or 1890. As you know, Leopardi was a remarkable Italian poet of extraordinary genius even though beset by great misfortune. These – Leopardi, Berthold Viertel, Stephan Hermlin and Hölderlin – make up the sequence. You'll ask me why Brecht isn't included and I have to admit it's a mistake of mine not to have included him, but I'd already set hundreds of Brecht's poems, so this time I left him out.[235] This doesn't mean that I don't think Brecht is the most important poet of our century.

When I looked through the manuscript I couldn't see any reason for the sequence of the seven poems. What was the general idea behind the composition?

The sequence is specific – it makes more sense the more you look at it. In order to raise hope, despair must be at its deepest. I think that today the young people of the GDR will hardly be able to understand the third song 'The Despair', but I needed to start from a low position in order to jump high. Or better, in order to jump at all I had to step back a few paces. 'The Despair' is of course a song that no composer in a socialist country would ever have considered composing. Imagine me, an old communist, suddenly setting 'The Despair!' People studying my work in better times will make sense of it.

You published Berthold Viertel's poem once previously under the title 'Chanson Allemande' in Volume II of your Songs and Cantatas.

Yes, I liked the poem very much. I set it to music before the 20th Party Congress. Berthold Viertel wrote the poem, I think, in 1936 during Hitler's dictatorship – but when you read it today.... And now I have set it to music and everyone can choose for themselves the dates that they want to be sad about.

Is it a new composition? Or did you make an orchestral version?

It's indeed a new composition with an additional prelude. Do you have nothing to say about it?

I haven't heard the songs yet and they were only read to me once. Stephanie Eisler: Maybe you could say something about the sequence?

I had the greatest of troubles with the sequence. It's so simple yet it took me a year to put the seven little pieces in an order. It is: reflection – consideration – depression – uplift – and again reflection. It's simply the normal course of human emotion or behaviour. You have to follow this cycle, any other order would be wrong. You can't write optimistic songs all the time. First, that would be terribly boring and second, it would be wrong. One has to describe (or sing or refer to, whichever you like) the ups and downs of actual situations.

You yourself identified the theme of our conversation right at the beginning when you mentioned two simultaneous events: the flight of two astronauts in space and your completing and delivering your Serious Songs.

That's a wonderful contradiction! Believe me, dear Doctor Bunge, we Communists live off those contradictions. Have a look at what I read the other day in *Neues Deutschland*. Page one: comrade Nikolayev making this colossal flight into space and on page two I read the following verse: 'Whether sunshine or rain – we must bring in our grain!' While our astronauts do those incredible things, we have a hard time with our farmers who finally have to get used to the fact that their working day doesn't end at five but can go on until eight in the evening when the people haven't got any grub. These are delightful contradictions. What I mean by delightful contradiction is that, as you know, there was a terrible struggle in our Republic before the collectivization of the farms and the land was accomplished, which we put through with very great sacrifices. And this collective agriculture stands in such stark contrast to individualistic capitalist farming. We need four Shakespeares and eight Brechts to describe the drama of the competition between the collective farmers in our socialist countries with the individualistic farmers of capitalism. This is an extraordinary state of affairs.

Believe me, there is no less contradiction in my songs than between the flight of the astronauts and my modest music. Isn't that interesting? For an old Hegelian, like me, this work is like a tonic, a refreshment. I thrive on such contradictions.

You find this contradiction embedded in my latest work – between the *Serious Songs* and today's situation. I think it is our responsibility to reflect on the past. He who desires the future has to come to terms with the past. He has to cleanse himself of the past to be able to look purely and cleanly into the future. I don't think we're doing enough about that. Perhaps it's the artist's job, and in the context of the modern world his job is a very modest one, to depict the past truly and clearly. Art is particularly well equipped to do that and to hand over the past to the future. If you don't, you'll be handing over a crude unchallenged optimism that doesn't ring true and is pointless. To understand the past everything has to be examined from a dialectical point of view.

I just repeated myself – I'm finding it very difficult to put my thoughts into words, but I think this statement is important: there is no future without the past. I have to tell myself this five times a day whenever I compose a heroic piece, because heroism is not a matter of gestus alone. Beethoven composed 'through night into light' once and for all. To repeat this today demands a special artistic intelligence, a special endeavour.

All this sounds a bit gloomy. Fortunately you're not an artist, dear Doctor Bunge and my pains in expressing myself – and what I mean by that is what artists feel and think – are very difficult to communicate.

You're also working on a symphony at the moment?

I can't tell you what hell it is for me. I actually don't know why I'm writing a symphony because there are such wonderful symphonies already. The reason is simple: The Gewandhaus Orchestra in Leipzig – as you know, I was born in Leipzig – commissioned a symphony for their 150th or 550th anniversary (I don't know how old these good people are) and, fool that I am, I have accepted. That is why I have been trying to write this symphony for some time now.

There no longer exists a true social reason to commission a symphony, of course, because for such an assignment you'd need an enormous audience, as for example Beethoven had. First, Beethoven wrote his symphonies for the big cities, not for chamber music evenings or special gatherings of an elite audience. No, Beethoven wrote his symphonies for the Jacobins, for the *citoyen* of the Republic. No such commission exists for me.

I'm only writing the symphony out of diligence, out of some kind of pedantry and because I also felt I had to write another symphony again since I have already written a few.[236] But if you ask me why, I answer: I don't know. This troubles me a great deal. I don't know who I'm talking to and who to reach. This idea 'through night into light' is certainly a magnificent heroic sentiment, but because we have been told it so often, shall I repeat it, with a weaker voice than Beethoven? No! Maybe I should reverse it just for a change, to please our listeners' ears a bit more.

But there are already some parts of the symphony in existence?

I've made lots of sketches over the past two years and I hope to get it in some order. I have to tell you frankly, I don't think it's an art form that you should actually carry on with today. It's just that because my friend Brecht is dead, I have nothing better to do than to write a symphony. My friend Brecht would have said: 'For God's sake write anything but a symphony!' Brecht was a courageous and great man who understood the complexities of such an art form better than the damned 'music lovers'.

In your opinion what should one write instead of symphonies?

The essential.

Stephanie Eisler: What is the essential?

I can't describe the essential to you as it changes from week to week. For example, my *Serious Songs* became essential for reasons lying in the past. I have no idea what's essential at the moment. Opera for me is daft – if only because of singers, who are unbearable – and, as you can see, symphonies are daft for me as well. There is only one thing that is essential: silence.[237]

At my age, silence is perhaps more appropriate than talking and that is why I'm stopping to let you reflect on what I'm now going to be silent about.

Conversation 14
26 August 1962[238]

Eisler and Bunge Compare Their Experiences as Soldiers

I think we're going round in circles, dear Doctor Bunge, and avoiding talking about our war experiences because in this good society, and by that I mean the socialist society, it isn't proper to talk about such things. What do you think?

To be frank, I don't like talking about it.

Why?

As you know, I was an officer during the last war. In 1943 I was captured in the Soviet Union, but not even my time as a prisoner of war made me any wiser. From today's point of view, of course, it's very easy to condemn this period. The views I have now are really totally different from the views I had then and that's why I don't think it's very productive.

I'm sorry but I think it's very productive to condemn this period. Like you, I was in a world war, in the earlier world war, but as an opponent of the war and for me it's very productive that this war is remembered for a very simple reason. You see, as the son of a petit bourgeois household, mother a worker, father a scholar, I learnt in the war for the first time who the so-called 'folk' is. It is the workers and the Hungarian farmers. Because I was politically suspect, I had to serve under the Hungarian regime. I wasn't allowed to enlist in an Austrian regiment. So, I was drafted into a foreign language regiment. That really educated me, in addition to what I got from the pamphlets about Karl Marx and Engels, which I read as a boy in

1912. For the first time I understood what really matters: the people who are actually fighting these wars, the ones who serve as cannon fodder. That was an enormous revelation, which really educated me and which I wouldn't want to have missed out on. Didn't you have similar experiences?

No, because when I went into the war, unlike you, I wasn't against it. I was talked into it and believed that fighting the war was justified. That's why I didn't learn what you did, under completely different circumstances.

But you've been with the so-called 'common people', with workers and farmers – that must have brought you some insights.

Maybe, but it didn't ever occur to me in that way. When I look back and recollect what I thought then, I remember a great, all-embracing feeling of comradeship. There were no differences between workers, farmers and me. We relied on each other and went through everything together.

As Germany is an industrial country, in your regiment, or the regiments you served in, the working class was probably predominant. I was lucky enough to serve in a regiment among Hungarian farmers. I really got to know the farmer, not as a tourist on summer trips, but because we were lying together in the trenches for many years, eating, sleeping, getting wounded and cursing together. Unfortunately, what we didn't do together was mutiny, because the Hungarian farmers with whom I served were royalists and were under the thumbs of the officers who in peacetime used to be the estate managers. In short, before the war the farmers were under the thumbs of the estate managers and during the war the farmer became the foot soldier, the estate manager became the officer and the Count had a seat high up at general headquarters.

The whole k.u.k. monarchical social structure was simply transplanted during the war. I could certainly have predicted that, but to actually experience it, was enormously educational. It didn't have to take a war to provide me with this education, I could, for example, have gone to a coal mining village or to a little Hungarian town, but the war was the fastest, cruellest and most brutal route to really mix with what was then called *narodniki*, the common people – and in a most unfortunate way, because I myself was oppressed in the same way as the Hungarian farmers with whom I served.

I'd like to be able to say something more sensible than I can, but I don't want to turn my attitude of those days into something else. Somehow, I never got the opportunity to realize what you did until I became a prisoner of war in August 1943. There were no differences in my troop. I didn't see any social problems.

That's interesting. In the summer of 1916, I think it was, I reported with my papers for duty to my battalion commander in the trench, the shelter. My military record gave details of my background. It reported that I was politically suspect and that I had already been disciplined twice for refusing to obey orders. My battalion commander said to me: 'See here: my revolver?' I replied: 'Yes sir, captain!' – 'If you, you stinking socialist breathe even a single word of your stinking socialism to my boys, I'll shoot you. Remember that!' I said: 'Yes sir, captain!' and made my exit. That was my first experience of the class enemy. It doesn't come much more brutal than that when you're only eighteen years old.

I couldn't experience things like that, of course, because nobody would have had a reason to point a revolver at me as they had with you. Before I became a soldier, I was a leader of the Jungvolk *in Dresden. (That's the organization for ten to fourteen year old boys; the* Hitler Youth *began at the age of fourteen.) When I became an officer and first led a troop as lieutenant, I behaved in the same way I had as a* Jungenführer [leader of boys] *and thought that my way of leading people was all right and that everyone liked it. It wasn't until much later that I had second thoughts about whether I had judged my behaviour correctly.*

I find that extremely interesting – how two wars can be so different. Between 1914 and 1918 the k.u.k. monarchy definitely retained its strong feudal characteristics, which Germany didn't have during Hitler's dictatorship. Instead, the Nazis invented some kind of illusory egalitarianism. It really was nothing more than an illusion but which negated those feudal characteristics.

In my company, for example, there were, besides the true Hungarian farmers from Groß-Kanizsa, a town in the middle of

Hungary, only three non-Hungarians. They'd been deliberately posted there as none of the three spoke Hungarian. First was me, then a Czech worker called Pelikan, and third was a Croatian worker. The Croatian was a bit shady and vulnerable and was later arrested. Today I would call him the anarchist type. The Czech worker, Pelikan, who turned up in this troop like a flower in a patch of weeds, was a socialist, a member of the Social Democratic Party. He and I, because I was a Young Socialist, were both transferred to Hungary for security reasons.

It's so interesting when you talk about war. Those three people met each other with the greatest mistrust. I couldn't get one word of interest to me out of Pelikan, the Czech soldier and, because I was an officer cadet, he didn't ask me anything either. The Croatian treated me as an enemy because I came from Vienna. This one anecdote encapsulates the entire division of nations and the extreme separation of the classes brought about by the k.u.k. monarchy. We knew only too well that when Pelikan and I went out on patrol together, even if it was just the two of us, we wouldn't say one single word to each other about politics. He thought, if he spoke against the monarchy I would immediately run to the battalion commander and I thought he'd go to the troop commander if I said anything at all.

We weren't able to achieve any kind of understanding while we were in the trenches. I blame it on my being a totally callow youth. I was very young then and Pelikan was thirty-five or thirty-eight and the Croatian worker was about forty-five. That's why in one company three opponents of the war – oppositional elements – for reasons of nationality or security, never made a connection with each other. All we felt for each other was, let's say, sympathy. We treated each other differently from how we behaved towards the stubborn Hungarian farmers, who incidentally had some brilliant qualities.

They are marvellous people, those farmers! I learnt more from the Hungarian farmers than from any of my teachers, even about music. They used to sing such wonderful folk songs. I became famous in my company because I was able to notate the tunes they sang to me and sing them back to them afterwards. They thought that was a wonder of nature. So, I did have some better company every now and then and sometimes I didn't need to go on guard duty. But the situation between those three oppositional elements obviously didn't exist in your time?

No, because first of all there wasn't this mixture of nations.

Didn't you have some Austrians?

No, not in our division. It was a Thuringian division.

Only people from Thuringia?

Most of them, yes, at least at the beginning of the war.

That's completely different then, of course.

It changed, of course, as the war progressed because substitute troops came in from other units. I can't remember having noticed any kind of antipathy to the Nazi regime within my company. And I was at the front line for many years.

I only noticed, or rather suspected, with those two blokes that they were against the Austro-Hungarian monarchy. Nobody came out and said it. We should keep our ears open to the subtleties of difference, because I can't imagine that this tank division from Thuringia was so homogeneous that there weren't any differences of opinion.

I won't deny that they didn't exist. I can only say that I didn't notice and that, as long as I was with the troop, until August 1943, no such problems became known to me.

That's sad.

There was no combat during which anyone refused to obey orders, no desertion in my regiment.

That didn't happen with us either.

There was just one occasion when I met someone who objected to the war. He was a journalist who was drafted to my unit as a soldier. I remember a discussion we had. I probably registered his ideas as cowardice, but that was so exceptional that I didn't take the incident seriously.

Well, I have to tell you that unfortunately, in spite of everything, I have to agree with you. You can see it also in *Secrets of the War* about which Lenin talks so well. If you had asked me two days before the putsch in Austria how much longer the war would last, even one day before the putsch (that was on Friday morning when we heard that the Czech people had rebelled), I would have said the war will last for as long as we fight it – that's how I phrased it then. I had been wounded and returned to the Personnel Regiment in Pilsen and there people asked when they could go home. I couldn't have pinned a date on it, say, the eighth of November. (I don't know when the putsch happened in Austria.) 'If it is up to the soldiers' I said, 'and the willingness of the people to be slaughtered, then it could go on for many more years'.

I couldn't see an end, but on Friday morning the end was there. Twenty-four hours later I saw that the monarchy and the army had collapsed. I couldn't have predicted it, even though I was connected to oppositional, revolutionary elements...with left-wing social democrats in Vienna. Nobody was able to pinpoint the end of the war. But there were others – factory workers and the national communities of the Czechs and of the Serbs who refused to participate in the war any longer. It is highly interesting that a not unintelligent boy like me would have been forced to fight in the war for another five years. Also, I hadn't understood that the war was over because the old monarchy was economically no longer up to it, leaving aside the business of national independence.

I think something similar must have occurred in the German army in 1944, when nobody could have known, say in December 1944, that at long last the war would come to an end in May 1945.

I remember the beginning of the war. People didn't exactly rush into the Wehrmacht *as they obviously did at the beginning of the First World War ...*

Headlong. But not me!

... but there were people who suffered if they weren't conscripted straightaway. A younger teacher had hardly any authority over his pupils if he wasn't called up.

Yes, such things happened. I remember a very poignant incident. We should also enrich our present conversation with anecdotes, otherwise it becomes too abstract. It was in 1916 in the trenches, it must have been in September or October, when I was shoved aside by a man while I was carrying rolls of barbed wire to the front line. I said to him in a hushed voice, because you had to be quiet: 'Get out of my way!' This man was a high-ranking officer but I didn't know that and I just started cursing away. 'What are you saying? Who is this?' He took his torch and shone it in my face and said: 'For God's sake! We have to wage this war with these children!' This man understood more than me and I was at the front. He looked into my face and saw a skinny young lad with a steel helmet and was shocked that this was the new recruit.

That's a good story. It must have been similarly shocking for the people in 1943/1944, when the seventeen-year-olds were called up. It's the most basic human feeling that you understand that such young people are in no way fit for these duties. Didn't people feel the same way in your time?

Unfortunately, again I can't agree. There wasn't this general opinion. You only had to look at the obituaries in the newspapers to find the answer was no. It was an SS-Division Hitler Youth, which was called into particularly critical situations. The boys who were conscripted into this division were not just unable to resist this call; most of them actually took pride in it. You grieved for the death of a relative or friend, but unfortunately you were ready to accept it as the price that had to be paid. It would be easier for me to tell you about it if I were able to leave myself out of it. The feeling of camaraderie among soldiers was of course fostered by the fact that nearly everybody was equally exposed to death. Under these circumstances class differences didn't materialize at all.

That's part of the secret of war, which we Marxists know all about: to be plucked out of a dreary petit-bourgeois existence, to be put into a big collective group and to feel yourself to be a member of the greater collective. It's astonishing and most horrible that a basic feeling which is in itself good should be exploited in that way. A lad from a miserable family, where his mother nags and his father is pissed or yells at him, suddenly, in a borrowed uniform, enters into a big collective group to fight for a common purpose. I think all wars abuse a kind of confused socialist instinct in people. Do you know what I mean?

Brecht calls it pretend social feelings.

Just as the railway is 'socialist' under capitalism, or the mail, so the bloody military possesses socialist characteristics. But it perverts and distorts them. It's like this: they appeal to a young man to leave his home in, say, Butchers' Alley Number 9 and immerse himself into a large collective group; it could be the Reich or anything else.

Today we must take advantage of these instincts and we do, as best we can. This feeling, to lift yourself above your own miserable circumstances into something greater could be the basic reason for young people rushing into the military and feeling better there than in their pitiful petit bourgeois or workers' homes. It's a difficult business that should be discussed seriously.

Strangely enough, those feelings persisted in the prison camps well after 1945. Even then, soldiers didn't become aware of their class origins although they had every opportunity to do so in the Soviet POW camps. Officers, for example, were in most cases still being treated as superiors.

Ridiculous. Those are not national matters, they are social. Apparently the soldiers saw in the officers ... I wouldn't know what, I thought they were dreadful ... The devil knows what they saw in them.

I believe that the human being's predisposition to belong to a collective group derives from primitive society. For example, it can't be a coincidence that all bourgeois young people have been reading stories about Red Indians for a hundred years. The Red Indians despise money and they're against trade because it's dishonest to trade, it's humiliating. You must be brave and stand by your tribe. So all these characteristics of a primitive, heroic and glorified tribal society are being absorbed by bourgeois youth as if it were 'the best'. They devour it like a bear eats honey. To tell the truth, when our young lads read stories about Red Indians, they are reading about some form of primitive ur-communism.

And that is why I also think that the military is the wrong collective group to satisfy the great yearning of the human beings who wants to achieve a change from a primitive single faith into a higher order. Militarism and capitalism have exploited this longing and we need to know how to make use of it, too, because the longing is something that can't be denied.

I remember the marvellous experience of it during the Spanish Civil War. Clever émigrés, people who fled over the border in great danger, enthusiastically participated in the Civil War. This made a huge impression on me. I had never seen this kind of behaviour in the old military. It was also there in the Resistance. Just think of the partisans! Here, the collective group was right. It would benefit our socialist state if we could recapture this collective group consciousness, this following the great idea, this human instinct to try to move from the individual into the general. Unfortunately, you didn't experience that. For you it remained an obstinate collective group.

If you see it from today's point of view. The question is whether and how I could have realized it earlier. You're absolutely right when you say we went into the war with stories of Red Indians in our heads. When we got ready for the attack on the Soviet Union, nobody showed fear or worried about what might happen.

It's not about fear, dear Doctor Bunge. You see, the crux of the matter is this: the absence of class consciousness. Hitler understood how to drive out class consciousness from the overwhelming part of German youth, and to orientate them towards the romantic idea of an early civilization, which was then applied to the military collective.

In simple terms it means that we have to take tremendous care that we don't lose class consciousness in whatever we do, because the readiness to join a wrong collective group is always there, it's biological. The primeval society within us is still there, it's a sort of inheritance deep inside us. In the Bible it says: 'It's not good if man is alone'. It's not only about marriage; it's also about the collective.

The human being is a product of society. He always moves forward and strives towards social being. We have to take care that the social aims are the right ones and that our struggle towards the general, the broad and those principles, to which we're committed, goes in the right direction.

AFTERWORD
For the first edition of the 'Conversations'[239]

by Stephan Hermlin

On the occasion of Hanns Eisler's sixtieth birthday, I wrote down this memory:

I saw Hanns Eisler for the first time in 1930 or 1931. I had heard of him. In the music shop I had leafed through his chamber music a few times which was published by *Universaledition* Vienna. To play this kind of music in our house was out of the question. We did play a lot of music at home but the modernists aroused suspicion. This Eisler, it was rumoured by the way, made political music. I was interested in him because I was interested in music and because I had just started to become interested in politics. I went to a meeting where Eisler songs were going to be performed.

The auditorium, somewhere in the north of Berlin, was actually just a big room at the back of a public house. Beneath streamers left over from the last dance, reserved men in caps and old leather jackets sat on iron folding chairs around small tables, and around each table four to six men drinking beer. In front of a backcloth of an idealized Greek landscape, like portrait photographers used to have once and like the surrealists love, somebody spoke about the Soviet Union. Then, to thunderous applause, an actor recited Walter Mehring's song 'In this Hotel on Earth' from Piscator's latest production *The Merchant of Berlin* and verses by Clément, the poet of the Paris Commune.

And then Eisler and Busch came onto the little stage.

I had already seen Ernst Busch on stage, namely in the role of the red baker in *The Weavers*, in a production by Karl Heinz Martin. It seems to me now as if Hanns Eisler looks the same today as he did then. In the same bashful way as he does today, he thanked the audience for the applause that greeted him. He immediately took his place at the piano that was pushed onto the stage; it was very out of tune. I heard for the first time those songs, which I, together with innumerable people, never forgot, and never ever could forget – 'Red Wedding' and 'Workers, Farmers'. Eisler and Busch turned to the audience and asked for their requests. From the tables they shouted to them titles of songs that they wanted to hear. The words were either from Brecht or [Erich] Weinert. I still remember how, with a kind of shock, I noticed that Eisler sometimes pounded the keys with his clenched fist. At the same time I was amused by my own outrage. I applauded and shouted along with everyone else in the audience, although up until that moment I never thought anyone could play the piano like that. With this insistent, uplifting music, a great hope had entered this dilapidated ballroom. Only later did I understand that this music for a new class came from the most formal school, from the school of the classics.

This memory of course doesn't convey an image of Eisler, but rather that of the atmosphere in which he operated. I got to know Eisler's music in more detail only slowly; slowly because it was seldom performed. An intelligent man once told me that among all the major contemporary composers, Eisler is the one who's least recognized. There are, I think, several reasons for this: hardly out of Arnold Schoenberg's school, Eisler dedicates his work and his whole being to the cause of the revolutionary proletariat; then followed the emigration; with the end of the emigration came the Cold War, of which, on several occasions, Eisler became a particular victim. In fact his political standpoint meant that Eisler turned his back on many opportunities in the bourgeois music business; even his revered teacher Schoenberg didn't understand this decision. In a letter to someone, Schoenberg writes that he would like to give this Eisler a good hiding, that he should concentrate on the music because that's where his real talent lies and only there.

But I believe that even certain positive aspects in Eisler's development have not always influenced how much of his work was really recognized. His collaboration for almost thirty years with the kindred-spirit Brecht, the significance of which for the art of this century can't possibly be overestimated, has made him in the minds of many people the definitive Brecht-composer, which he by no means is. Eisler's magnificent songs, almost as numerous as Schubert's, indeed consist mainly of texts from Brecht. But they are only a part of his whole oeuvre that needs to be listened to and understood in its entirety.

In the GDR a substantial part of his work has been made accessible, although I don't want to imply that enough has already been done for Eisler here. As far as West Germany is concerned, in this respect we can only say it's a huge scandal. For the audience there, Eisler is at best the composer of Brecht's *Schweyk* or *Galileo*, and for certain newspapers the composer of a detested national anthem, the significance of which is only whether it can be played at sporting events or not. It is a further scandal that when anyone speaks of the Schoenberg-school, two names are mentioned, the third coequal, though, is omitted. In a letter of January 1945, the old Arnold Schoenberg names as his most important pupils three men and in this order: Alban Berg, Anton von Webern and Hanns Eisler. As far as Eisler's oeuvre is concerned, of course one has to acknowledge the songs set to texts from Hölderlin, Goethe, Leopardi, Mörike, Brecht and Tucholsky; but one has also to get to know the early piano works, the orchestral pieces and suites, the quintet *Fourteen Ways of Describing Rain*, the septets and nonets, the wind quintet, the violin sonata, the *Little Symphony Op. 29* and the *German Symphony*.

Nevertheless, even when Hanns Eisler had become known only through one defining part of his works, in Germany, in the Soviet Union, in England, France, and the United States there was, in addition to the revolutionary workers who knew of him, an intellectual elite who understood where Hanns Eisler belonged: in the front rank of contemporary artists. When Eisler was under threat from the Rankin-Committee in the United States, Chaplin immediately spoke up for him, and Thomas Mann, Einstein and Stravinsky added their voices. A manifesto describing Eisler as one of the most important contemporary composers bore the signatures of Picasso, Matisse, Cocteau, Jean-Luis Barrault, Aragon and Eluard, among others.

Of all the very intelligent people I have met throughout my life, Hanns Eisler was probably the most intelligent. This intelligence was for the interlocutor in no way intimidating or oppressing; on the contrary, it was encouraging, demanding and supportive. Everyone tried to give their best in his presence. Eisler's enormous philosophical and literary education corresponded with his musical genius, with his highly trained compositional technique. I admired his diligence, his constant readiness to fulfil artistic tasks, to rehearse with singers, to teach his – very few – pupils. And he did all this in a lively, polite and courteous manner. Even his mockery was never malicious but always friendly. I had the privilege of working with him a few times, although my contributions were rather small. 'Don't you notice', he used to say, 'how old fashioned you are? Imagine this man is sitting in the corner waiting for inspiration! Rubbish! A real musician or writer has always to be able to deliver what is asked of him! And at the highest level!' He went on and on about how outdated my ideas were. I listened in delight. He was absolutely right.

I loved the writers that were dear to him: Horace, Lucretius (whom he always read in Latin), Goethe, Hölderlin, Stendhal, Rimbaud, Apollinaire and Proust. For him, Thomas Mann and Bertolt Brecht were and remained the two greatest contemporary German authors; he said that, even though for each of them the name of the other was anathema but both of them knew Eisler very well personally. Eisler was unwavering in his admiration and was not an opportunist.

He read Hegel, Marx and Lenin almost daily. He knew them better than most of those people who constantly drop their names. For him – the Schoenberg-pupil – music was virtually governed by the great German masters from Bach to Brahms with Bach and Mozart occupying pride of place. Once we were talking about Händel. 'A magnificent fellow' said Eisler, 'a kind of Jacobin, something the more brilliant Bach unfortunately wasn't.' He demonstrated to me Händel's wonderful ideas, but how Mozart, for example, corrected him in *Alexander's Feast*. 'He crossed out his sequences.' In terms of contemporary colleagues he spoke with the highest admiration of Schoenberg and Stravinsky. Richard Strauss was for him the incarnation of 'stupidity in music'.

When I visited him in the evenings, and the chess match with his brother Gerhart was taking too long for me (I don't play chess), I liked to steer the desultory conversation onto Wagner, whom I praised. Upon which, the game was immediately broken off and Eisler, sometimes complemented by Gerhart's philosophical and political observations, began to prove at the piano the enormous ridiculousness of, for example, the overture to *Meistersinger*. My rejoinders drove the brothers to more and more passionate eloquence. Finally, Eisler leaned back exhausted and concluded: 'Scandalous rubbish! But what a genius…' When Eisler died, *Tristan*, the last score he had read, lay open beside his bed.

He enthused; he stimulated everyone who came into contact with him. He was no stranger to grief. He endured it and experienced it all too often; the slow movements of his chamber music bear witness to that. But the fundamental motif of his being, his music, was the energetic 'a new battle is at stake', to quote a famous Heine poem. He could never separate or divide his art from the struggle of the working class. He has left, in the conversations with Bunge, that wonderful confession that he ever only saw himself as a go-between, as the exhausted messenger who 'delivers the message'.

This book cannot and will not replace the knowledge of true revolutionary music. However, it makes known important prerequisites on which a great oeuvre is based. It belongs among the most moving documentations of art that I have ever read. Hans Bunge, as an excellent pupil of Brecht's has drawn the conclusions from the famous poem of 'Tao-Te-Ching' and played the role of the customs officer who extracts the wise man's wisdom. And for that, as it is written, we owe him our gratitude.

NOTES

Abbreviations

GW   Bertolt Brecht, *Gesammelte Werke* [Collected Works], Frankfurt am Main (= werkausgabe edition suhrkamp); after the abbreviation volume and page number, i.e. *GW* 2, 450.

J   Bertolt Brecht, *Arbeitsjournal*, Frankfurt am Main 1973. For this translation the following source was used: *Bertolt Brecht Journals, 1934–55 (Diaries, Letters and Essays)* by Bertolt Brecht, John Willett and Hugh Rorrison, London 1993 (= Methuen Drama); after the abbreviation date of the entry, i.e. 10 December 1941.

SuF B2   *Sinn und Form, Beiträge zur Literatur* [Title of a literary journal published by the Academy of Arts], Berlin 1949; Volume IX (1957), Second Special Issue Bertolt Brecht; after the abbreviation page number, i.e. *SuF B2*, 57.

1   *Hanns Eisler Gespräche mit Hans Bunge. Fragen Sie mehr über Brecht.* Übertragen und erläutert von Hans Bunge [Hanns Eisler Conversations with Hans Bunge. Ask me more about Brecht. Transcribed and edited by Hans Bunge], Deutscher Verlag für Musik, Leipzig, 1975.

2   Houben, H.H., *Gespräche mit Heine* [Conversations with Heine], 1st ed. Frankfurt am Main, 1926; 2nd ed. Berlin, Rütten & Loening, 1948.

3   This is a slightly amended version of Bunge's original foreword to the 1975 edition.

4   See note 1.

5   *Bertolt Brecht Journals, 1934–55 (Diaries, Letters and Essays)* by Bertolt Brecht, John Willett and Hugh Rorrison, London 1993 (= Methuen Drama).

Conversation 1

6   Hans Bunge writes: 'The recording of the conversation during our
    first meeting on 9 April 1958 was inadvertently deleted due to a
    technical mistake. The text before you is a reconstruction from
    memory of the first conversation on the basis of prepared written
    questions. This recording took place on 2 May 1958.' The only
    passage preserved on tape is a discussion about a title change to
    Brecht's song 'In Praise of Communism'. With Brecht's knowledge,
    Eisler changed it to 'In Praise of Socialism'. Eisler remarks that
    the title of a song is not the important issue, although Brecht
    would certainly not have allowed him to change it to 'In Praise of
    Reformism'. The passage has not been included in this edition.

7   'Tui' is an invention of Brecht's. The word 'intellectual' is
    reassembled as 'tellect–ual–in' and the initial letters form the
    new word 'tui'. By 'tui' Brecht means 'the intellectuals in the age
    of buying and selling.' The intellectuals who occupy themselves
    as 'whitewashers', 'brainy timeservers', 'intellect merchants',
    'formulators' and 'apologists'. Instead of investigating the matter
    of the ownership of property, which is the root of all evil, and
    instead of criticizing the entire social structure and wishing to
    overthrow it, they offer only an assortment of intellectual solutions
    to the economic and social problems. Brecht's 'tuism' questions the
    philosophical 'tuism', which, being opposed to egoism, is concerned
    with what is 'beneficial for the fellow human being' examining only
    personal moral behaviour rather than the social being.

8   See full text J, 24 April 1942.

9   *Hegel's Aesthetics. Lectures in Fine Art*, translated by T.M. Knox,
    2 Vols., OUP, 1975.

10 Eisler means the short-lived *Groupe des Six* who based their ideas on
    the aesthetics of Jean Cocteau and the music of Eric Satie. The group
    comprised the composers Arthur Honegger, Darius Milhaud, Francis
    Poulenc and others.

11 See full text, J, 20 July 1942. By 'hostage story' is meant the Fritz
    Lang film *Hangmen also Die*, produced in America by United Artists.
    The final version of the script was created without Brecht. Hanns
    Eisler wrote the music for the film and was nominated for an Oscar
    Award for Best Score in 1943.

12 See full text J, 27 April 1942.

13 On 4 May 1935, in connection with his paper 'On Experimental
    Theatre', Bertolt Brecht writes in his Journal that he owes a great
    debt to the stimulus provided for his theatre by the epic elements in
    Charles Chaplin's silent films. It is known that Brecht had seen at

least the following Chaplin films: *The Gold Rush* (1924/25), *City Lights* (1928/29), *Modern Times* (1932/35), *The Great Dictator* (1938/40) and *Limelight* (1951/52).

14 Eisler is probably referring here to a declaration of 1 August 1943, which (according to Brecht's Journal) was signed by Thomas Mann, Heinrich Mann, Lion Feuchtwanger, Bruno Frank, Bertolt Brecht, Berthold Viertel, Hans Reichenbach and Ludwig Marcuse, relating to the founding manifesto of the National Committee for a Free Germany, in the Soviet Union. See J, 1 August 1943 for wording of the declaration (see also Journal entries on 2 August and 9 September 1943).

15 Eisler is referring to the content of a particular chapter in Thomas Mann's *The Magic Mountain* entitled 'Political Suspect!'

16 Such 'spiteful things' are not verifiable.

17 After the hearing before the House Committee on Un-American Activities in May 1947, Eisler was questioned for a second time on 24 September 1947. It was planned to prove that Eisler was a communist or a member of the Communist Party of Germany or that he had collaborated with communist organizations in the Soviet Union and the United States and had, therefore, infringed the immigration law of the United States. These hearings took place under the pretence of a thorough cleansing operation against liberal Roosevelt-supporters in the Department for Foreign Affairs. Already several months before the hearing, some sections of the American press had mounted a smear campaign against Hanns Eisler, alongside the campaign against Eisler's brother Gerhart, who was under investigation as a Moscow spy. In October 1947 a Committee for Justice for Hanns Eisler was founded with Aaron Copland and Leonard Bernstein as its chairmen and on which Charles Chaplin and Thomas Mann worked as well as others. They also mobilized support abroad. In France, twenty-three intellectuals, among them Pablo Picasso, Henri Matisse, Jean Cocteau, Jean-Luis Barrault, Pierre Brasseur, Louis Aragon, Paul Eluard and Louis Jouvet protested at the American Embassy in Paris. See also footnote 84.

18 See full text J, 2 May 1942.

19 In 1935 and 1938, respectively (but published for the first time in 1957), Brecht wrote two essays: 'On the use of music for an epic theatre' and 'On gestic music'.

20 This refers to Erwin Ratz who wasn't Eisler's pupil but a friend of the same age.

21 Brecht collaborated with Fritz Lang on the film *Hangmen also Die*. See notes 11 and 42.

22 Eisler probably means here his letter from Ahrenshoop on 13 August 1952.

23   Brecht and Weigel had a country house in Buckow, by Lake
      Schermützelsee, about an hour's car journey east of Berlin.
24   See full text J, 9 May 1942.
25   This is a play on words in German. In Brecht's entry in the Journal
      (see 9 May 1942), he uses the word *Schlachtpferde*. 'Pferde'
      means horses and 'Schlacht' means battle but 'Schlachten' means
      to slaughter, so 'Schlachtpferde' can be warhorses but also horses
      assigned to be slaughtered.
26   All the material that has been found so far is contained in GW 12,
      p. 589. The founder of the Institute for Social Research, which Eisler
      mentions is Felix Weil.
27   In 1939, Eisler wrote the score for Clifford Odets' play *Night Music*.
      In 1944, he was nominated for an Academy Award for Best Score
      for the second time for *None But The Lonely Heart* (Screenplay and
      Direction Odets). In 1946, Eisler wrote the score for *Deadline at
      Dawn* by Odets and Harold Clurman.
28   The play in German is called *Furcht und Elend des Dritten Reiches*,
      which is also known in English as *The Private Life of the Master
      Race*.
29   In the Aurora edition (New York 1945) is a footnote explaining that
      the American stage version (entitled *The Private Life of the Master
      Race*) contains seventeen scenes (out of twenty-four) and is divided
      into three parts. The introduction to the third part gives the verse
      incompletely quoted by Eisler.
30   *Katzgraben*, the name of a German rural village, is the title of a
      comedy by Erwin Strittmatter.
31   The notes have not been found as yet.
32   In Brecht's melodies the intervals are marked only with crosses on
      the stave but not the rhythmic value.

Conversation 2

33   The error on the programme was corrected in time.
34   See note 2.
35   The letters have been published in the meantime in: Arnold Bronnen,
      *Tage mit Bertolt Brecht. Die Geschichte einer unvollendeten
      Freundschaft* [Days with Bertolt Brecht. The Story of an Unfinished
      Friendship], Vienna 1960 and Berlin 1973.
36   See full text J, 13 August 1942. For Brecht on Huxley, see also J, 20
      September 1943.
37   Not Hermann but Hans Reichenbach (1891–1953). Eisler used one
      of Reichenbach's texts for the canon 'Peace on Earth' but also, there
      too, gave his first name wrongly as Hermann.

38   Austro-Hungarian Army; k.u.k = kaiserlich und königlich [imperial and royal].

39   See full text J, 21 August 1942. Brecht records a slightly different account of this story. The inconsistency between Eisler's and his story can't be explained.

40   There are so many variations in the number of poems assembled under the collective title Hollywood Elegies that it is impossible to define them as one compilation. See Bertolt Brecht Archive BBA 16/57 or BBA 98.

41   Hanns Eisler, *Lieder und Kantaten* [Songs and Cantatas], Leipzig 1955.

42   See also notes 11 and 21. Brecht writes in his Journal between 5 June 1942 and 24 June 1943 about the ups and downs of working on this film.

43   This refers to Brecht's and Eisler's appearances before the House Committee on Un-American Activities.

44   The actor Paul Henreid was actually born Paul Georg Julius Freiherr von Hernried Ritter von Wassel-Waldingau. Brecht always wrote 'Hernried'.

45   Retold as in J, 29 December 1941.

46   The full title of the play is *The Vision of Simone Machard*.

47   For details on the preliminary work on the play, see Journal entries from 25 November 1942, 2 December 1942 and 8 December 1942. Brecht and Feuchtwanger worked from October 1942 until February 1943 on the play. Feuchtwanger sent Brecht his final version of the play in August 1955.

48   Hanns Eisler, 'Brecht and Music', SuF B2, p. 439.

49   For many plays, several years of preparatory thinking preceded the writing. Then the work was completed in a surprisingly short time. For example, Brecht needed only two weeks for *The Trial of Lucullus*, three weeks for *The Resistible Rise of Arturo Ui*, and for each of the plays *Mother Courage and her Children*, *The Vision of Simone Machard* and *Schweyk in the Second World War* he needed four weeks, for *The Caucasian Chalk Circle* two months and for *Life of Galileo* he needed three months.

50   *The Good Soldier Švejk and his Fortunes in the World War*, novel by Jaroslav Hašek.

51   It is a play on words. The word 'Krug' [jar], as in the original title of Kleist's play, is replaced with 'Giesskanne' [watering can], which is a pun on the surname of Therese Giehse.

52   See full text J, 26 September 1943.

53   The 'Moldau Song' is from *Schweyk in the Second World War*. The text has been found and was published in1968. English translation by William Rowlinson. Brecht Collected Plays Vol.

7, ed. John Willett and Ralph Manheim, London, Eyre Methuen 1976.

54 See full text J, 4 September 1943. The song is not part of Brecht's original manuscript.

Conversation 3

55 See full text J, 29 July 1942.

56 Thomas Mann writes about Schoenberg in *Die Entstehung des Doktor Faustus. Roman eines Romans*. Bermann-Fischer Verlag, 1949. In English translation: *The Story of a Novel: The Genesis of Doctor Faustus*, Alfred A. Knopf, 1961.

57 This information could not be verified. The first edition of the book Eisler is referring to was published as: Arnold Schoenberg, *Style and Idea*, New York: Philosophical Library, 1950.

58 See SuF B2, 440. Eisler retells Schoenberg's story, the model for Brecht's cantata-text, like this:

> I once went up a hill and because I have a weak heart the gradient became very difficult for me. But in front of me went a donkey. He didn't go directly up the steep way but trotted in zig-zags, left and right of the direct route and in this way evened the gradient out. And so I followed his example and can say: I learned from a donkey.

59 The cantata has not as yet been found.

60 The oratorio *Jacob's Ladder* was first performed in 1961 as part of the 10th International Music Festival of the Vienna Concert Society. Though left unfinished by Schoenberg, the piece was prepared for performance by Schoenberg-student Winfried Zillig at the request of Gertrud Schoenberg.

61 *Six Little Pieces.*

62 This occurred on 2 August 1946. Schoenberg died on 13 July 1951 in Los Angeles.

63 The Anacreon poems (Eisler calls them 'Anacreontic fragments') and the Hölderlin poems or fragments have not been published as cycles as such in the edition of *Songs and Cantatas*. They are scattered throughout Vols 1 and 2. Only the 1972 edition *Selected Songs I, Anacreontic Fragments, Hölderlin Fragments for Solo Voice and Piano*, Leipzig 1972, reflects Eisler's original manuscript.

64 Eisler means Mörike.

65 This date is too early by far. It is possible to detect references to the 'gestus' in Brecht's *Augsburg Theatre Critiques* (1918–1922),

but as a component of epic theatre and with that also as a defined theoretical term, the word surfaces for the first time in the spring of 1926 (see Elisabeth Hauptmann, 'Notes on Brecht's Work', in SuF B2, p. 241). Hanns Eisler got to know Brecht in 1927. Brecht didn't put anything down in writing about the gestic/gestus in music until the mid-thirties.

66 Paul Dessau composed the music to *The Caucasian Chalk Circle* in 1953 and 1954 in Buckow and Berlin. A first, unfinished, version was rejected; the second and final one was completed on 4 March 1954.

67 In German this play on words is clearer: 'history' in German is 'Geschichte' and derives from the word 'Geschehen' [happening].

68 They were published in 1959 as Vol. XI of Brecht's *Stücke* [Plays].

69 See full text J, 25 July 1943.

70 This is possibly a movement from the *Sonata No. 3 for Piano* from 1943.

71 See full text J, 26 September 1944.

72 A collective farm in the former USSR.

73 Chinese classical zaju verse play in four acts with a prologue by Li Qiantu from the Yuan dynasty (1259–1368). Also translated as (The/A) 'Circle of Chalk'.

74 A sentence had to be omitted here for personal and legal reasons.

Conversation 4

75 This refers to the music for *The Private Life of the Master Race*.

76 The title of the film was *The Spanish Main*.

77 Eisler calls this film genre in German 'Freiheitsfilm' [Freedom Film].

78 *4 Norwegian Moods* (1942).

79 Eisler probably means Alexandre Tansman.

80 This again refers to the music for *The Private Life of the Master Race*.

81 This is now published in a slightly amended later version under the title 'Prologue to the American Production'. See J, 1 December 1945 and GW 10, p. 936.

82 The letter, without a date but probably from the end of August or beginning of September 1935, has been preserved.

83 Brecht worked with Charles Laughton on the American version of *Galileo* from December 1944 until December 1945. See full text J, December 1944, also 10 December 1945.

84 Brecht left America immediately after his hearing before the House Committee on Un-American Activities on 31 October 1947. Eisler appeared before the same committee on 24 September 1947, was subsequently subjected to repressive measures and finally expelled on 6 February 1948. See note 17.

85   See full text J, 4 March 1945.

86   See J, 22 December 1948.

87   Eisler never got round to setting Mao Tse-tung's Ode 'Thoughts during a Flight over the Great Wall'.

88   Brecht's hearing exists as *Stenographic Transcript of hearings before the Committee on Un-American Activities House of Representatives, testimony of Berthold Brecht in the Matter of Un-American Propaganda*, Vol. 9, Washington, D.C., 30 October 1947, Washington Reporting Service. The manuscript is 32 typewritten pages long. Brecht had his hearing recorded on vinyl; Eric Bentley used the recording in 1963 for a sound documentary with commentary (Folkways Records FD 5531). The hearing and Bentley's comments are published in an accompanying magazine.

89   Brecht has written an essay with the title 'We Nineteen', which investigates the results of the hearings on un-American activities (GW 19, p. 490).

90   Eisler's hearing is published. *Hearings Regarding Hanns Eisler. Hearings before the Committee on Un-American Activities, House of Representatives*. 18th Congress 1st session, Public Law 601, 24, 25 and 26 September 1947, Washington 1947, 209 pages.

91   Protocol of the Hearing, p. 57.

92   Protocol of the Hearing, p. 58.

93   Protocol of the Hearing, p. 49.

94   Eisler refers here to the celebrated discussion on plagiarism, which began after the critic, Alfred Kerr, reproached Brecht for using, without attribution, verses by François Villon (in the translation by K. L. Ammer – real name Karl Klammer) in *The Threepenny Opera*.

95   In fact, Eisler neither revealed the names of the authors nor did he claim that the works had been written by him. To the formulaic question 'Did you write those songs?' he replied: 'I wrote the music to them' and to the question, 'Did you write the lyrics?' he said: 'I never write lyrics.'

96   In 1957, one year after Brecht's death.

97   The text to the song 'The Sack Throwers' is by Julian Arendt.

98   Eisler refers to the words 'Get Up!' in the song. Brecht writes,

        The dilettante director's disregard for the composer's instructions concerning the use of music achieved ... a damaging political effect in the play. During the scene 'The Party is in Danger' for example, the piece of music actually represents the party's appeal to the revolutionary proletariat. This music therefore has to be sung directly to the audience or broadcast, invisibly, through a loudspeaker. During the song, the old and sick Wlassova gets up and, like the other revolutionaries, follows the call of the party. In the misconceived production of the Theatre Union, a group of workers storm Wlassova's sickroom and order her, in shouting and commanding tones, to go to work. This is an inhuman attitude and is therefore an enormous political mistake. Had the composer thought it right to compose a dialogue between the party members and an old, sick comrade, he would have written a completely different piece of music which would contrast in intonation, rhythm, melody from the way in which the party had to appeal in a dangerous situation.

99 Brecht sailed from New York on 29 December 1935.

100 Brecht was in London from October until December 1934. He didn't live 'opposite' though but 'in a pension in Calthorp Street' where Karl Korsch was also staying, about 4 km as the crow flies from Eisler's apartment in Abbey Road. See *Brecht-Chronic, Dates to Life and Work*, compiled by Klaus Völker, München 1971, p. 31.

101 Probably Frederick A. Voigt.

102 The Italian title of Leoncavallo's opera is *Pagliacci*. Karl Grune directed the film based on this opera in 1936. Eisler adapted the score.

103 Eisler miscalculated. It is of course still only 10,000 Marks.

104 Material from Brecht's work on the *Bajazzo* film has not been found yet.

105 A meeting with Elisabeth Hauptmann did not happen. It is most probable that Eisler and Brecht met for the first time in 1927 at the 'Deutsche Kammermusik' [German Chamber Music] festival. Their actual collaboration started with the play *The Measures Taken* in the spring of 1930.

106 Eisler means the creation of the American version of the play in 1945 in Santa Monica. See note 83.

107 See note 10.

108 See full text J, 15 May 1942 and 20 May 1942.

109 The 'scandal' refers to the hearings before the House Committee on Un-American Activities (HUAC).

110 Mordecai Gorelik, *New Theatres for Old*, Samuel French, New York, 1940. Brecht writes about this in his Journal. See full text J, 4 March 1941.

111 Margarete Steffin worked with Brecht from 1932. He credited her as his co-author on eight of his plays and they worked together on other projects as well. Hanns Eisler added in the autograph of his 'Variations for Piano' above the 1st Finale, 'Funeral March (for Grete)' and a footnote saying, 'Died, during the flight, from tuberculosis'. From this note it is clear that the composition can't

have been finished in 1940, as printed in the published edition (Edition Breitkopf) but in 1941 at the earliest.

112 Eisler means the philosopher Ernst Bloch, who had a chair in Philosophy in Leipzig. When the wall was erected in 1961, he did not return to the GDR, but went to Tübingen in West Germany, where he received an honorary chair in Philosophy. He died in Tübingen.

113 Wieland Herzfelde and John Heartfield are brothers. Helmut Herzfelde adopted the English name in 1941 in protest against German war propaganda.

114 Annual Award for Achievement in Science, Technology, and the Arts in the GDR.

115 Wieland Herzfelde was the manager of the famous Malik publishing house where the first two volumes of Brecht's Collected Works were published in 1938. John Heartfield designed this edition, as well as the editions of Brecht's *Plays and Poems* published by Aufbau, Berlin.

116 Wieland Herzfelde corrected this mistake in a later edition.

117 Hanns Eisler means the first volume of his *Songs and Cantatas*, which was published in 1955.

118 It is possible that there is a version of the manuscript with the text that Eisler set. All published versions of Brecht's, though, are as they appear in Wieland Herzfelde's edition.

119 Hermann Budzislawski told Bunge that he and Brecht rehearsed in advance the hearing before the House Committee on Un-American Activities.

120 Unfortunately, the planned conversation with Elisabeth Hauptmann (1897–1973) did not take place because of Eisler's long sickness and stay in Vienna, which was also the reason why these conversations with him were suspended for three years. Elisabeth Hauptmann worked with Brecht from 1924. Brecht credited her as his co-author on nine of his plays.

Conversation 5

121 Karl Marx and Friedrich Engels, *Manifesto of the Communist Party*, 1848.

122 Eisler means the book by Werner Hecht, Hans-Joachim Bunge, Käthe Rülicke, *Bertolt Brecht. Leben und Werk [Life and Work]*, Berlin 1963, which had not been published at the time of the conversation.

123 It is the fourth scene.

124 The full title of the play is *St Joan of the Stockyards*.

125 That's correct with reservations. It's true that the gods disappear on a pink cloud, but in the Intermezzo before it says, 'The signs of a long journey are unmistakable, deep exhaustion and manifold bad experiences. One has had his hat beaten off his head, one lost his leg in a fox trap, and all three are barefoot' (GW 4, 1595).

126 Hanns Eisler refers to Gerhart Hauptmann's *The Beaver's Coat* (1893) and maybe also to its sequel *The Conflagration* (1901); in both plays Mutter Wolfen or Frau Fielitz are the main characters.

127 A quotation from Marcel Proust, *Le temps Retrouvé*, NRF 1927.

128 It is possible that this is meant in the sense of 'Literature will be examined (For Martin Andersen Nexö)' or the motto to the Steffinische Sammlung.

129 Brecht writes about this in his Journal. See full text J, 7 December 1939.

130 Eisler surely means Georg Friedrich Wilhelm Hegel, *Lectures on the Philosophy of World History*, 1837.

131 See Brecht's comments on Hegel in J, 26 February 1939.

132 This is a quotation from Hegel's *Phenomenology of Mind*, 1910.

133 See Brecht's comment in J, 25 September 1938.

134 See full text J, 26 February 1939.

135 Me-ti also Mozi or Mo-Ti or Mo-Tzu (479–391 BC), famous Chinese philosopher who was the first to challenge Confucianism. The works of Me-ti were published for the first time in German translation in 1922. Brecht's fragment *Me-ti. Buch der Wendungen* [Me-ti. The Book of Changes] was inspired by them.

136 Brecht's adaptation of Jakob Michael Reinhold Lenz' play *The Private Tutor*.

137 Eisler means the book *Tao-Te-Ching* by Lao-Tzu (also Laozi or Lao-Tse).

138 The full title is *Tales of Mister Keuner*.

139 The first poem in Brecht's *Handbook for City Dwellers* (about 1926) is called 'Obliterate the Traces'.

140 There are not many, but occasional references to Augsburg and his youth in Brecht's poems and notes.

141 But there is one poem 'Song of my Mother', which belongs to the *Psalms*. Brecht's mother died on 1 May 1920 and his father on 20 May 1939.

142 A term that Brecht uses to describe a certain theatrical effect, which is translated into English as alienation or distancing or de-familiarization, or estrangement or making strange.

143 A wire-fabric-wall. This term denotes a very common Berliner method of constructing a wall that has no real function, i.e. more a partition than a real wall and has a function of deception.

144 This is a term that Brecht consistently used to describe bourgeois theatre: a theatre that merely gives an experience, mental refreshment as a meal is a bodily restorative. Brecht despised theatre that provides mental foodstuffs but makes no difference to audience. He believed that the audience should be made not to feel, but to think.

145 Brecht initiated the foundation of a Diderot Society in March 1939.

146 Eisler probably means Denis Diderot's (1713–1784) essay 'Le Paradoxe sur le Comedien', 1769.

147 See full text J, 25 January 1942.

148 Parts II and III were set by Eisler in April 1937 with the title 'Zwei Elegien' [Two Elegies] (*Songs and Cantatas* 1, p. 191) and part I two years later with the title 'Elegie 1939' (*Songs and Cantatas* 1, p. 124).

Conversation 6

149 Hanns Eisler accompanies himself on the piano. He played and sang only Part II of Brecht's poem: the first of the 'Two Elegies'.

150 See here especially Eisler's essays 'On Stupidity in Music' in Sinn und Form X, p. 442, p. 541 and p. 763. Translated into English in *Hanns Eisler A Rebel in Music*, ed. Manfred Grabs, London, Kahn & Averill, 1978.

151 Cities in the north-east and south-west of the former East Germany.

152 This is probably the composer Alan Bush.

153 This is probably the conductor Hermann Scherchen.

154 A fictitious hamlet in the back of beyond, on the river Unstrut.

155 *Mrs Flinz*, comedy by Helmut Baierl.

156 The work remained a fragment.

157 Certain dance forms, which originated in the West, were fiercely debated in the GDR at the end of the 1950s and the start of the 1960s. Dance events at the West Berlin venue Die Waldbühne sometimes ended in riots in which all the furniture was destroyed.

158 Bishop Friedrich Karl Otto Dibelius, President of the Council of the Evangelical Church in Germany (EKG), together with Konrad Adenauer and Franz Joseph Strauß, had signed on 22 February 1957 a 'Contract for Pastoral Care in the Military' in West Germany. As a result of this contract, a military church was established, financed, and governed by the state. Dibelius's provocative request to extend this contract to East Germany as

well was rejected by the GDR government on 4 March 1957. The request was rejected because, according to the nature of the GDR's National People's Army (NVA), the Evangelical Church has no business with the NVA. Negotiations between the EKD representatives and the GDR government were broken off. In July 1961 the Vice-president of the EKD, Bishop Lilje, declared on West German radio and television that Christians in the GDR had an 'active right to resist'. When, in the same month, the EKD planned to hold a pan-German church congress in the GDR, the GDR government prevented the anticipated provocations, by banning it.

159   The premiere of *The Mother* under the direction of Ruth Berlau and designed by Caspar Neher, took place in January 1950 at the Volksbühne in Leipzig. This was one year before Brecht's production with the Berliner Ensemble at the Deutsche Theater in Berlin, where the so-called 'bible-scene' wasn't cut.

160   See J, 16 May 1942.

161   Hans Reichenbach. See note 37.

162   The full title of the play is *Rise and Fall of the City of Mahagonny*.

163   A secular ceremony that was introduced in East Germany as an alternative to Christian confirmation. It takes place at the age of fourteen and is a rite of passage from childhood to responsible adulthood.

Conversation 7

164   The composition shows a variation of the text compared to Brecht's poem. It belongs to the *Steffinische Sammlung*, to the cycle *1940*. English translation from: *Bertolt Brecht, Poems 1913–1956*, edited by John Willett and Ralph Manheim, London: Eyre Methuen, 1976.

165   The poem 'On a Chinese Tea Root Lion' was set to music in 1961.

166   Wedding is a district of Berlin, historically inhabited by working class people.

Conversation 8

167   Eisler and Bunge had agreed to meet on 24 August 1961 to continue the conversation they had to break off two days before, because Eisler was caught up in other work. But as soon as they

withdrew into Eisler's office, visitors came and one phone call followed the other. The measures taken by the GDR government to secure their border by erecting the wall occupied Eisler and his friends more than any other matter and the discussions about it were endless. The actual meeting was preceded by a conversation between Eisler and Bunge about the formulation of a reply to an 'Open letter', which Günter Grass had written one day after the erection of the wall on 13 August 1961. Eisler dictated a letter at the end of the conversation, which was subsequently published in the journal *Die Weltbühne* XVI, Number 35, 30 August 1961, p. 1096. See Appendix for the full text of Eisler's letter.

168   See note 150.

169   The conversation took place at an unusually late hour, following one of Eisler's long working days. The following day, at the beginning of the ninth conversation, he points out himself that he, and his voice in particular, wasn't on best form. Consequently, transcription of the conversation was a little difficult.

170   Sidonius Apollinaris, actually Gaius Sollius Modestus Apollinaris Sidonius, born about 430 in Lugdunum (Lyons), died about 489.

171   Eisler tried to quote from the poem in Latin but broke off because he couldn't decipher his own handwriting.

172   Perhaps Eisler means the sentence from the first complete version from July 1930 (*Bertolt Brecht, Die Maßnahme, Kritische Ausgabe mit einer Spielanleitung* von [The Measures Taken Critical Edition with Instructions for the Actors by] Reiner Steinweg, Frankfurt am Main 1972, p. 8, line 18 and following): 'But I know, that the classless society can only be realized through the dictatorship of the proletariat and that is why I am for the radical enforcement of our slogans.' In later versions this text was replaced by 'And I am for the measures taken by the communist party, which fights for a classless society against exploitation and misinformation.'

173   See GW 8, p. 314, written about 1930, that is at the time of the work on *The Measures Taken*.

174   There is no such note in Brecht's Journal. But in the general sense it says in Brecht's preface to the edition of Hanns Eisler's *Songs and Cantatas*, 'He is not just mining his texts to the full, he adapts them and gives them everything that is inside Eisler.'

175   Brecht wrote about the music for *The Mother*: 'Hanns Eisler's music is in no way what one would call easy. As music it is quite complicated and I don't know any music that is more serious than his. In a most admirable way, the music enables certain simplifications of the most difficult political problems, the solutions

of which become indispensable for the proletariat [...]' See full text GW 15, p. 479.

176 After Hölderlin's poem 'Heidelberg'.

177 This is a line from a poem by Heinrich Heine 'The Lorelei'.

178 Eisler probably means Karl Marx' and Friedrich Engel's 'Letter to the Committee of the Social-Democratic Workers' Party' at the end of August 1870.

179 Eisler's intervention in 'Song of a German' is considerable – of the fifteen verses by Hölderlin he uses four: the first, the second, the fourth and the sixth. See *Songs and Cantatas* 1, p. 76.

180 Eisler says eight lines but in reality there are sixteen lines.

181 The Hölderlin fragment mentioned here was set to music on 2 August 1943 in Pacific Palisades (California).

182 Brecht does not mention this in his Journal. See J, 25 June 1943.

183 The thought is not wrong if history is corrected: the poem was written between the battle of Stalingrad and the last attempt of the Nazi army to delay its total defeat by advancing into the Kursk Arch (Summer 1943).

184 This refers to Brecht's poem 'On Germany', which was written around 1940 and is partly quoted in *Refugee Conversations*.

185 Eisler refers to the motto of the 'Svendborg Poems' (1939).

186 Military March by August Högn, published in 1905. Herms Niel added the text to the March around 1930. Niel's marching songs were widely employed as Nazi-propaganda and were enormously popular, particularly during the Second World War.

Conversation 9

187 Hans Mayer, *Bertolt Brecht and the Tradition*, Pfullingen, 1961.

188 Hans Mayer, p. 74.

189 The First International Congress of Writers for the Defence of Culture took place at the Théâtre de la Mutualité in Paris, 21–25 June 1935.

190 The First Preparatory Conference for the Establishment of a German Popular Front met in August 1935 in Paris.

191 In the sense of 'deception'. See also note 143.

192 In fact, at the latest on the 7th World Congress of the Comintern (25 July–20 August 1935).

193 Eisler means the Berliner Ensemble, which was called 'Theater am Schiffbauerdamm' until Brecht and his company moved into the building in 1954.

194 Mayer, p. 75.

195   Hans Mayer (p. 51) obviously thought Brecht was the author of
      this poem. The 'Hour's Song' is by Christian Weise. Brecht adapted
      it only a little and used it in *Mother Courage and her Children*.
196   Mayer, p. 77.
197   It is the seventh scene.
198   The play *The Mother* was written in 1931.
199   Mayer, p. 82. The chapter is called 'Texte in der Sklavensprache'
      [Texts in Slave Language]. There he refers to Lenin's phrase.
200   The fact can't be traced any more.
201   See the chapters 'Formalism and Realism' and 'On Realistic
      Writing' in GW 19, p. 290 and p. 339 and all of the references to
      Lukács in Brecht's Journal.
202   See full text J, 15 August 1938.
203   Georg Lukács wrote an article for the Hanns Eisler memorial issue
      of the journal *Sinn und Form* in 1964. Bunge, who edited this issue,
      was not allowed to publish it because of political objections from
      the party.
204   Literary section of a newspaper devoted to criticism, light fiction etc.
205   See Mayer, p. 107. He had actually stated the facts correctly.
206   Hans Mayer corrected this oversight later.

Conversation 11

207   An ironic remark of Eisler's. In fact, the Tübinger Germanist, Prof
      Dr Friedrich Beißner was one of the close advisers for the then
      proposed historical-critical edition of Bertolt Brecht's works.
208   Here, and also later, Eisler refers not to Hölderlin's poem but to the
      montage he made from it.
209   'Antagonism' probably has to be understood here in its original
      Greek meaning: opposition.
210   Eisler highlighted this paragraph in the margin of the typed transcript.
211   The remark refers to an earlier conversation, in which a
      contemporary composer had been mentioned. He had set to music
      a poem by Goethe in the style of Schubert, as though that should
      be the standard way of setting Goethe's poems. Eisler protested
      against this 'mechanical way of doing music' and was also annoyed
      because he found the imitation to be 'dreadful'.
212   Eisler imitates in tone and manner someone gloomy.
213   Johannes Brahms set to music a text by Detlev von Liliencron
      ('Five Songs', op. 105/4).
214   The text of the song, published in 1955, is in *Songs and Cantatas* 2,
      p. 81 under the title 'L'automne Prussien'.

215 See Brecht's poem 'Sounds' in GW 10, 1014. It belongs to the
   Buckow Elegies, 1953. Eisler somewhat misquotes the poem,
   which, in turn, of course affected the conversation.
216 In the transcript Eisler put a question mark after this passage and
   then crossed it out again.
217 Eisler set the poem 'Come! Into the Open, Friend!' as the sixth of
   the *Serious Songs* his final work, completed 14 August 1962. By his
   saying on this day, that 'it cost me nearly a year to write these songs
   beside many other works', it can be assumed that the conversation
   of 6 November 1961 was an important, maybe even the crucial
   stimulus for this project. (See also Conversation 13.) In response to
   the question (during dinner, 14 August 1962), why he had deleted
   the verse that we discussed in such detail, 'the knowing have no
   doubts' Eisler's laconic reply was: 'It was too long for me'. The
   work at that time had been 'preparatory'.

Conversation 12

218 On 24 April 1959 – the same day on which Eisler's *German
   Symphony* had its premiere – a cultural conference (the so-called
   Bitterfeld-Conference) took place at the Culture Palace of the
   Nationally-owned Bitterfeld Electro-Chemical Factory. In his
   speech, Walter Ulbricht (the then First Secretary of the Socialist
   Unity Party and Head of State of the GDR) pointed towards a
   socialist German national culture and characterized its essential
   features. The Conference emphasized as priorities for the task of
   achieving the socialist cultural revolution: art's movement towards
   the creation of a hero of our time, particularly drawn from among
   the socialist workers and farmers, who is in touch with the people
   and who follows the party line; the forging of new relationships
   between artists and working people through the artists changing
   their way of life and methods of creation; the manifold creative
   activities of workers, farmers and other working people. The
   participants appealed to all artists to connect more closely with
   the socialist way of life and, in particular, to demonstrate and to
   create artistically the coming into being of the new, socialist people.
   These principles, directed towards the continuous development of
   socialist-realistic art in the GDR, formed this particular cultural-
   educational methodological system, which was summarized by
   the term 'The Bitterfeld Way'. The Conference orientated towards
   the development of lay artistic creativity and the expansion of the
   Writing Worker movement. The people of the GDR were called

to participate in the creation of a socialist national culture. As result of the Bitterfeld Conference there began a major movement of workers writing, painting and making music. The phrase 'Let's conquer the summits of culture' can be found in Walter Ulbricht's closing remarks to the first Bitterfeld Conference.

219 In German this is a play on words: 'class aim' [Klassenziel] means to reach the required educational class standard in school and for the working class, to achieve their political aim: the dictatorship of the proletariat.

220 William Makepeace Thackeray and Charles Dickens were the main representatives of critical realism in England in the nineteenth century.

221 Eisler might have been thinking here of the following authors: Jonathan Swift, Henry Fielding, and Tobias George Smollett.

222 From the wealth of significant French writers of the eighteenth and nineteenth centuries there are mentioned here a few of those whom Eisler knew and from whose works he loved to quote: Alain-René Lesage, Charles de Montesquieu, François des Voltaire, Jean-Jacques Rousseau, Denis Diderot, Stendhal, Honoré de Balzac, Victor Hugo, George Sand, Gustave Flaubert, Émile Zola and Guy de Maupassant.

223 Also from the period of Russian literature to which Eisler here refers, a few authors should be mentioned most of whose works it is clear that Eisler knew very well: Alexander Pushkin, Nikolai Gogol, Mikhail Lermontov, Ivan Turgenev, Feodor M. Dostoevsky, Mikhail Saltykov-Shchedrin, Leo Tolstoy, Anton Chekhov, Maxim Gorki, and the great theoreticians Vissarion Belinsky, Alexander Herzen and Nikolay Dobrolyubov.

224 Eisler probably means here the introduction to *Critique of Political Economy*, 1857 in the unpublished manuscripts of Karl Marx (Marx/Engels, *Werke* [Works], Vol. 13, Berlin 1961, p. 615 and in particular p. 641).

225 Eisler is probably referring to Charles Singer's *Short History of Scientific Ideas*.

226 Bertolt Brecht, *A Short Organum for the Theatre*, GW 16, p. 661. In the Appendix (of the 1954 edition, p. 701) it says, '...when the production is unbridled, then learning can turn into pleasure and pleasure into learning.'

227 This exact quotation can't be found.

228 Eisler had read at that time in particular the pamphlet by Z Rovensky, A Uemov, EK Uemova, *Machine and Thought. Philosophical Problems of Cybernetics*, edited by Georg Klaus, Leipzig 1962. He also obtained, Georg Klaus *Cybernetics from a Philosophical Viewpoint*, Berlin 1961; I A Poletajev *Cybernetics*,

Berlin 1962; Norbert Wiener *The Human Use of Human Being*, Frankfurt/Main 1959; Wolfgang Wieser, *Organisms, Structures, Machines*, Frankfurt/Main 1959; Pascual Jordan, *The Image of Modern Physics*, Frankfurt/Main 1958; and Luis de Broglie, *Light and Matter*, Frankfurt/Main 1958.

229   The first chapter of the *Manifesto of the Communist Party*.

230   From a poem by Heinrich Heine 'The Migratory Rats'.

231   As well as everything else he was doing, Eisler read the almost 4000 pages of Napoleon's memoirs in two weeks. He usually read such books in bed before falling asleep. His bed was surrounded by towers of books, piled high. At dinner parties Eisler thoroughly enjoyed retelling Napoleon's stories. He'd have his audiences in stitches and quite incapable of eating. I used the next appropriate opportunity to encourage him to record some of these stories, and this presented itself after our twelfth conversation – to a certain extent like a Satyr Play following the serious matters we'd discussed before. And to cap it all, it was the eve of Eisler's sixty-fourth birthday and he was in an especially good mood.

Conversation 13

232   The premiere took place on 6 September 1963.

233   They were published in Vol X of Eisler's *Songs and Cantatas*, Leipzig 1966.

234   See here also Conversation 11, 6 November 1961.

235   Eisler has set about 200 of Bertolt Brecht's poems or other texts.

236   In 1932: *Kleine Symphonie op. 29*; from 1935 onwards: *Deutsche Symphonie für Soli, Chor und Orchester, 2 Sprecher*; in 1940: *Kammersymphonie für 15 op. 69*. The symphony for the Gewandhaus exists only in very few sketches.

237   In spite of his dislike of the form, Eisler wrote three symphonies, and in spite of his dislike of opera, he wrote several plans for operas, although they did not get beyond the draft stage. He had broken off work on his opera *Johann Faustus* – he had written the text himself and had the libretto published in 1952 in the Berliner Aufbau-Verlag – but in the late Fifties he did once more consider using Brecht's play *Turandot or The Whitewashers' Congress* as the basis for an opera. He didn't go through with it because he thought Brecht's text not suitable for an opera at that point in time.

Conversation 14

238   Eisler was unable to see the transcript of the fourteenth
conversation that took place twelve days before he died.

Afterword

239   Written for the first edition published as Hans Bunge, *Fragen Sie
mehr über Brecht. Hanns Eisler im Gespräch*. Rogner & Bernhard,
Munich 1970. Stephan Hermlin (1915–97), author, poet, translator,
editor and critic, is one of the most highly regarded and significant
writers of the GDR. He held influential positions on the board of the
Writers' Union of the GDR, as secretary of the poetry section of the
Academy of Arts, and as Vice President of the International PEN.

APPENDIX

Open Letter to Günter Grass

Mr Günter Grass
Berlin-Grunewald
Karlsbaderstrasse 6

> Because at night all flowers
> Look like grass.
> (From *The Awkward Age* by Jean Paul)

Without mission and prospect for success of this Open Letter, the signatory asks the writers in West Germany to think about the consequences of the sudden action of 13 August. Nobody should come along later and say that although he has always supported this action, he was prevented from speaking because he couldn't get a word in or not even a loud pronouncement.

When West German writers set themselves the task of writing against Hans Globke remaining in position and retaining authority; when West German writers call the planned Emergency Acts of the Minister of the Interior, Gerhard Schröder, an un-democratic law; when West German writers start warning of an authoritarian clericalism in the Federal Republic, then they must at least try to understand our measures of 13 August.

I ask of you to answer my Open Letter, either by approving the measures taken by our government or at least by condemning the dangerous hate campaigns against the GDR. There is no 'inner emigration'. There was also no such thing between 1933 and 1945. Who is silent, is guilty.

This is how far I'd got when my friend Dr Bunge interrupted. 'Eisler, you can't send such a letter. That's demagogy, currying favour with our government – which certainly doesn't need it; and you don't need that either, Eisler. And what is it with those dark threats? Who threatens whom and with what? Besides, the letter is dreadfully formulated, and the German, Eisler, is below your standard.'

'Bunge, this is the Open Letter from Grass, politically reversed. I'm just quoting him! It's plagiarism!'

'Eisler, did you quote Grass word for word?'

'I left a paragraph out, changed just a few things and tried to correct the German: I didn't like the "herewith"; in "Open Letter answer openly" I was irritated with the assonance; out of the strict "you have just as much the duty", I made, toned down, "you should at least try".'

'But Eisler, in "without mission and prospect for success", you should have added at least another "without". And what's with the "loud pronouncement"? Can you pronounce quietly? That's some kind of pleonasm and reminds one of "Lohengrin". And you don't set great store by that.'

'You've got me there, Bunge. I was already tired. German is a difficult language.'

Mr Grass, it simply won't do. We can't tell each other the political positions we should take, although it might be useful to suggest to you what would be necessary for you to do at the moment in the Federal Republic. I could give you a few ideas.

But if you take that line with my friends – I only mention Bredel, Renn and Apitz – then I have to object. We can't even hold a candle in terms of morality to those people – to quote a favourite slogan of our minister Bentzien, with whom you have already been annoyed. Bredel, Renn and Apitz have shown so much morale, courage and steadfastness in the torture cellars of the Gestapo, in prison and in concentration camps, that both of us can learn a thing or two from them, Mr Grass.

But about the actions which necessitated the measures of 13 August, about – according to you – illegal emigration and human trafficking, and altogether about democracy and freedom, one should debate seriously instead of writing Open Letters which create only annoyance or even offence.

I expect your answer.

Hanns Eisler
Berlin, 23 August 1961

INDEX